Fort Center

The Ripley P. Bullen Series
Florida Museum of Natural History

Florida Museum of Natural History
Ripley P. Bullen Series
Jerald T. Milanich, General Editor

Aboriginal Subsistence Technology on the Southeastern Coastal Plain during the Late Prehistoric Period, by Lewis H. Larson (1980).

Cemochechobee: Archaeology of a Mississippian Ceremonial Center on the Chattahoochee River, by Frank T. Schnell, Vernon J. Knight, Jr., and Gail S. Schnell (1981).

Perspectives on Gulf Coast Prehistory, edited by Dave D. Davis (1984).

Archaeology of Aboriginal Culture Change in the Interior Southeast: Depopulation during the Early Historic Period, by Marvin T. Smith (1987).

Apalachee: The Land between the Rivers, by John H. Hann (1988).

Key Marco's Buried Treasure: Archaeology and Adventure in the Nineteenth Century, by Marion Spjut Gilliland (1989).

First Encounters: Spanish Explorations in the Caribbean and the United States, 1492–1570, edited by Jerald T. Milanich and Susan Milbrath (1989).

Missions to the Calusa, edited by John H. Hann, with Introduction by William H. Marquardt (1991).

Excavations on the Franciscan Frontier: Archaeology at the Fig Springs Mission, by Brent Richards Weisman (1992).

The People Who Discovered Columbus: The Prehistory of the Bahamas, by William F. Keegan (1992).

Hernando de Soto and the Indians of Florida, by Jerald T. Milanich and Charles Hudson (1993).

Foraging and Farming in the Eastern Woodlands, edited by C. Margaret Scarry (1993).

Tacachale: Essays on the Indians of Florida and Southeastern Georgia during the Historic Period, edited by Jerald T. Milanich and Samuel Proctor (1978, 1994).

Fort Center: An Archaeological Site in the Lake Okeechobee Basin, by William H. Sears, with contributions by Elsie O'R. Sears and Karl T. Steinen (1982, 1994).

Fort Center

An Archaeological Site in the Lake Okeechobee Basin

William H. Sears

with contributions by

Elsie O'R. Sears and Karl T. Steinen

University Press of Florida
Gainesville/Tallahassee/Tampa/Boca Raton
Pensacola/Orlando/Miami/Jacksonville

Library of Congress Cataloging-in-Publication Data

Sears, William H. (William Hulse), 1920–
Fort Center: an archaeological site in the Lake Okeechobee Basin / William H. Sears with contributions by Elsie O'R. Sears and Karl T. Steinen.
p. cm. — (Ripley P. Bullen series)
Originally published: 1982, in series: Ripley P. Bullen monographs in anthropology and history; no. 4.
Includes bibliographical references and index.
ISBN 0–8130–1298–8 (pbk.: alk. paper)
1. Fort Center Site (Fla.) 2. Hopewell culture—Florida. 3. Calusa Indians—Antiquities. 4. Florida—Antiquities. I. Sears, Elsie O'R. II. Steinen, Karl T. III. Title. IV. Series.
E78.F6S413 1994 94–4231
975.9'51—dc20

The University Press of Florida is the scholarly publishing agency for the State University System of Florida, comprised of Florida A & M University, Florida Atlantic University, Florida International University, Florida State University, University of Central Florida, University of Florida, University of North Florida, University of South Florida, and University of West Florida.

University Press of Florida
15 Northwest 15th Street
Gainesville, FL 32611

Contents

Foreword

IN this volume William Sears describes his long-term archaeological investigations at the Fort Center site in southern Florida. Over a six-year period his excavations unlocked the secrets of what is surely one of Florida's most intriguing archaeological treasures. The information he gathered and reported here is a mainstay in understanding the Belle Glade culture.*

Like other of the large Belle Glade sites, Fort Center is made up of a complex of earthworks which extend along Fisheating Creek for a mile. In addition to mounds, linear embankments, extensive middens, and

---

*Studies of the Belle Glade culture completed since *Fort Center* was published include David Allerton, George M. Luer, and Robert S. Carr, "Ceremonial Tablets and Related Objects from Florida," *The Florida Anthropologist* 37(1984): 5–54; Robert S. Carr, "An Archaeological and Historical Survey of Lake Okeechobee," *Miscellaneous Project Report Series* No. 22, Florida Bureau of Historic Sites and Properties, Tallahassee (1975); Robert S. Carr, "Prehistoric Circular Earthworks in South Florida," *The Florida Anthropologist* 38(1985):288–301; Stephen H. Hale, "Environmental Exploitation around Lake Okeechobee," *Southeastern Archaeology* 3(1984):173–187; Stephen H. Hale, "Prehistoric Subsistence Strategies and Settlement Patterns in the Lake Okeechobee Basin of the South Florida Peninsula," Ph.D. dissertation, University of Florida, 1989; William G. Johnson, "Remote Sensing and Soil Science Applications to Understanding Belle Glade Cultural Adaptations in the Okeechobee Basin," Ph.D. dissertation, University of Florida, 1991. Jerald T. Milanich and Donna L. Ruhl, *Fort Center and the Belle Glade Culture, Florida*, Pictures of Record, Weston, Connecticut (1986), is a slide show with accompanying text about the site.

several overlapping circular ditches, Fort Center also contained a large burial mound adjacent to a small pond which had been dug by the people who lived at the site.

Sears determined that the earthworks dated from different times and had different functions. The site was first occupied in the late Archaic period, sometime between 1000 and 500 B.C., when the circular ditches were constructed. That people were living in the Okeechobee Basin by 500 B.C. was not as surprising as the identification of maize pollen grains from several early contexts at the site. The contention that maize—native American Indian corn—was cultivated at such an early time in the Lake Okeechobee Basin remains controversial.

From the artificial pond beside the burial mound, both built about A.D. 1, Sears excavated a large number of wooden carvings of animals, many larger than life. The carvings, which had adorned a wooden platform erected in the pond, are one of the most extraordinary single collections of precolumbian art ever found in the United States.

In this volume Sears describes these carvings, as well as a number of rare objects found at Fort Center and made from silver and gold. These objects were apparently made from metals salvaged from Spanish ships, indicating that the site continued to be used into the colonial period.

Fort Center: An Archaeological Site in the Lake Okeechobee Basin offers modern readers a chance to glimpse the world of the Belle Glade culture, a world that existed hundreds of years ago.

Jerald T. Milanich
General Editor
Ripley P. Bullen Series

Preface

MY practice of archaeology began with five years at Kolomoki, a large and complex site in Georgia, and it ended at Fort Center, an even more complex site, where we worked for six full field seasons and parts of two more. I regret that ten years passed between the end of the fieldwork and the completion of this report. Some of the delay may be explained by the complexity of the material, and my efforts to teach, administer a department, and do research simultaneously accounted for more delay. In any event, like Kolomoki, the site will not need a "salvage" or "mitigation" program.

The Fort Center site is named after a Second Seminole War fort, which certainly existed not too far from the big mound, Mound B. No trace remains of the fort; I am quite sure that it was washed away by Fisheating Creek.

Much of the work at Fort Center was done by teams from the University of Florida and Colgate University. The University of Florida Field School, directed by Charles H. Fairbanks, worked in the springs of 1966 and 1967 for six to seven weeks. Colgate's student group, directed by John Longyear, worked in January, often wet and cold, in the years 1966–68. Contributions of these field excavations are appropriately noted in the text. Both these scholars, together with their students, worked hard, long, and effectively, under often difficult conditions.

Everyone involved in the entire Fort Center project owes an immeasurable debt to Lykes Brothers, Inc., which owned the land, and particularly to Charles Lykes and Parke Wright. The Lykes organization, often through its local representatives in the ranch unit where the site is located, contributed money, equipment, surveying services, the use of a building, protection, and too many other services to list. I offer my thanks for all of them. Without their cooperation, the research program would have been impossible.

The Florida State Museum provided institutional support and services at the beginning of the program when I was employed there. The late Ripley P. Bullen and the director of the museum, J. C. Dickinson, Jr., facilitated equipment use, bookkeeping services for the Lykes grants, and laboratory assistance. Without these aids, later provided by the Department of Anthropology at Florida Atlantic University, the fieldwork could not have been done.

The main progam, from 1966 to 1971, was supported by the National Science Foundation. Research Grants GS-910 and GS-2534 provided funds for operations; GS-980 provided custom-built trailers, which served us admirably for dormitories, labs, offices, dining room, and kitchen, a generator to electrify these facilities, and the equipment we used to provide water and sewage disposal. A further grant in 1980, BNS-7914008, provided assistance for the preparation of this report.

I am indebted to many people for help and support of all types during the years of fieldwork, lab analysis, and writing. Foremost among these has been my wife, Elsie, who added to her usual tolerant and supportive role by becoming a most competent palynologist and operating an all-purpose laboratory. Her explicit contribution will be found under her name as chapter 8.

The late James A. Ford showed up during a number of field seasons with some regularity. He parked his travel trailer next to ours, plugged in his refrigerator, and went to work. My gratitude was, and is, immense.

Many students worked for me on this program. Some of them—the late David Wallace, Karl Steinen, Melbourne Thurman, and Anthony Austin—were or became assistant archaeologists. Others were less formally recognized and rewarded but they made major contributions nonetheless. James MacLaury, William Williams, and Michael Sears come to mind. For their work in my labs, Donna Ruhl and Diane Nagel deserve special thanks.

The shop might have had to close in the first years of the program if it had not been for the late Dorothy Barton. Department secretary, confidante, keeper of the books, den mother—she did it all. I was, and remain, most grateful.

A note on two classes of data should be included here. The human skeletal remains in the charnel pond were studied by the late Dr. Audrey Sublett, then a member of the anthropology faculty of Florida Atlantic University. Her long illness and subsequent death prevented the preparation of her report. Collections and data are stored at FAU, and it is hoped that a report can be prepared in the future.

Dr. Elizabeth Wing, curator in zooarchaeology at the Florida State Museum, graciously undertook curation and analysis of the voluminous faunal collections. Only two specialized techniques were used by the Fort Center archaeologists for the recovery of faunal remains. First, residues from some Mound A units, primarily very small bones and bone fragments that would not wash through window screen, were sacked by units and sent to the lab. Second, Dr. Wing, feeling that our trowel techniques in the basal midden in the pond were missing more than micro-fauna, brought a team down for a day and processed quantities of the muck through window screen with water.

I was trained to recover only the joint ends of bones big enough to see easily. Early in my career I had been chided in the field by a senior archaeologist, who has been associated for many years with one of America's leading institutions, for doing even that, and wasting time and funds. There has been much progress in zooarchaeological recovery techniques, and Dr. Wing and I would like to see even more. She appreciates even more than I do the fact that more would require a zooarchaeologist on the job in the field, a contingency perhaps possible at Fort Center but beyond my conception and budget at the time.

I have had information from Dr. Wing that has helped my understanding of the site. Detailed presentations of the Fort Center zooarchaeological data will appear elsewhere in a report prepared under her direction.

Once more, thanks to all of the organizations and people who, through their contributions and their labor, made the work possible.

1

South Florida and Fort Center

FOR the last 6,000 to 8,000 years, the climate and the varied environments of the southern half of the Florida peninsula have remained essentially stable (ignoring those recent massive modifications produced by our society). During these millennia, three distinguishable major environments or ecosystems have characterized South Florida: Glades, Gold Coast, and Lake Okeechobee Basin. The physical characteristics of each environment supplied an economic base for a long-lasting cultural tradition, which adapted to and exploited the system.

The Glades actually contains two environmental regimes, saltwater and freshwater. The former, the mangrove country of the western and southern coasts, is marked by huge bay and estuary areas bounded by sandy offshore islands. Tidewater penetrates for miles inland (if indeed one can determine where "inland" starts). The major economic item is shellfish, including many common species rarely eaten today. There are great quantities of fish, particularly easy to catch with traps and nets in the shallow waters, and turtle and snake occur. Sites also exist in the freshwater glades; almost every tree island seems to have served as an aboriginal camp. There are similar sites in the Big Cypress Swamp.

The Glades tradition (Goggin 1949b: 28–32) represents an aboriginal adaptation to these environments. Within the tradition, changes in the archaeological record through time are limited virtually to changes in the decoration on a small percentage of the sand-tempered bowls.

The southeast coast, called today the "Gold Coast," was characterized by beach and by dunes that used to grow grasses and sea grapes rather than concrete buildings. There are narrow, often very narrow, bays and mangrove swamps inland from the dunes and beach. Behind the saltwater bays and swamps lies a belt of sandy soil, old beach ridges in most cases, covered with pine and palmetto scrub, which in turn leads to freshwater muck and grass. There never was, except on occasional riverbanks, any significant occupation of the pine–palmetto scrub belt, here or anywhere else in the eastern United States. It has few food resources and low natural fertility. On the southeast coast of Florida, there is some occupation of hammocks, many significantly increased in size and fertility by human use, at the edges of the freshwater muck and grasslands.

The sand dune and beach zone was occupied to any extent only near the bays that provided shellfish; the larger bays, such as Biscayne Bay and Lake Worth, were particularly significant in this respect, seemingly in direct proportion to their size. The so-called Tequesta culture area apparently extended northward from Dade County, at least to the New River in Fort Lauderdale. Considerable use of undecorated pottery occurred within this area. Belle Glade Plain and St. Johns pottery is also found but in much smaller amounts than the generic type Glades Plain. As one moves farther north, the occurrence of St. Johns pottery increases gradually until the St. Johns cultural region is reached, in Brevard County. Unfortunately the practice of classifying all sand-tempered plain sherds from the coast (and elsewhere in South Florida) as Glades Plain has obscured our ability to sort out the cultures of this transition zone between the St. Johns and the Tequesta areas. Although we have a growing corpus of data on Broward and Dade counties, we know little about the coastal region immediately north of them.

Numerous marine resources were available along the Gold Coast, and fish, turtles, and other aquatic animal species could be caught at the inland camps. Lewis H. Larson (1980:23–34) has studied the food resources of all of South Florida in his overview of prehistoric aboriginal subsistence. When analyzed, data from the Granada site in Miami probably will increase our knowledge of Gold Coast aboriginal subsistence.

One portion of the Lake Okeechobee Basin, with some variation in its boundaries, has been called the Kissimmee area (Goggin 1949b), but usually all or most of the basin is included in the Glades area. Even some of its archaeological features, the mounds and earthworks, have been associated with the Calusa (Goggin and Sturtevant 1964), who seem to have been, at best, a regional variant of the Glades tradition. The Kissimmee area, one of low-lying savannah and saw-grass marsh, surrounds Lake Okeechobee and extends up such stream valleys as the Kissimmee, the Caloosahatchee, and Fisheating Creek. To the south, the saw-grass marshes, underlain by thick peat, were the "River of Grass" through which fresh water moved slowly to the saltwater glades to the south and west. Today the area has been diked and often drained, impeding and redirecting the water flow, and the mucklands are used to grow sugarcane and vegetables. Once thought to have had little habitation in aboriginal times, we now know that the Everglades contain numerous hammock sites.

The savannahs, areas of low-lying sandy soil with poor drainage resulting from an impervious humite hardpan, have occasional fair-sized hammocks, occurring particularly on old natural levees in the river meander systems. Now they are used primarily for cattle raising, but human occupation in this peculiar ecosystem goes back at least to 1,000 B.C. Available natural food sources were, and are, turtles (present in vast quantities), snake, fish, turkey, probably some zamia, and some mammals, particularly deer. Today, as in the past, the area harbors large numbers of wading birds. Most important, the basin savannah could and did support specialized horticulture by the Belle Glade culture, a fact borne out by the presence of many Belle Glade middens, mounds, and earthworks, often of considerable size, throughout the basin.

The savannah ecosystem can be divided into three subsystems, each of which was occupied and was used in differing ways by the culture with which we are concerned at Fort Center: the *river meander belt*, which has cut down below the humite hardpan; the *hammocks*, characterized by the cabbage palms and oaks, often located on old natural levees and on Indian mounds and earthworks; the flat, grassy *savannah*, dotted with ponds, sloughs, and small hammocks, and flooded as frequently and unpredictably in the past as in the present.

Fortunately, Fort Center's location is not cut off from Lake Okeechobee by a dike or by drainage ditches, an engineering stratagem designed to use the Fisheating Creek system as an emergency reservoir for floodwaters. It is, then, the best archaeological site available for our study of these culture-ecosystem relationships. A site map drawn from an aerial photograph with modifications from the ground (fig. 1.1) and the aerial photograph (fig. 1.2) show parts of these three subsystems. They are, of course, characteristic of a larger area today than in the time of the Fort Center culture and one that was even larger before dikes and ditches were built.

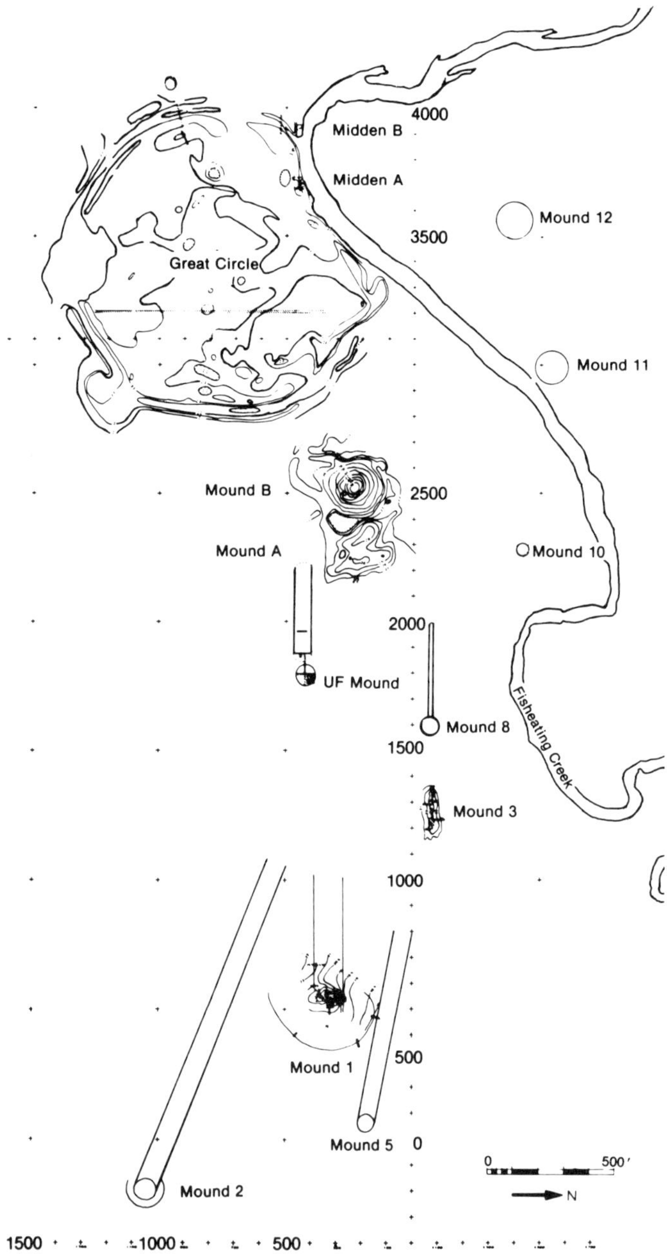

Fig. 1.1. Map of the Fort Center site, which extends along the south side of Fisheating Creek for approximately one mile; north to right.

The Fort Center site seemed to be a good choice for the study of human cultural adaptation to a wet savannah environment. It was hypothesized, based on the presence of the linear earthworks at the site, that this adaptation included a productive agricultural system to supplement or replace the food resources available through hunting, gathering, and foraging (which I call "extraction"). For some time I have been interested in the change from extraction to production, that is, to the level of village agriculture (indicative of the Formative stage) (Sears 1971a). I regard the Hopewell phenomenon or "cult" (Prufer 1968b) as the major indicator of the presence of Formative cultures in the eastern United States. But what does a wet site with earthworks and plain pottery have to do with food production?

First we must consider the earthworks. At Fort Center and at other sites in the area, there are a few single mound occurrences and there are three types that may be physically connected in various ways: long, narrow linear earthworks; circular ditch formations; and mounds of various forms and sizes. One unique variant at Fort Center is the low "wall" (fig. 1.1), which partially encloses an area in which there was a low platform mound and an artificial pond; the area and the platform mound eventually were partially covered by Mound B.

Though there has been little study and certainly little published information, there has been a tendency to assign these earthworks to the Calusa (Goggin and Sturtevant 1964), thus implying a late date, and to class them as "ceremonial." Even in advance of our fieldwork, neither of these ideas seemed acceptable. Collections of pottery were dominated by an areal specialty, Belle Glade Plain, and differed very much from pottery collected from the Fort Myers estuary (Sears 1967; collections at the University of Florida and Florida State Museum). Nor are the Fort Center linear mounds, with low platforms adjacent to one end, likely candidates for any ceremonial function we could imagine. The same is true of the great circle (but the Mounds A–B complex is a different matter).

The linear earthworks, at Fort Center and elsewhere in the Lake Okeechobee area, usually have adjacent to one end a small, single-house-sized platform mound with a normal midden on its surface. The linear earthworks seem to have been agricultural plots; the elevation would have been necessary to keep the growing area above the frequent floodwaters. The linear shape is the result of producing a particular number of square feet of elevation with the minimum amount of labor. Soil could simply be scooped up along both sides of the earthwork and deposited without having to be transported very far.

This hypothesis came from Denevan and others who have observed ridges and circles in most of the tropical savannahs of the New World (Denevan 1970). The circles at Fort Center, only one of which existed or functioned at a time, appear best explained by a practical economic hypothesis, similar to the earthwork hypothesis: they were drainage ditches. Ditch bases were dug below the hardpan so that water would drain across the hardpan and into the ditch, drying the surrounding area. The Fort Center circle was rebuilt at least two times, the second rebuilding increasing its area greatly, from 300 to about 1,200 feet.

These hypotheses have been tested with, I believe, positive results. In order to test them we had to develop a chronological scale, first, to relate the earthworks to the settlement patterns and, second, to place the artifact assemblages associated with phases of human activity in the correct sequence. Then we could approach the problem of what kind of food was being produced in the linear and circular fields.

In addition to hypothesizing that food production accounted for the presence of most of the earthworks, we thought that, because the site was a village occupied by a Formative population, there would be earthworks associated with agricultural or mortuary ceremonialism or both. Mound B, the pond, the enclosure, and the attached living area (Mound A) were the most likely places. If our hypotheses were valid, there should have been Hopewellian connections with those structures (Sears 1971a)—and indeed there were.

There was little information on the Lake Okeechobee area, or on the Fort Center site itself, at the time that they came to my attention. There had been some speculation about one of the large earthwork complexes that occur in the area (Allen 1948). Of the Ortona Works, west of the lake on the Caloosahatchee River, and Big Tony's Mound to the southeast (Allen 1948), we have only aerial photographs or descriptions, either published or in files. A small surface collection made at Big Tony's Mound seems, as a collection, to fall entirely in the Period II range at Fort Center (see chapter 7). There are few formal similarities between the circle and linear arrangement at Big Tony's and that at Fort Center.

Data on Big Mound City, excavated as a Works Progress Administration (WPA) project and reported by Willey (1949b) as completely as he could from surviving remnants of inadequate notes and partial collections, do not provide much help in evaluating Fort Center. (At least we know that there was a lot of dirt in the mounds there.) Fortunately, the site is now protected by a government agency and will not be further disturbed except in the course of properly conducted excavations.

The situation with respect to the Belle Glade site is equally confused. Using inadequate notes and incomplete and badly selected collections, Willey (1949b) could not determine with any precision what, structurally and geographically, had been there. The artifact samples had been sorted and discarded many times before Willey worked on

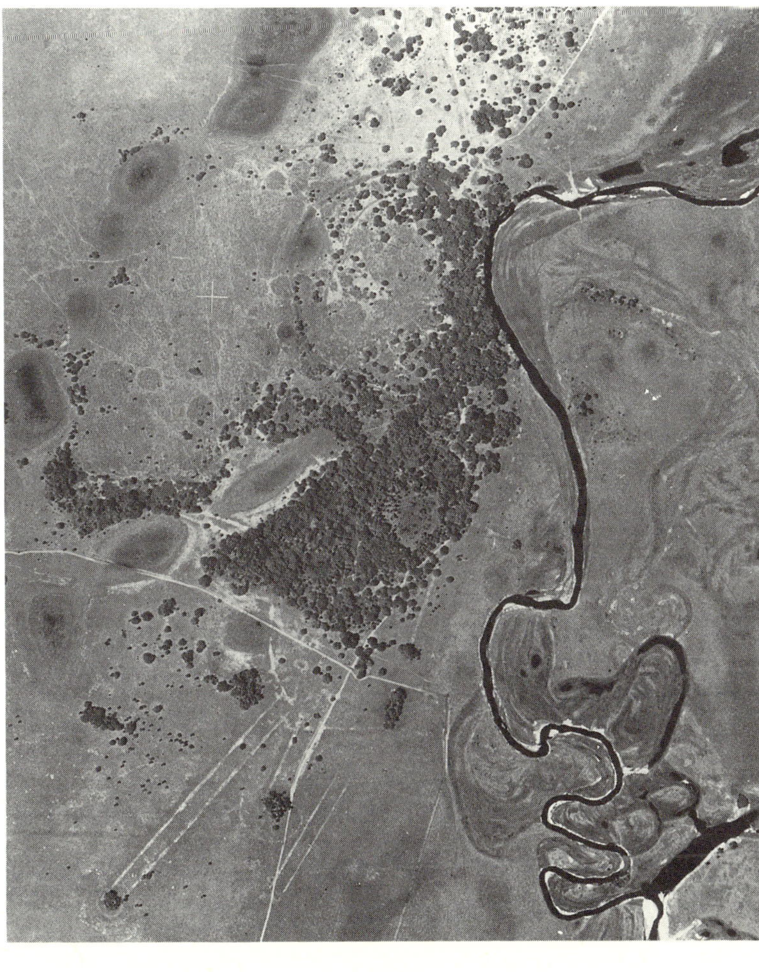

Fig. 1.2. Aerial photograph of Fort Center.

them, but they give some idea of the ceramic assemblages present in the Okeechobee Basin. The pottery type, Belle Glade Plain, was characteristic of the site, but proportions of types and variants have been grossly distorted (Willey 1949b: 62). The pottery collection contained more decorated sherds, for example, among its 1,350 specimens (Willey 1949b:24) than were present in the entire sample of over 65,000 sherds from Fort Center.

The WPA work, summed up by Willey, did make clear that something special and different had occurred around Lake Okeechobee. Describing what had happened remained for others to do.

John Goggin worked at the Fort Center site and the nearby Platt site, a mile closer to Lake Okeechobee up Fisheating Creek (Goggin 1952a). His description of Fort Center, deliberately vague, is even more deficient because he did not have aerial photographs available, and many of the earthwork features cannot be found without guidance from such photographs. His interest might have been enhanced, as mine was later, by verbal communications from John Griffin concerning presumably early fiber-tempered sherds found in pottery collections from the creek bank. My first pit in Midden A overlapped Goggin's back-filled test pit slightly; we had both selected a high point on the midden, hoping for deep deposits that result from a long period of occupation. Goggin's report is adequate for the work he did at Fort Center and the Platt site. As it happens, his test covered a limited time range, Periods III and IV, in the Fort Center chronology. It can be plugged into the Fort Center chronology easily but adds little to the available information.

The final piece of useful information was provided by a carved wooden bird in the Florida State Museum collections. Records suggest that the 1926 collector, and donor, had found it at Fort Center. This supposition made it necessary that we prepare for the excavation and preservation of muck- and water-preserved materials and allowed us to hope that the record would be expanded by such finds.

In advance of the major excavation program, I was able in 1964 and 1965 to survey the site and to make some test pit excavations with funds provided by Lykes Brothers, Inc., and the Florida State Museum. Tests were scattered around the site in locations chosen to maximize information acquired for the dollars spent. Pits and trenches of various sizes were placed in low mounds, in several parts of the complex consisting of Mounds A and B and the charnel pond, in part of the riverbank midden, and in the edge of the big circular ditch. (The Mounds A and B and charnel pond complex will be referred to hereafter as the mound-pond complex.) The program was intended to ascertain structural function and, if possible, to develop a time scale, using artifact seriation and radiocarbon (C-14) dates. The program was adequate for planning purposes, and its results are incorporated into this report. On a site with human activities limited almost entirely to concentrated use of human-made earthworks, occupying only a fraction of the site's total area, no form of overall sampling would have been of any use except, of course, the sampling of occupational units by excavation.

An archaeological report must contain descriptive and interpretative material. If it is presented in the plainest terms from a simple site, the sequence of presentation is clear. The sequence in this report is less obvious, because the analyzed artifacts are from a number of classes. Artifacts and structures were made and used through a long period of time, about 2,000 years, a fact that compounds analytical problems. We also gathered and analyzed floral and faunal data, and all of these descriptive and analytical segments must be organized to achieve some semblance of order leading to final attempts at synthesis.

Frequently, it is necessary to discuss methods of classification and to describe the classes derived and used, or to present the results before the descriptions of the data. My choices were made to achieve the semblance of order noted, to allow the student to locate data as required, and, again, to lead logically to conclusions.

Thus we proceed directly from this introduction to the chapters on field methods and the system of artifact classification. A statement on problems peculiar to this site and the prehistoric culture area in which it is located is followed by the descriptions of the excavated collections and data. This presentation allows us to proceed, in turn, directly to the development of a seriation that provides temporal controls for this multicomponent site which was occupied for over 2,000 years. This seriation is supplemented by data from pollen analysis and some information from the continuing zooarchaeological analysis, followed by a description of the physical characteristics of the site's various units, structures, and deposits. Analysis of these features illuminates the site's settlement patterns and provides sufficient information for attempting to understand the economic system's role in those settlement changes. Settlement patterns are composed of occupied or utilized units of space, each located in a specific ecological system, and built or used in a limited period of time. That is, a physical component has the space and time dimensions cherished by the now old "new" archaeologists and so obvious to many old "old" archaeologists and cultural anthropologists that, in the past, formal statements did not seem necessary. Finally, with data organized in a fashion, some attempt at processual interpretation is made in the last sections of the report.

By this time the reader will have noted a dearth of statistical treatment and references to statistics and to computer programs. At no point did I seem to be dealing with material or problems that could be approached more efficiently with sophisticated quantitative techniques. I did not feel that the use of such methods would increase knowledge at a rate commensurate with the time and effort expended. My views have not changed greatly since, from my graduate student's desk at the University of Michigan, I watched the Arzeberger site cards being punched.

But, to reassure myself that neither stubbornness nor senility had dictated my approach, informal discussions, presentations of data, and sessions of questions were carried on with some of my archaeologically naive but quantitatively sophisticated colleagues in the social sciences. They agreed with me. I found, I think, further support in a recent article by David Hurst Thomas (1978).

There are many raw quantities, measurements, and crude percentages herein. They, the field notes, and some 70,000 to 80,000 specimens are available for such quantitative manipulation as may seem appropriate. All are housed at the Florida State Museum.

2

Field Methodology

IT is a truism that the selection of field methods to be used in archaeological excavations, not just the excellence of their execution, affects directly the quality and quantity of data recovered. Current texts and reports do not always accept this premise. If the archaeologist is to find out what happened in the past, the methods used must be responsive to several factors, including research hypotheses, recording procedures, and efficiency.

Methods chosen must test hypotheses that both account for all of the observed data and attempt to predict what is under the surface. Unless the archaeologist is gifted with second sight or the archaeological site is so predictable as to render excavation unnecessary, the hypotheses must be modified continually to account for new data. Data include all artifacts—from portable specimens suitable for elaborate quantitative manipulation to soil zones, strata, lenses, and so forth, which are products of human behavior—as well as associations among them, which frequently contain the most important data of all.

Field methods determine, in turn, which data are recorded. A vertical profile does not reveal the same data and associations as does a stripped and planed floor, even though both may produce the same artifacts. Use of any method destroys some data. Recording is not a substitute for inappropriate methods and cannot replace the use of scientific method in the field.

Excellence cannot be achieved by a single "best" method: staking out a perfect grid system and excavating all squares in thin arbitrary levels or in "natural" or "cultural" zones; recording all artifact locations; using the cell block technique, in which balks are left between squares; slicing vertically with the profile recorded at frequent intervals; or combining some or all of these methods. Even filling out large quantities of prepared forms will not guarantee success for the field archaeologist.

Rigid adherence to any of these methods often simply regularizes data destruction (as opposed to capricious destruction by the pot hunter). It does not matter whether destructive methods and techniques are applied by students using brushes and trowels or by illiterate laborers using shovels. Unfortunately, training students sometimes results in selecting methods and techniques for teaching purposes rather than in accordance with the demands of science. The results can be as damaging to the archaeological record as an uncontrolled effort with a bulldozer.

Consequently, excavation methods used at Fort Center, selected each time for a specific reason, include textbook blocks, test pits, and trenches. Stripping to peel off layers or strata or zones—not simply removal of the plow zone by power machinery as the term has been restricted by some writers—was frequently done. Single test pits, bore holes, short and long trenches, continuous stripping over large areas controlled by continuous level determination, occasional vertical slicing, and excavation by arbitrary levels were among the techniques used. Tools for excavation also varied: We used toothpicks and brushes, trowels, water jets and sprays, shovels, and a crawler tractor. Long trenches and mound fill layers were cut or stripped entirely by a crawler tractor equipped with a Drott 4-in-1 bucket-clamshell-scraper-bulldozer attachment. Artifacts were recovered and recorded by hand-cleaning in place, washing off in place with water, sifting with hand- and power-operated screens of several types, and other methods.

Recording was based on a grid system. An east-west row of capped pipes at 100-foot intervals, with a north-south row running through the eastern portion of the great circle, was placed by a professional surveyor, courtesy of Lykes Brothers (fig. 1.1). Each pipe cap was numbered and its precise elevation above sea level recorded.

In spite of the loss of pipes in working areas of the ranch, and consequent damage to mowing machines, the system saved a lot of trouble and enabled rapid development of local grids for the various excavation units. Stakes and squares were numbered; squares bore the number of the stake in the lower right-hand corner of the square when facing up the grid (north). But despite this care, a number of grid identification errors were made. They have simply been perpetuated, and corrections have been filed in the notes.

Recording included the usual notes, supplemented with many photographs from an automatic Polaroid Land Camera. Photos were stapled to final copies of the notes, typed each night. In most cases the photographs are far superior in quality to my usual sketches or scale drawings. Basic recording, of course, includes many scale drawings of profiles and floors, supplemented and reinforced by black and white photographs made with a 4-by-5-inch view camera or one of several 35-mm cameras.

Most floors in the Mounds A and B complex were photographed from an oversized tripod ladder with 20-foot legs, also invaluable for seeing minor stains and other variations in floors. Color photographs in large quantity were routinely made, for special purposes, as a running record, and as a backup to other recording techniques.

In summing up our approach to excavation, we viewed the site and its components as an organism to be dissected scientifically. Any single excavation might be seen as the careful dissection of a complete organ or system for further study. This approach, guided by constant hypothesis formulation and testing in the field, with feedback from observed phenomena and continuing analyses, enabled us to select or develop methods and techniques suited to the organism and to our evolving concepts of what it was and how it functioned.

We made mistakes, but we did not destroy parts of the record, trusting that meticulous vertical walls, flat floors, and accurate recording of what we observed would, via laboratory computer-based analyses, save us from error. Specific decisions on which method or technique to use in which instance will be found in the description of each unit, with the reasons for initial choices and for changes in those decisions.

The way in which specimens are collected and treated, particularly until they are analyzed in the laboratory, has more effect on the information published than I had once thought. So peer evaluation and use of this report, as well as future use of the Fort Center data, demand some description of collection, cataloging, and information transfer processes.

Varying with the unit, our most common specimens were either animal bones or potsherds. Most of the few artifacts of chipped stone, ground and polished stone, shell, or other materials were collected from the middens with the bones and sherds. Virtually all of the bones and sherds were recovered from midden deposits with shovels or trowels, from mounds, or elsewhere. Most of the deposits, excepting trowel collections from wet muck, were sifted through ⅜-inch mesh, diamond- or square-shaped. Florida Atlantic University and Colgate used a screen I devised; it slants down to an open lower end and deposits the material that does not go through the mesh on a piece of plywood or plastic, from which final sorting and packaging take place. The University of Florida used horizontal closed screens from which specimens were removed and packaged manually.

All specimens were placed in heavy, custom-made plastic bags. Full location data were marked on the bag with a black fade- and waterproof marking pen.

The University of Florida group maintained a field catalogue system, so that only bags bore a field catalogue number. My crews, and Colgate's, did not use this system but placed permanent catalogue numbers on specimens and entered location data directly on prenumbered slips of paper daily. These slips, when completed with analytical information, served as the basis for final typed catalogue cards.

There were exceptions: recording and bagging, with precise location data, of single specimens, such as shell tools and clay pipes in Mound A; the omission of screening and dependence on thin shovel-slicing in Mound B and elsewhere; complete trowel excavation in the flooded or flooding muck at the base of the charnel house pond; and similar minor exceptions in or on features, floors, and unusual deposits. No specimen left the field without having full location data attached to or wrapped around it.

All collections were washed in the field laboratory, using traditional basin and brush techniques. Florida Atlantic University collections were cleaned by a hard-working and reliable laborer, who, though illiterate, followed instructions and became fast and efficient. All other collections were cleaned by students, who tended to overscrub some specimens, unfortunately eroding surfaces to the point where one cannot differentiate Belle Glade Plain and sand-tempered plain surfaces, a most important point. Such collections are not considered in this report. While specimens were being washed and were drying, workers maintained a tight one-to-one association between specimens and data on waterproof bag labels. Numbers were assigned to dried specimens. Prenumbered slips were placed in a tray with the specimens and the assigned numbers placed on the specimens and on the box, as were all locational data. While mistakes were made, essential data were recorded with little or no loss by use of the waterproof bag labels and by tight control over data-specimen identities in the cleaning process.

In the 1965 season, devoted to extensive test pitting, we excavated several hundred square feet of the pond area between Mounds A and B. This excavation was based on the knowledge that a wooden eagle had come from there and on the fact that there had been some slump and wash from Mounds A and B into the pond. These facts could have required simultaneous excavation of all three sites. The test, more extensive than originally intended, was designed to help develop excavation techniques for a permanently wet medium of mud, sand, and cow manure and to develop techniques for the possible collection and preservation of wooden and other perishable materials.

On this first job I borrowed equipment from Lykes Brothers, including two small rotary pumps, an assortment of steel, plastic, and aluminum hoses and pipes ranging from ¾ inch to 4 inches in diameter, a well point, and a 55-gallon steel drum cut in half lengthwise to make two vats in which wood specimens could be treated. Preservatives on hand included carbowax and white glue, the latter suggested by Albert Spaulding.

We started excavation by conventional shovel and trowel techniques in a 5-by-10-foot cut. We began in an unusually dry spell, and this first hole was, apparently, well over toward the northern edge of the original pond basin. Nothing was wet until we got down about 18 inches and were thoroughly involved in a mass of wood and bone. We did develop usable excavation and preservation techniques.

Eventually, as work continued over several seasons, we developed the techniques to be described. With National Science Foundation support, we purchased three rotary pumps, long lengths of drain hoses, intake hoses, screens, and our first large wooden vats. We also had carpentry and plumbing tools and an assortment of pipe nipples, fittings, and valves.

Water control was attained by excavating one square to natural soil and using it as a sump to pump out of. Throughout the work in the pond, over several seasons, every bit of excavation had to be designed to permit water flow toward the sump. Dewatering with well points would not have been practical since a permanently wet layer of coarse gravel lay just under the pond. The excavation and cleaning in place of wooden specimens and a lot of human bone was done best with carefully controlled water jets, produced from garden sprayers with modified nozzles and from garden hoses attached to the output end of one of the water removal pumps through a complex "Christmas Tree" valve assembly. Shovels and trowels were used in conjunction with the water jets.

When an approximate outline of a carving had been determined by using shovels and trowels, it was further outlined, cleaned off, and then undercut with water. Jet size and strength were modified according to the apparent size and strength of the carving and any other wooden or bone pieces directly over, under, or adjacent to it. It was possible to produce specimens which had not suffered from drying at all and which were completely clean, without scratches or gouges from tools. This technique did not solve the problem of masses of cabbage palm roots on and in the surfaces, but nothing could have. After the end of work every day, the excavation was reflooded to prevent damage to specimens from uncontrolled drying. Pumps were started at dawn each morning, using up to three pumps, which pulled the water level down sufficiently for work to begin at 7:00 or 7:30 A.M. A minimum of two vats was needed for treatment of specimens, and we used as many as four, depending on the rate of recovery and the size of the objects, the latter, of course, also determining the minimum size of the vats. One or more vats was kept full of water and changed frequently. Another was filled with a 50 percent solution of white glue. As a specimen was removed from the pond, a tag with a field catalogue number was tied to it with nylon string. Tags were made from the plastic bags we used for smaller specimens, marked with the same fade- and waterproof felt-tipped markers. Immediately, until there was room for them in the treatment tank, the clean specimens were placed in the water vat to prevent any damaging moisture loss.

We tried various methods for making vats, ranging from cutting up oil drums to lining wooden vats with sheet plastic. We finally made all of them from heavily framed ⅜-inch plywood, 8 by 4 by 4 feet. All seams were sealed inside with fiberglass tape and resin, and the entire interior was resin-coated to waterproof it. This method worked well, and it would be readily adaptable to larger or smaller vats.

The white glue posed a problem. It tended to settle out, becoming much thicker in the bottom of the vats. At first we simply removed all of the specimens quickly, stirred up the glue, and put the specimens back, a technique that produced tangled tags and glue-coated personnel, particularly as the number and size of specimens increased. The solution was a manual marine diaphragm pump with 1½-inch intake and outlet. The intake hose was placed at the bottom of the tank and the outlet hose just under the surface at the top. The volume of fluid moved and the current produced by two or three 15- to 30-minute pumpings daily gave us a uniform solution in which to work. An electrically operated diaphragm pump, readily available on the marine market, would have worked even better. Care had to be taken to run clean water through the pump at the end of each use.

Specimens were kept in the treatment tank from several days to several months, depending on our estimate of thickness and porosity, factors affecting penetration, and attainment of solution equilibrium inside and outside the object. One large carving started to crack a month after removal; it was reimmersed for an additional month.

White glue, a plastic emulsion, was chosen over any of the water-soluble waxes or other wax treatments for two reasons. First, after soaking, the specimens have, when dried, regained strength and abrasion resistance to a level approximating that of fresh wood; plasticizing the wood by replacing water in pore spaces with plastic not only prevents checking but also strengthens the object. Second, after drying, resoaking the material in a white glue solution softens the plastic already present and permits further absorption, although this technique is not possible with some materials.

A number of people as well as some of the literature suggested alum treatment. In my experience with it in the Florida State Museum, the process was messy, and, since heat is required to warm the solution until penetration is complete, specimen damage was probable.

White glue was easy to handle, simple to purchase, and low in cost when purchased in bulk. Having seen the results of most other methods, from alum and paraffin to carbowax and its relatives, I believe this treatment best for these specimens in results and in cost. This would not be so for all specimens; a flexible substance, delicate matting, for example, seems to respond well to the more flexible carbowax. But for heavy wooden pieces, including all of the ones from Florida sites, white glue seems best if the specimens have not been dried. If specimens have already suffered from damaging dehydration, only strengthening is physically possible; it is best achieved with other plastics and volatile solvents.

After removal from the vats and careful brushing with soft brushes and glue solution or water to remove any surface buildup, specimens were dried in the shade. (A few showed slight cracks ten years later.) Permanent catalogue numbers were painted on as soon as possible and the catalogue cards completed.

For anyone excavating wet deposits, it is simpler to use electricity. We had three to five small gasoline engines operating in the field and at times could have used more, but a diesel-powered generator mounted on a trailer would have been easier to use. Three to seven kilowatts, depending on the job, would have permitted operation of more dependable electric pumps for clean water and use of sealed electric motors for the power sifter. We could also have used the electricity and the simpler, cheaper motors for heaters, drying fans, air compressors, and so on.

A major hypothesis of the Fort Center research was that horticulture—plant unknown—had been practiced at the site. This practice would account in one way or another for the several kinds of earthworks. The most useful test for horticulture appeared to be pollen analysis, which would also produce data on plants of economic value other than those cultivated as well as on any environmental changes. But our primary interest was in cultigens. The most probable were corn (the North American staple) and manioc, possibly coming from South America along with the building of earthworks.

In either case, as in the cases of squash and beans, we would be dealing with heavy pollen, normally spread by insects and not likely to have been moved any distance by winds. It would have fallen nearly straight down when separated from the plant. Manioc, unfortunately, could not really be expected to flower in this climate, but we were hopeful that we would find some.

For collecting purposes, we had to identify and collect samples from surfaces on which pollen might have fallen: garden plot topsoil, house floors, storeroom floors, and food preparation areas. Samples collected at regular horizontal and vertical intervals, or randomly sampled from mound, earthwork, or midden, would be more likely to miss key surfaces than to hit any of them.

Almost all of our samples were collected from profiles on which we could identify surfaces, ditch bottoms, or floors. To these samples we usually added others from modern topsoils and old muck deposits. In every case, after the profiles were scraped clean, the sample or samples in a vertical series were cut out with a clean trowel and placed directly into a clean, new, labeled plastic bag. Contamination from other dirt or the atmosphere was thus almost eliminated.

We added a few other samples to these from the soil, human feces, preserved by contact with quicklime in Mound A, a notable example. Other additions included strips of pigment from one of the carved wooden birds associated with the charnel house, samples of unusual soil types, and a number of sets of samples taken at arbitrary intervals from thick midden deposits, such as zones in Mound A between probable floors.

3

Ceramic Artifacts

THE most lucid and pointed statement on artifact classification that I have seen is by J. O. Brew (1946:65): "We must not be satisfied with a single classification of a group of artifacts or of a cultural development, for that way lies danger and defeat. We are, or should be, in search of all of the information our material holds. Even in simple things, no single analysis will bring out all of that evidence."

I have elsewhere (Sears 1960a) stressed the point that there is a difference between analysis and classification and that, by definition, any classification used should be the product of analysis. Classification alone can only mean—and usually does—the pigeonholing of units, whose dimensions may vary from those of the original analyst, creating "classes" of predetermined dimensions. This system, at best, may facilitate some limited communication between archaeologists. At times, such classes or "types" will be used for that purpose in this study. But classification without analysis, as often practiced, does not increase our knowledge of how any group of people were living or what they were doing.

Analysis and the classes it produces, whether varieties, types, or units labeled with physically descriptive terms, are our tools for understanding parts of prehistoric cultures. The way we organize our data is designed to accomplish specific tasks.

In analyzing potsherds from Fort Center, we paid attention to all attributes or modes "which the archaeologist's grasp of his business tells him are of potential utility" (Sears 1960a:328–29). This statement does not mean that I have fallen into the common semantic trap of producing my "classes" or "types" as artificial entities, devoid of cultural reality. That theoretical approach founders on the rock of reality; that is, if a prehistoric group had not been cognizant of the same combinations of attributes that we recognize, those combinations would not have existed for us to study. I realize, of course, that I am abstracting attributes, and combinations of them, from the specimens themselves and from the realities of a culture undergoing constant changes in space and time. But only in this way can we answer our questions. And my classes are not sacred. I do not doubt that different analyses—even those merely using larger or smaller samples—would produce different results. But when my heliocentric view of the prehistoric cultural universe changes, I do not believe that the change will be brought about by the tedious input of subjective factors into an electronic device which makes millions of objective decisions per second and coughs out numbers. In the case of the Fort Center material, by the time I knew which factors were important and which were not, I had the answers I could use.

All of the vessels made by the Belle Glade culture, at any time, were simple bowls. Size varied somewhat, and wall angles varied from slightly outflaring to slightly incurving. This restriction of vessel forms is characteristic of southern Florida's utility pottery throughout prehistory. At Fort Center, as around Tampa Bay, across the state to the headwaters of the St. Johns River, and apparently to the state's northern borders—areas that in the earlier periods were characterized by fiber-tempered pottery—pottery collections from midden deposits indicate similarly restricted vessel forms. This "Florida Bowl Tradition" stands in distinct contrast to the vessel form traditions north of the peninsula and, I think, suggests relationships with early cultures in southern Central America and northern South America, a subject we will consider after more evidence has been presented.

Formal pottery type descriptions for the Fort Center ceramic collections follow.

Pottery descriptions

Belle Glade Plain

Temper: Large amounts of coarse sand to very small amounts of fine sand. Variation is through time, small amounts of fine sand latest.

Method of manufacture: Probably segmental fillet. Few sherds have informative fractures.

Texture: Varies with amount of temper, color, and hardness, all of which change with time. Darker, thicker specimens have large amounts of sand and angular fracture. Thinner, harder, and lighter-colored specimens are late and have even fracture and texture.

Color: Early specimens are consistently in the gray-brown-black range. Color becomes lighter through time with increased control of firing. Latest and hardest specimens are consistently off-white to dirty light gray.

Thickness: 6 to 10 mm early, consistent change to thinner specimens through time, latest range 4–7 mm. Thicker often near rims. As predictable, a few specimens are thick or thin at wrong points in time.

Surface: Tooled and compacted. A wooden tool picked up grains of sand and dragged them for some variable distance, leaving the surface, frequently faceted because of tool size and shape, scratched and pitted. The effect resembles a brushed surface at times, except for the frequent pits left by the removal of sand grains. The tool often loaded up or was applied to an overly wet surface, and the scratching or pitting is missing in spots. This scratched and pitted finish is the only characteristic that permits Belle Glade Plain to be consistently sorted from other types with which it shares vessel form, color, temper, hardness, and faceting. That is, unless analysts use this single characteristic as the major class determinant, the type is not a useful tool, a fact that emerged as some 65,000 plain sherds were analyzed and reanalyzed in an effort to find a consistently useful time marker.

Hardness: Around 2.5, occasionally to 3 early in the period of manufacture. Most specimens can be scratched with the fingernail. Late, light-colored specimens with small amounts of temper run to around 4 on the Moh scale.

Vessel form: Bowls, most 8 to 15 inches in diameter. A few are larger or smaller. Depth appears to be approximately one-third to one-half the diameter. A fair number of specimens appear to have vertical upper walls, and a few are slightly to markedly incurved in the upper part of the wall, usually beginning high enough to be considered, strictly speaking, a rim phenomenon. A few specimens have outcurved upper walls.

Rim lip: Most rim features per se, as required on bowl forms, described under vessel shape. Number of lip forms present. See seriation chart (fig. 7.1) for variation in lip shape through time.

Flat: appears to be cut rather than modeled on most specimens. Frequent groove on top, rarely for full circumference. Apparently produced by grain of sand or other object caught by cutting tool.

Direct rounded: usually sloppily executed. Range from slight taper to slightly expanded. Occasionally, lip on a single pot will show both flat and rounded areas.

Late: elaboration on the simple flat and direct rounded forms is restricted to the later periods.

Expanded flat: often near "T" form, usually a distinct wedge with flat side uppermost. Might be considered a rounded version of T-shaped lips. Both T and comma-shaped lips appear to be directly molded. There is little or no suggestion of added strips or folds.

Miscellaneous: large variety, few specimens of any single variant. Include tapered lips, a few true "T" shapes, rim folds, modeled rims, and so on. Variation appears to lack temporal significance.

Base: Rounded bases only.

References: Willey 1949b: 25–26. Goggin and Sommer offer another description (1949: 46–47); it is not of the same kind of pottery described by Willey. I cannot account for this, but the definition should not be used.

Geographical distribution: As dominant type, the marker for a culture found primarily on the sand lands, the savannahs, around Lake Okeechobee, north up the Kissimmee, and west perhaps halfway to the coast down the Caloosahatchee. It is also dominant in several locations on the east coast, including a site in Boca Raton (Furey 1972), and occurs in some quantity in a few sites on both coasts that are dominated by other complexes, as the Grant Mound near Cape Canaveral (Sears 1958) and small sites in the Caloosahatchee estuary (Sears 1967). Unfortunately, well-made and hard St. Johns Plain pottery, and some sand-tempered plain, has been classified as Belle Glade Plain.

The Okeechobee series

I had intended, when analysis started, to use Willey's Okeechobee series (Willey 1949b: 29–30). I decided, after working with collections and restudying the type description, that the specimens so classified would today be classified as St. Johns Plain and Dunns Creek Red. All relevant specimens are so classified in this report.

Sand-tempered plain

Temper: As with Belle Glade Plain, there are large quantities of sand in some thick, smooth, early specimens. Occasional sherds have coarse sand.

Method of manufacture: Same as Belle Glade Plain.

Texture: Same as Belle Glade Plain. Thick sandy specimens that occur early have a very even fracture.

Color: As with Belle Glade Plain, same variation through time excepting a few off-white late in time. Thick, sandy early specimens tend to be reddish brown.

Thickness: Same as Belle Glade Plain.

Surface: Variable, apparently due to lack of effort or care. Most sherds have an irregular surface with protruding grains of sand, but surfaces improve technically with time, as does Belle Glade Plain generally. Some of the earliest specimens, which are thick, heavily tempered, and reddish-brown, have well-smoothed surfaces. Frequent smooth facets suggest sloppy use of flat smooth pebbles, common in middens, as finishing tool.

Hardness: Same as Belle Glade Plain.

Vessel form: Same as Belle Glade Plain, including late rim lip variants.

Base: Only rounded bases known.

Discussion: Most practitioners have been classifying the plain sand-tempered sherds from this area as "Glades Plain" following the lead of Willey (1949b) and Goggin (1949a). Over some years, it has become increasingly apparent to me that I could not sort out plain sherds from this area from those found around Tampa Bay or in much of Central Florida. Use of the term Glades Plain gives a spurious illusion of control over time, space, and even ethnic identity, as indicated by references to Tequesta and Calusa.

There are more variations in plain pottery than the Belle Glade Plain and laminated-contorted used in this report. With careful analysis, some of the variation might be useful, such as the thick sand-tempered variant I isolated some years ago at the Bayshore Homes site in St. Petersburg (Sears 1960b:6). We need further analysis to classify the variations. At Fort Center, the thick, reddish-brown, heavily tempered pottery grades imperceptibly into the rest of the sand-tempered plain. I was not able, in many trials, to sort for it consistently and had to abandon the effort.

Semi-fiber-tempered pottery

Semi-fiber-tempered pottery is thick, most specimens measuring nearly 10 mm; it is soft, consistently 2.5 on Moh's scale, and very sandy. The fibers or fiber holes in the soft, dark, sandy paste vary from a few to perhaps one-quarter of the volume. The few rim sherds are direct rounded except for several nearly flat specimens. There is no suggestion of any form but the simple bowl.

I have chosen to use Bullen's somewhat descriptive term "semi-fiber-tempered" (Bullen 1959:45) precisely because it is a bit ambiguous and suggests to me Bullen's implicit hypothesis that the fiber is being replaced by sand as the transition from fiber-tempered pottery to later varieties was taking place. The sherds contain both fiber and grains of sand. Phelps (1965) and others would probably classify these sherds as Norwood Plain. Judging by the type description and photographs of that type, the few soft, heavily fiber-tempered sherds that I have classified as Orange Plain would also be included. Having handled some of the sherds from the northeast coast of Florida that have been classified as Norwood Plain, I am not sure that the type exists except as a label for an assortment of variants of Orange Plain. In any event, the descriptive term is used here in preference to one that is beginning to accumulate an overload of undocumented, even undigested, semantic baggage.

On the other hand, I am not sure that this pottery in the Lake Okeechobee basin is really a development from Orange Plain, as Bullen's hypothesis requires. As I have suggested elsewhere (Sears 1977b) there are many traits, including fiber-tempering, in the Southeast, in Florida, and in this area specifically, that appear to have Middle and South American origins. Without more data than we have, we cannot rule out such a source for semi-fiber-tempered pottery.

Laminated-contorted plain

Temper: Small to moderate amounts of fine sand. Many specimens appear to be temperless until examined closely.

Method of manufacture: Probably segmental fillet. Little data.

Texture: Laminated, contorted. Appears to have been worked very dry so that folds, bends, and layers did not adhere well and did not blend into each other.

Color: Most light tans, browns, ranges to dark gray. Cores usually dark gray. Poorly controlled firing.

Thickness: Most about 8 mm, some thicker, to 10 mm. A few of the flatter sherds included may be bases from sand-tempered plain bowls.

Surface: Well smoothed. Tooled sufficiently with hard, smooth tool to produce a "wet" float. Produces a smooth, thin, superficial layer, a self slip. Grains of temper often protrude through surface. Self slip usually cracks in random fashion on drying or during firing so that many specimens have a surface crackle.

Hardness: 2.5–3.5, most too hard to be scratched by fingernail.

Vessel form–lip rim–base: As Belle Glade Plain.

Discussion: Most sherds of this pottery are similar to normal specimens of Pinellas Plain (Willey 1949b:482), a late type in the Tampa Bay area. I do not believe that there is any relationship. These bowls at Fort Center, as suggested by the seriation chart (fig. 7.1), appear to represent a step in the development of paste qualities from fiber-tempered and semi-fiber-tempered wares into those that are normal for the sand-tempered plain and Belle Glade Plain pottery.

Trade ware

In table 3.1 most of the trade pottery and a few informative unique specimens found at Fort Center are summarized. Specimens are lumped by periods in order to permit evaluation of sources of contact from quantities large enough to permit perception. St. Johns Plain is omitted because it is often present in quantities large enough to be significant on the seriation chart (fig. 7.1). Most of the raw data will be found in unit descriptions in chapter 9. More precise sources for some specimens will be given in the discussions of periods that follow.

Period I

Little trade ware is present in Period I. A few sherds of Orange Plain and a few of Orange Incised, outnumbered considerably by St. Johns Plain, are found in several small collections, but these collections are not included in seriation because the small quantities clearly covered long periods of time. In each of them, along with the Orange series fiber-tempered sherds, there are quantities of semi-fiber-tempered plain. Certainly the Orange and St. Johns series sherds demonstrate intensive relationships with the St. Johns area from the time of the earliest occupation.

Table 3.1 Trade pottery by period

Type of sherds by period	Number	Percentage
Period I		
Semi-fiber-tempered, like Simple Stamped—Mossy Oak	1	1.7
St. Johns Paste		
1. Simple Stamped	2	3.3
2. Cord Marked	57	95.0
Total sherds	60	
Period II		
Pasco Plain	7	5.1
Belle Glade		
1. red interior	5	3.6
2. curvilinear incised	2	1.5
Sand-tempered		
1. incised	12	8.8
2. red interior	4	2.9
3. brush or rocker stamped	3	2.2
4. fine knotted fabric	1	.73
5. deep horizontal grooves	1	.73
6. modeled	1	.73
7. polished	1	.73
8. punctated	1	.73
9. tetrapod, distal end	1	.73
Deptford		
1. Check Stamped	3	2.2
2. Check Stamped or Cartersville Check Stamped	1	.73
3. Check Stamped or St. Johns paste	1	.73
4. Simple Stamped	8	5.8
5. Simple Stamped or St. Johns paste	2	1.5
Orange		
1. Plain	1	.73
2. Incised	2	1.5
Mossy Oak Simple Stamped	1	.73
Booger Bottom Check Stamped	8	5.8
Crystal River		
1. Plain	12	8.8
2. Punctated	5	3.6
Fine limestone-tempered plain	5	3.6
Dunns Creek Red	1	.73
St. Johns		
1. Incised	5	3.6
2. Simple Stamped	7	5.1
3. Cord Marked	6	4.4
4. Check Stamped	1	.73
5. tetrapod-hard St. Johns Plain	2	1.5
Unclassified		
1. incised	1	.73
2. punctated (1 hemi-punctated)	2	1.5
3. sand-tempered plain	3	2.2
Miscellaneous	21	15.3
Total sherds	137	

(*continued*)

Table 3.1.—*Continued*

Period III		
Dunns Creek Red	7	14.0
Belle Glade		
1. red interior	2	4.0
2. incised	15	30.0
3. zoned	1	2.0
Sand-tempered		
1. direct rounded, extruded edge nicked	1	2.0
2. smooth	2	4.0
3. incised (five lines, 3; four lines, 7; modeled lip, 1)	11	22.0
4. excised	1	2.0
Pinellas Plain	4	8.0
St. Johns Check Stamped	1	2.0
Complicated stamped, flat lip	1	2.0
Contort laminated, Belle Glade finish	3	6.0
Pasco Plain	1	2.0
Total sherds	50	
Period IV		
Pinellas Plain	5	35.7
Belle Glade Incised	1	7.1
Englewood or Safety Harbor	1	7.1
Contort laminated, fiber tradition	1	7.1
Okeechobee Red	1	7.1
Fibrous plain-chalky	2	14.2
Pasco Plain	1	7.1
St. Johns Simple Plain	1	7.1
Unclassified punctated-sand-tempered	1	7.1
Total sherds	14	

Period II

Some of the trade sherds from Period II came from the surface midden on the small platform mound under Mound B (table 3.2). This collection clearly demonstrates intensive contact with the St. Johns cultures who were manufacturing pottery in the St. Johns, chalky-ware tradition. The plain sherds also document contact of some intensity since they are relatively more numerous than in other earlier and later periods at this site. However, the decorated ware resulting from the indicated St. Johns Ia Early contact should be St. Johns Incised, if anything (Goggin 1952b). Instead, we have copies of Deptford Check Stamped and Simple Stamped, with tetrapods. These copies are present in St. Johns burial mounds of the period, such as Murphy Island (Goggin 1952b).

The Deptford complex is also represented by simple- and check-

Table 3.2 Period II trade pottery from platform mound under Mound B

Type	Number
Deptford series	6
Simple Stamped	4
Check Stamped	1
Mossy Oak Simple Stamped	1
St. Johns series	71 (including Plain)
Dunns Creek Red	1
Deptford-like Simple Stamped	4
Tetrapod, plain	2
Deptford-like Check Stamped	2
St. Johns Plain	2
Pasco Plain	4
Fine limestone-tempered plain	5
Crystal River series (or clearly related to it)	3
Polished, fine, mica	1
Complex broad-line incised, polished, mica, rim	1
Crystal River Punctated	1
Sand-tempered miscellaneous	7
Punctated	1
Fine knotted fabric	1
Modeled	1
Fine incised parallel lines	1
Miscellaneous incised	1
Brushed or rocker stamped	2

stamped sherds, frequently represented in non-Deptford burial mounds of this period. The limestone-tempered Pasco Plain and the more finely tempered variant, perhaps Pasco Plain, tell us only that the west coast of Florida, particularly that area of coasts and islands dominated by the Crystal River site, was also known to the society that used the Mound B ceremonial complex.

Finally, but certainly not least in importance, there is an odd collection of sand-tempered sherds with a variety of features that are not normal locally. These include polishing, light or deep incision, modeling, and fine punctation. Their affiliations are with the oddities presented as the types of the Crystal River series (Willey 1949a), which are not native there either. Not only are they fine-sand-tempered whereas the resident ware in middens is the limestone-tempered Pasco Plain; the paste also shows the fine mica flecks characteristic of northwest Florida and southwest Georgia. In any event, at Crystal River, even more than at Fort Center, they come from a sacred rather than a secular context (Sears 1973).

Table 3.3. Period II trade pottery from Mound A redeposited in charnel pond

Type		Number
St. Johns series		32
Plain	24	
Cord Marked	4	
Simple Stamped	2	
Incised	2	
Crystal River series		8
Punctated	2	
Plain sherds from 1 dark, polished, egg-shaped vessel with fine mica in temper	6	
Cartersville Check Stamped		4
Tetrapod, heavy, plain, probably plain Deptford		2

All in all, relationships of this group appear to be with ceramics that usually appear in sacred associations, specifically Yent complex (Sears 1962), rather than in midden deposits.

Another collection of Period II sherds comes from the first deposits on the floor of the charnel platform pond, washed there from the low platform mound (Mound A) or from areas immediately adjacent to it (table 3.3). The wash layer, and the specimens, were in place under mucky midden redeposited in the pond from Mound A.

This assemblage differs little from that on the low platform mound, substantiating the stratigraphic evidence that says it was derived from there. Deptford pottery is not demonstrably present but may certainly be inferred from the two plain sand-tempered tetrapods.

Since relationships with the Yent complex have been suggested, the Cartersville Check Stamped (the stamping on which is a little fuzzier than Deptford, probably because the stamping was done on a wet surface) is no surprise. One short, angled rim with a rounded lip fits the type variation well.

Cord marking on chalky St. Johns paste does not have much significance. I have found it in most sites in Florida at almost any time level when St. Johns pottery was also present. Sherds of the type St. Johns Incised, missing from the surface of the platform mound collection mentioned, are indeed the defined type (Goggin 1952b), not just chalky sherds with incised lines.

Sherds representing about half (from lip to base) of a dark, egg-shaped vessel are not, of course, a Crystal River "type." But at this time level in Florida, well-polished, thin, finely made pottery with fine

Table 3.4 Period II trade pottery from floor of charnel pond

Type		Number
Deptford series		3
Deptford Check Stamped	2	
Deptford or Cartersville Check Stamped	1	
St. Johns series		98
St. Johns Plain	94	
Simple Stamped	2	
St. Johns Incised	2	
Orange Incised		1
Miscellaneous, sand-tempered		9
Possibly Crystal River Incised and Punctated	1	
Lug handle, fingernail punctates top and bottom	1	
Red interior	1	
Raised interior nodes	2	
Miscellaneous incised	2	
Hemi-conical punctates interior, dimples exterior	1	
Exterior triangular area raised by excision of adjacent areas	1	

micaceous temper is certainly related to the Crystal River series of decorated types, wherever the vessels of that series may have really been made.

The remarks concerning the trade sherds from the surface of the platform mound also hold for this context. These sherds, apparently resulting from the trade of ceremonial items, are from the St. Johns IA Early, Deptford, and Yent complexes. Basically, this is the Hopewell period in Florida (Sears 1962), which fits well with our radiocarbon dates of the first five centuries A.D. associated with the ceremonial structures and associated artifacts.

Other trade sherds came from midden on the floor of the charnel pond (table 3.4). Stratigraphically, they overlap the wash deposits. This midden deposit, ultimately derived by redeposition from Mound A, underlies all the charnel platform wood and bone artifacts.

While this collection certainly suggests the same sources and time period as the last two units described from Mound B, it does so less emphatically, even marginally. There are Deptford and St. Johns paste simple-stamped sherds, but there are no tetrapods in this reasonably large collection nor are there any certain specimens of the

Table 3.5 Period II trade pottery from Mound A

Type		Number
St. Johns series		42
St. Johns Plain	42	
Deptford series		2
Simple Stamped	2	
Pasco Plain		1
Crystal River series, probably		3
Fine line incised, fine paste	2	
Punctated	1	
Miscellaneous sand-tempered		5
Zoned, "Z" or rocker stamped	1	
Red interior	2	
Deep horizontal grooves, finger tip?	1	
Deep incised line, curvilinear	1	
Orange Plain (fiber-tempered)		1

Crystal River series. Instead, we have an assortment of odd, apparently one-of-a-kind sherds.

Trade sherds also came from levels in Mound A deposited in time just before or after those that the midden redeposited in the pond. These sherds are listed in table 3.5.

Obviously, except for the three possible Crystal River sherds, this assemblage is much like that from the basal midden deposit in the pond. It differs from the Mound B collections in the same way noted in the discussion of the basal pond midden material; I presume these differences are for the same reasons.

Periods III and IV

In the units from Periods III and IV—the upper levels of Mound A midden deposits and various house mounds—the common trade ware is St. Johns Check Stamped. With these few check-stamped sherds there is a small quantity of the chalky plain ware. There are a few other odds and ends. Trade wares, including Pinellas Plain, fall temporally where they should. A few unclassifiable incised sherds, mostly from Mound A near surface levels, are on a local paste. All in all, contacts with the St. Johns and with the west coast near Tampa, neither of any real intensity, are indicated. We should expect more west coast contact, particularly in Period IV, which is historic. There is no evidence to support Calusa dominance.

Summary

Starting with a few Orange Plain fiber-tempered sherds in Period I and ending with a few check-stamped and plain sherds in periods III and IV, St. Johns contacts are continuous. Materials obviously acquired through trade, such as the shell tools and sharks' teeth of Period II, indicate intensive contact with coastal populations, probably the west coast. But, except for a few Pinellas Plain sherds in Period IV context, we cannot document this contact with the trade pottery that we have because the relevant east and west coast areas are, through most of their history, dominated by the "Glades Plain" sand-tempered bowls of most reports. We cannot recognize these at Fort Center. We can isolate Belle Glade Plain, when properly classified, in coastal sites. I noted in the discussions of pottery types a few sites on each coast with quantities of Belle Glade Plain. But there is reason to be wary of this identification since, if my observations of some extant collections are correct, it often means only that the collections had light-colored pottery with facets.

Possibly the lack of Glades series decorated types is significant, suggesting a lack of contact with the saltwater Glades—the mangrove coast—in the area where these decorated variants are most common, from Marco Island south. But even in that area, the decorated sherds are a distinct minority. Willey (1949b) did find Glades decorated types in the Belle Glade site collection, but we do not know the sizes of the collections from which the decorated specimens were abstracted. The discard policy at the U.S. National Museum before Willey worked on the collections makes it possible that the total decorated sherds represented less than 1 percent of the total.

We do have evidence for external contacts during Period II at Fort Center in the form of Deptford series sherds, Deptford copies on chalky paste, Crystal River series specimens, and other sherds. All indicate culture contacts on a sacred or ceremonial level. Many of the "types" or features occur in the strictly ceremonial Yent complex at this time level. We may interpret their presence in sacred context at Fort Center as evidence of at least fringe participation in the Hopewell phenomenon.

Pipes

We recovered 74 fragments of pottery pipes representing at least 50 pipes. Most of the fragments are, or appear to be, from equal-armed

Table 3.6 Characteristics of platform pipe fragments

# Frags.	Elements present			Decoration		Stem shape			Modeled mouth-piece	Location in fig. 3.1
	Stem	Bowl	Spur	Incised	Punct.	Squared edges	Rounded edges	Triangular cross sect.		
1	X	X	X	—	—	—	X	—	—	A
1	—	X	X	X	—	—	X	—	—	D
3	X	—	—	—	—	—	X	—	—	—
1	X	X	—	X	—	X	—	—	—	F
15	X	—	—	—	—	X	—	—	—	—
1	X	—	—	—	X	X	—	—	—	—
1	X	—	—	X	—	—	—	—	—	—
1	—	—	X	X	—	X	—	—	—	—
6	—	—	X	—	—	X	—	—	—	—
2	—	—	X	—	—	—	X	—	—	—
1	—	X	X	X	—	X	—	—	—	B
1	X	X	X	X	—	—	X	X	—	E
1	—	—	X	X	—	—	X	—	—	C
1	X	—	—	—	—	—	—	—	X	—
36 total										

Table 3.7. Characteristics of elbow pipe fragments

# Frags.	Plain	Incised sides	Flat base	Arched top	Circular cross sect.	Location in fig. 3.1
1	—	X	X	X	—	I
1	X	—	X	X	—	G
1	X	—	—	—	X	—
3 total						

monitor or platform pipes of several variants. A number of obtuse-angle elbow pipes were also found.

All of the paste is sand-tempered. Finishes range from as sloppy as the worst sand-tempered plain pottery through several specimens with a Belle Glade Plain finish to several that are polished on the surface. I can see no consistent trend except that most are simply smoothed.

Most specimens are either stem fragments or are unperforated fragments from the other side of the bowl of the two-armed, if not always equal-armed, style. These unperforated segments are referred to here as "spurs." Many other fragments are from bowls, and the base or stem type cannot be estimated.

Tables 3.6–3.8 list the characteristics of the various pipes, examples of which are shown in figure 3.1. All specimens in all cases are broken and fragmentary to some degree.

Pipes were found only in the dense midden with the lime deposits in Mound A and with the midden were moved intentionally from there to the bottom of the charnel pond. The only exceptions are several fragments from equal-armed platform pipes that were found in an odd midden deposit on the old ground surface under the University of Florida Mound (which derives its name from its excavators) and a spur from an appropriately dated context in Mound 3.

No other deposits contemporaneous or nearly contemporaneous with these (contemporaneity is established and visible on the seriation chart, see fig. 7.1) contained any pipes, nor did the Mound B deposits from the surface of the little platform mound.

I have studied the data carefully, and the only suggestion of a change through time in the Mound A pipes is that the definite elbow pipes come from the last Mound A levels along with some platform pipes but after the major occurrence of platform pipes in Period III. This is a reasonable conclusion, but the elbow pipe sample is too small for generalizations to be made.

Table 3.8. Characteristics of miscellaneous pipe fragments

	Elements present			Decoration				Stem shape			
# Frags.	Stem	Bowl	Misc.	Incised	Excised	Engvd.	Punct.	Squared edges	Tapered	Cylind.	Oval cross sect.
6	X	—	—	—	—	—	—	X	X	—	—
4	X	—	—	—	—	—	—	—	X	—	X
8	X	—	—	—	—	—	—	—	X	X	—
5	—	—	X	—	—	—	—	—	—	—	—
1[a]	X	—	—	—	X	—	—	—	—	X	—
8[b]	—	X	—	—	—	—	—	—	—	—	—
1[b]	—	X	—	—	—	X	—	—	—	—	—
1[b]	—	X	—	—	—	—	X	—	—	—	—
1[b]	—	X	—	X	—	—	—	—	—	—	—
35 total											

a. Fig. 3.1, H.
b. Bowl shapes for these 11 fragments are distributed as follows: 5 cylindrical; 4 flared with narrow midpoint; 2 squared.

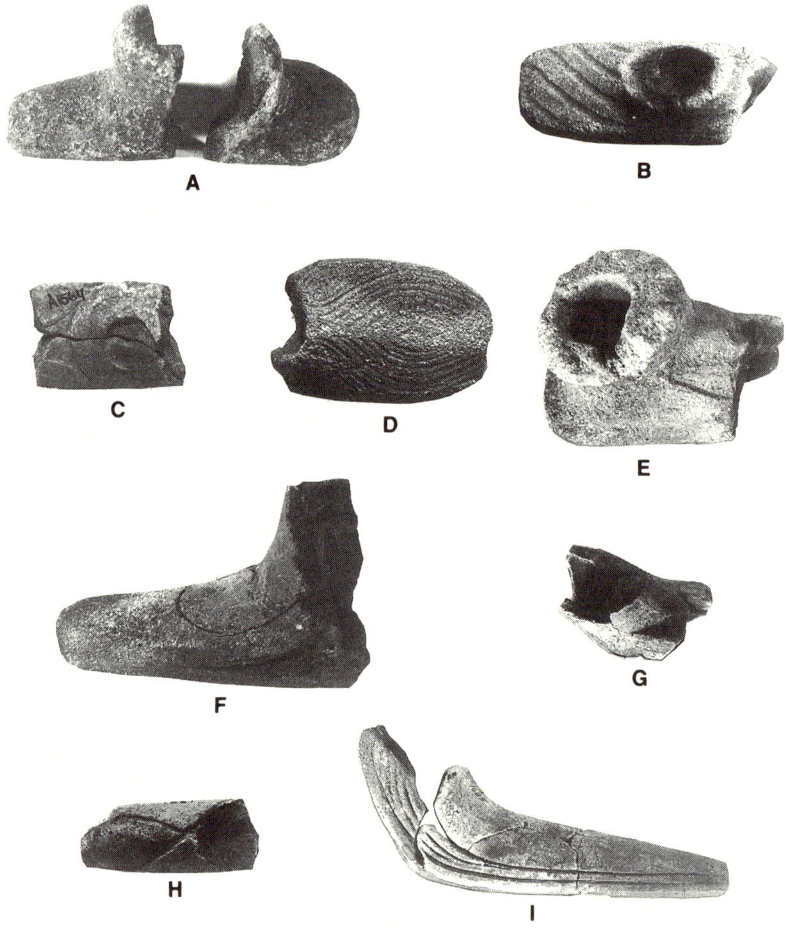

Fig. 3.1. Pottery pipe fragments from Mound A and the pond (see tables 3.6 and 3.7 for identifications).

I had thought that finding these pipes on midden deposits suggested everyday rather than ceremonial smoking, as suggested by the associations of platform pipes in Ohio and Illinois. Now I have doubts about this conclusion. Restriction of the pipes to a single locale and a restricted time period—a period characterized otherwise by intensive ceremonial-mortuary activities—suggests that both the pipes and Mound A had related ceremonial functions.

Sherd hones

The inhabitants of Fort Center, like most other prehistoric pottery-using Indians, were well aware of the fact that sherds of sand-tempered pottery would serve as excellent tool sharpeners. None of the wear, exhibited as one or more grooves, seems to have resulted from use on or with shell tools. Most of it, by width and shape of grooves, could easily have resulted from sharpening bone awls, particularly the common bipointed variant described in the chapter on other nonceramic artifacts (chapter 6).

4

Wooden Artifacts

REPRESENTING mostly large birds and other animals, 100 to 150 wooden artifacts and fragments (the precise number depending on the number of fragments demonstrably parts of wholes) were recovered from an artificial pond between Mounds A and B. Details of the pond and its relationship to the mounds, and a reconstruction of the structure associated with the wooden carvings, will be found in chapter 9. Some references to the structure, apparently a "D"-shaped platform a couple of feet above the water, used for deposition of the dead, will be found in the discussions that follow. It appears that most of the carvings were structural parts of the platform as well as ornaments or symbols.

Some of the earliest work at the site produced evidence that we would be working with the remains of a complex structure, intermingled in water and muck with human remains. Consequently, locations of all of the wooden and human remains were plotted with unusual care, often redundantly in notes, scale drawings, and several photographs of different kinds. All of our preparation helped in reconstruction but did not provide any definite answers to questions about the site and its purposes. The data obtained do allow us to make some inferences.

Specimens 10 feet long or more had been erected vertically. They could and did fall in various directions, and some may have floated for some time. Many had rotted completely, leaving only masses of waterlogged, root-penetrated fiber, the surfaces and even deeper layers permeated by palmetto and cabbage palm roots. Some specimens had burned.

All of the objects except the two double-ended pestles were carved from pine. Pine logs up to 30 inches in diameter were used; these were large logs but not abnormally so for single trees in ideal situations. Judging from the best-preserved pieces, such as the large turkey head (fig. 4.1, B) and from certain aspects of others, the rendition of detail was superb, although all pieces were somewhat stylized.

One might ask why cypress was not chosen, since it was at least as available as pine. I suggest that pine has certain characteristics that made it more suitable for shaping with the tools and skills available, particularly for the larger carvings. In turn, some of the stylization is the result of these characteristics.

The most significant of these distinctive features of pine is, I think, the well-defined grain and its tendency to split readily along this grain. This tendency could cause problems, but the artisans appear to have taken advantage of it by cutting across the grain at the ends of sections to be removed and then splitting off the delimited segments, probably one carefully defined splinter after the other. This method would have facilitated removal of the great quantities of wood between the erect wings of the large birds or the segments behind the legs in the two-legged style. There is little evidence remaining for the use of this technique, but evaluation of the styles makes its use, and effect, quite apparent. Other characteristics of pine are the reasonably hard surface of the wood, enabling the artist to cut and scrape details into being, and its durability, which facilitated shaping and permitted shape and surface details to last.

In many instances, knots and twisted areas in the grain of the wood formed around knots, branches, or root swells were used to make shaping easier and to add strength. Grain was turned 45 or even 90 degrees, particularly for some of the tenoned carvings. Knots were used for detail on other specimens. Some of these details will be noted. Presumably, the artist had a shape in mind and then found a piece of wood that could be adapted, just as builders of wooden boats for centuries, even today, take their patterns to the woods to find just the right crook or oak branch for rib or knee.

The tools used are clearly those found on the site, particularly in the Mound A midden context. These tools were made from flint, other stone, shell, and sharks' teeth as described in chapter 6. Flint points used as knives, shell celts, shell adzes of several varieties, and the harder and heavier stone celts would have been used for most of the cutting and finishing. Sharks' teeth, hafted and unhafted, obviously made superior cutting tools for delicate detail work and func-

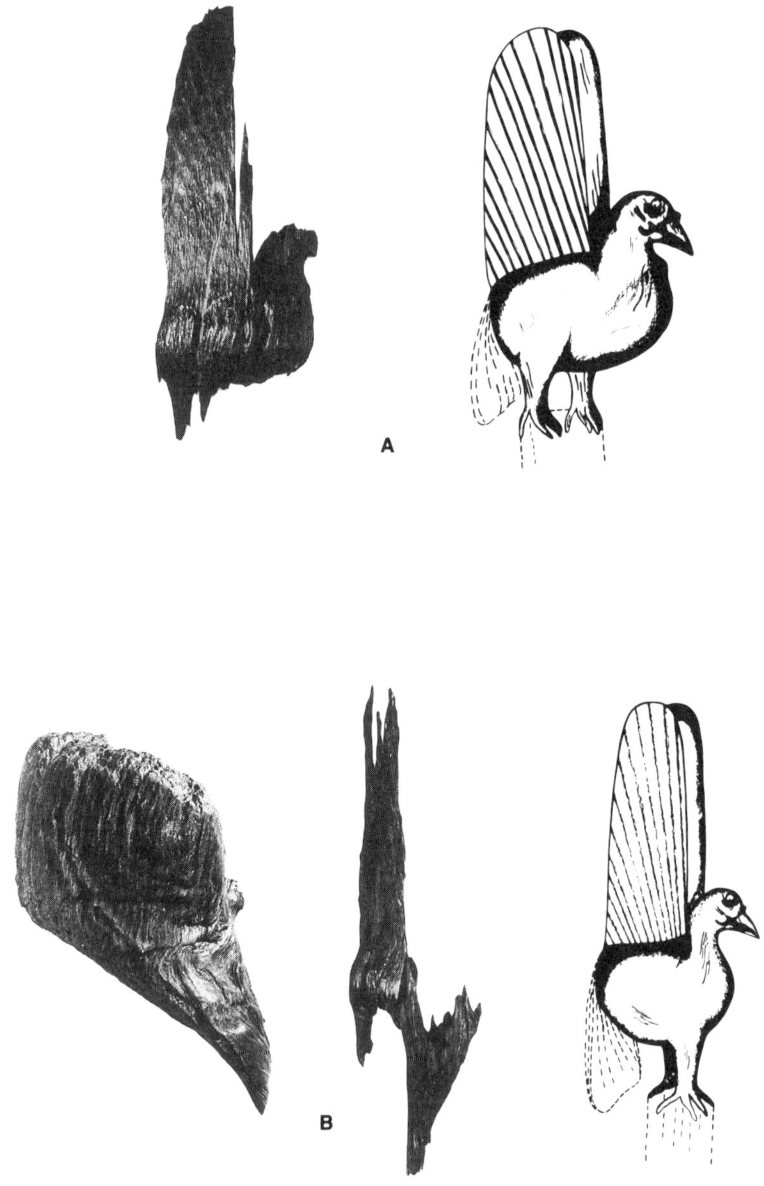

Fig. 4.1. Large bird carvings, both turkeys: *top* specimen, 41½ inches tall; *bottom* head, 15 inches long, height of wings and post 58¼ inches. (Measurements in fig. 4.1–4.11 refer to wooden specimens, not to artists' drawings, and give maximum measurements unless otherwise noted.)

tioned admirably as finishing scrapers to bring the hard pine surface to final form and finish.

Reconstruction

There are two kinds of reconstruction: artistic and physical (gluing fragments together and adding material to replace that which is missing). Not a great deal of physical reconstruction of the wooden artifacts was possible. Generally, the carvings were either intact or we did not find pieces. In a few instances, it was clear that a number of fragments belonged to a single creature, but large connecting areas were not present. There was some breakage in place or in the laboratory. Clean breaks, new or old, were mended with white glue. A few specimens broke because the amount of sound wood remaining was not sufficient to carry the load. Material was added to strengthen these glued or weak joints, restoring them to something resembling original form and dimensions. Acceptable results were obtained with mixtures of white glue, sawdust, and sanding dust of various grades and pigment trowled on and finished to the desired surface after drying.

Artistic reconstructions are another matter. Results of drawing the specimen and adding obviously missing parts such as legs and ears would not have been useful or informative. After excavating, cleaning, treating, photographing, and otherwise becoming familiar with the specimens, I had some sense of basic styles and artistic conventions. I communicated, shared, and amplified these feelings with the artists and other persons working on the project. Further handling, measuring, photographing, production of scale drawings, and discussion of style conventions added to the descriptions we were accumulating. Finally, we used books with good photographs and paintings of wildlife to help identify the creatures represented by finding characteristic features chosen for depiction or accentuation by prehistoric artists. All of these factors were used in producing the drawings that accompany the photographs of the wood carvings. I believe that publication of only photographs of the carvings would have been inadequate, even misleading.

The descriptions and discussions that follow are based on the sample of reconstructable specimens. A few bird and animal heads for which we lack bodies are included, as are some wings for large birds and a few somewhat enigmatic bits.

We also recovered about 50 fragments; these are definitely carved but cannot be assigned to category or class and will not be described.

Locations for specimens or groups of at least physically related specimens that seemed to be the remains of one carving will be found on figure 9.13. Locations of the carved pieces were measured horizontally and vertically to the approximate center of the creature or that part of it remaining. Sketches and photographs accompanying the notes furnish some information on observed size and orientation. The larger creatures could have fallen in any direction. There is a suggestion that the rear arc of two-legged creatures fell outward, to the west, and it is possible that the entire platform slumped to the west when it collapsed.

The carvings can be separated into two categories, ceremonial and utilitarian, each of which can be further divided into classes of artifacts. The categorization is based on probable function and inferences about style.

The three major classes of carvings in the ceremonial category (large birds and beasts, two-legged style, and tenoned birds) appear to have been regarded as distinct realities by the manufacturers. Classification on the basis of style automatically produces size and location correlations that are consistent.

Ceremonial carvings

The ceremonial specimens clearly were associated with at least 150 and probably as many as 300 human bodies on the charnel platform. Description of the platform and its immediate associations will be found in chapter 9. The evidence suggests that at least two classes of carvings (large birds and beasts and two-legged style) functioned in an engineering sense as parts of the platform structure. Probably all of the bird and other animal carvings served also, and perhaps primarily, as religious symbols or totems. I cannot see a way to test this hypothesis, but, certainly, except possibly for a specimen or two in the miscellaneous class, the wooden replicas of birds and other animals do not have any function in the everyday affairs of the community.

Large birds and beasts

The carvings of large birds and beasts were located on, and were structurally a part of, the straight front (east) edge of the platform (fig. 9.13). Carvings in this class are about 4 feet high for that part that depicts the bird or other animal and would have risen above the platform level. The longest base section is 4½ feet long. I estimate that all bases, that part of each carving below the creature, were about 6 feet long. These measurements are based on the fragments themselves, on field observation of them, on pond depth below unaltered ground surface in the vicinity, on normal water depth, and on an allowance for the base of the carving to have sunk or been forced a little way into the pond bottom.

Birds

We have the remains of three large birds with vertical, erect wings and parts of bodies, wings, and pedestals still joined (figs. 4.1, 4.2, B). One large head, beautifully preserved and clearly a turkey, was found separately and is included in figure 4.1, B, as part of that restoration. Size and bulk of the separate parts suggest this relationship.

None of the three large birds has more than one wing remaining. Wings illustrated in figure 4.3 (E and F) appear to belong to two of them: E to figure 4.1, A, and F to figure 4.1, B. There are seven more wings, the locations of which help to define the straight front edge of the platform. One of these could belong to the bird in figure 4.2, B. All this leaves six wings plus two more observed in the field that were too rotted to remove. So there were at least four more of the large birds with vertical wings and possibly even more, since the wings do not sort into pairs particularly well. The artist's drawing of the reconstructed platform (fig. 9.14) shows seven birds, and there is room for one or two more in the front row.

All of the birds were carved from single pieces of pine. Minimum diameters are 18 to 24 inches, and some probably were as much as 30 inches. Heights appear to run around 4, possibly 5, feet for the large turkey (fig. 4.1, B) and down to 3 feet for a creature represented by a single wing.

More wings were preserved than bodies or heads, and in the more intact specimens wings are better preserved, considering their thinness, than are bodies or heads; see figure 4.1, A, for one of the best preserved figures. The reason for the differences in preservation is, I think, that the thin vertical wings seasoned quickly, and then, shedding water, stabilized and escaped rot. Heads, particularly bodies, with the center growth rings of the trees and all grain facing up, did trap water eventually and, like fence posts, rotted from the top down and the inside out. This course suggests long exposure before immersion in the pond, an assumption which is in accord with other available data. Well-established rot would also tend to continue after the collapse of the platform.

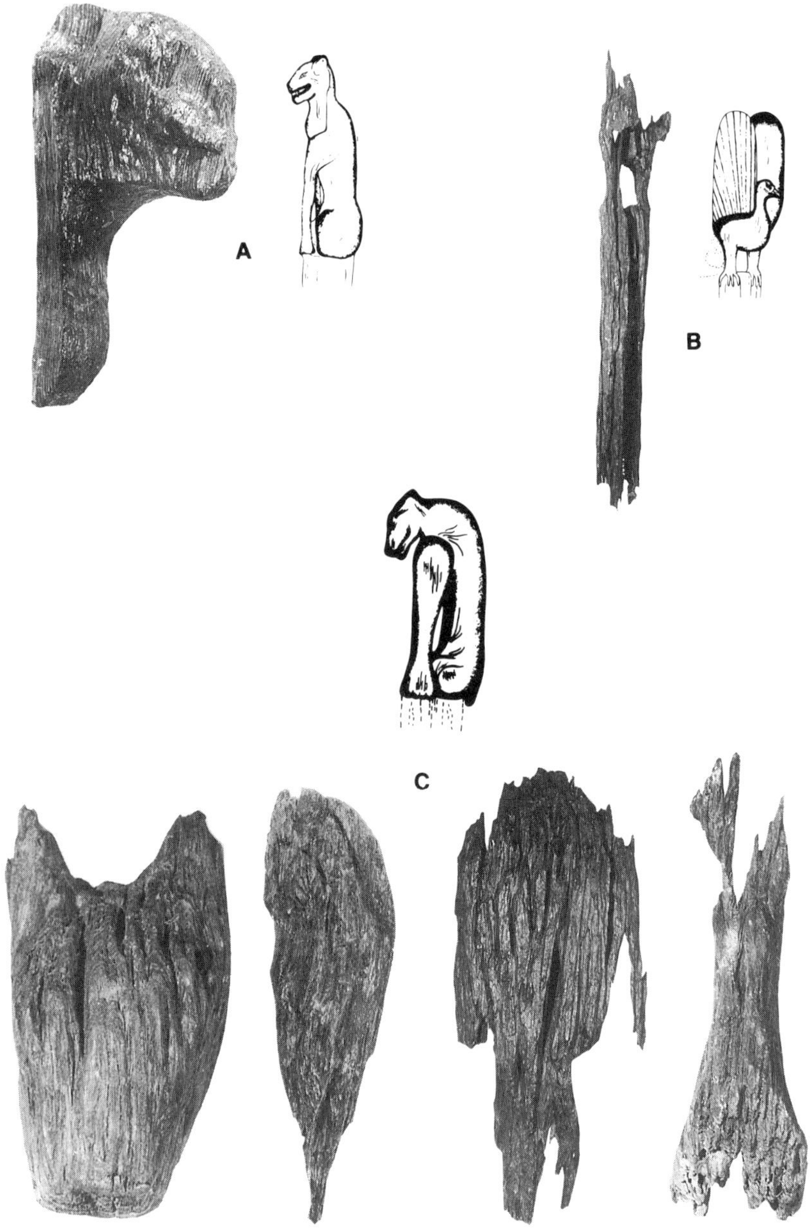

Fig. 4.2. Large bird and mammal carvings: **A**, cat with head, 13 inches high; **B**, turkey, 74¾ inches; **C**, probable bear: (*left*) head, 12½ inches tall, (*left center*) shoulder, 23¼ inches, (*right center*) back, 36 inches tall, and (*right*) leg, 26½ inches.

Bear

Figure 4.2, C shows what might be a dog but looks more like a bear; certainly a bear is far more likely than a dog to be represented in sacred context in prehistoric or historic North America. The head and associated parts, those illustrated in figure 4.2, plus the other leg and paw were the southernmost wood specimens in the pond. Some sand from the embankment that caps that end of the pond edge had washed down over the pieces. All of the pieces except the head show some charring, as do several other fragments of wood (which may or may not have been parts of the bear) from the immediate vicinity.

The largest fragment, part of the back, is 36 inches long. Reconstruction of the creature as 48 inches high is reasonable; a height 5 feet or a little more is possible.

Cat

We found only the head of a cat (fig. 4.2, A). It had split off from the body of the carving before much decay had taken place. Probably more of the creature was in the nearby large masses of decayed wood mixed with less decayed wood and a large quantity of human remains. The reconstruction is based on the head, which has more detail than we were able to bring out in the photograph, and on style data for larger creatures, particularly the bear just described.

Two-legged style

All of the two-legged style animals that were restorable to any extent are illustrated in figures 4.4 and 4.5, a total of nine animal carvings including three birds. As the photographs and drawings show, the creatures seem to be paired. There are two cats, probably bobcats. The separate head shown in figure 4.5, C, is part of the restoration in figure 4.10, D. There are also two dogs or bears, differing somewhat in details, two foxes, two birds, which have owl body conformation although heads are missing, and one eagle in an odd style. One eagle head (fig. 4.6, E) could come from a creature in this size range, completing that pair.

Four or five specimens observed in the field, collections of root-penetrated wood fragments lying in alignment, were too fragmentary and decayed to be removed. Apparent size, shape, and location suggest that they belonged to this class of two-legged creatures.

The stylistically unifying feature of this type is that the front legs in the quadrupeds or the legs in the birds have been cut free of the body from shoulder to foot. Rear legs or birds' tails remain attached and

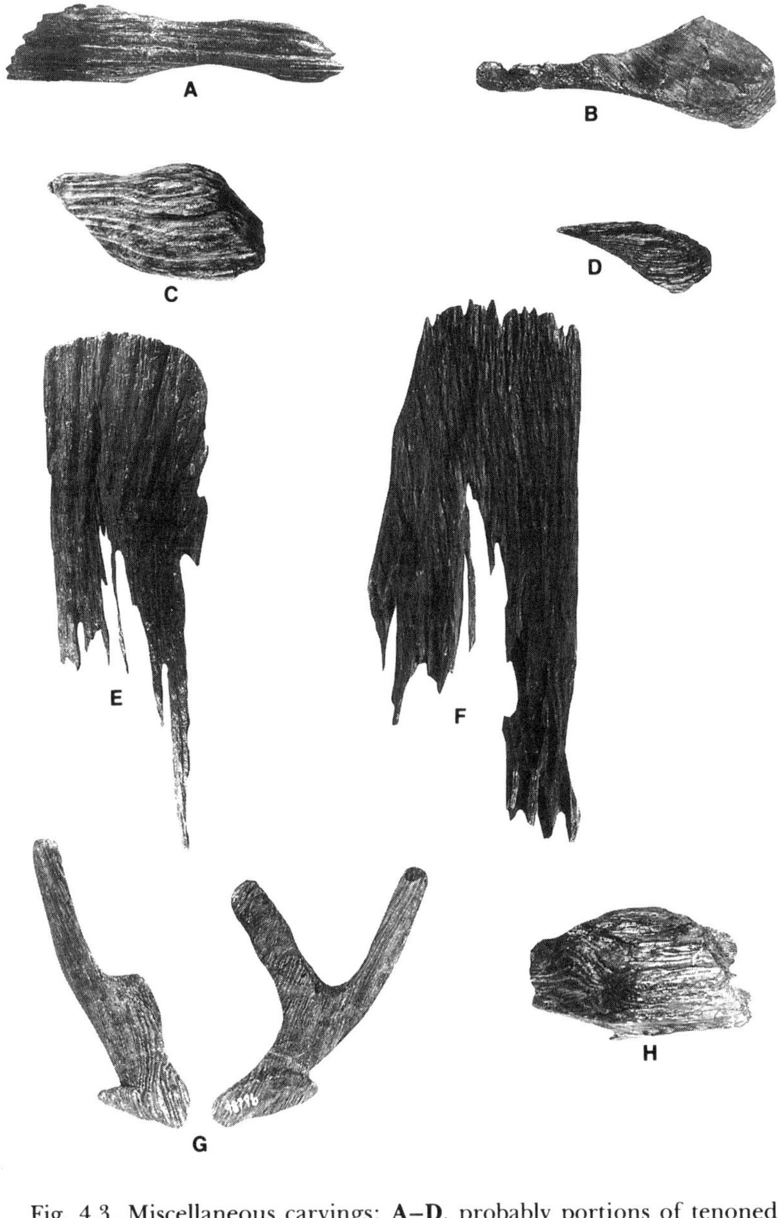

Fig. 4.3. Miscellaneous carvings: **A–D**, probably portions of tenoned birds, 6¾, 6¼, 4¾, and 3¾ inches long, respectively; **E**, **F**, wings from large birds, 38½ and 89 inches tall; **G**, antlers (left one is 8½ inches long); **H**, cat head, 8½ inches.

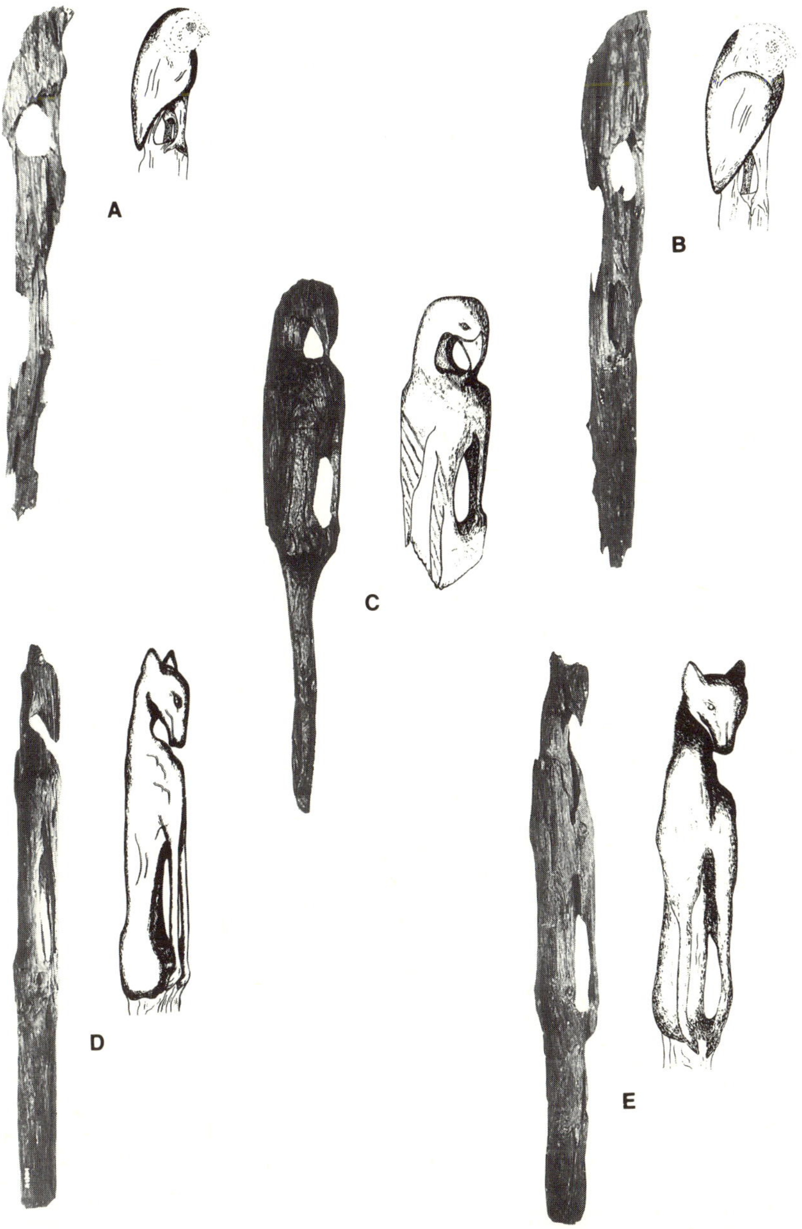

Fig. 4.4. Carvings in two-legged and tenon styles: **A**, **B**, owls, 52½ and 54 inches; **C**, eagle, 39 inches; **D**, **E**, foxes, 58¾ and 60 inches.

are, legs and animal tails especially, carved in relief. The rear legs tend also to be proportionately undersized. This treatment produces an effect quite different from the freestanding birds and animals of the preceding class or the smaller but stylistically similar tenoned class.

These two-legged animals are much smaller than the large birds and beasts. The carved creatures, excluding bases, range from 18 inches tall for owls through 24 inches for dogs (or bears) to 30 inches for foxes. These measurements reinforce the concept of pairs. All of these carvings were used in, or as supporting members for, the rear part of the platform; locations where they were found (fig. 9.13) define the western arc of the platform.

Tenoned birds

Birds in the tenoned class are somewhat smaller than the two-legged creatures. The body and legs of the water bird (fig. 4.7, B) stand only 9 inches high and the hawk (fig. 4.7, D) 7 inches. Style does not seem to be particularly uniform; the consistent feature is the tenons, which are 19 and 13 inches long, respectively, for these two birds.

The largest tenoned carving, an eagle or hawk, is a miniature of the large birds with erect wings and is, at 22 inches tall, the largest of these tenoned creatures. It is also unique; when found, some strips of rubbery white pigment, 3⁄16 to 1⁄4 inch in diameter, adhered to the wings, where they accentuated the feature markings. Many of the strips had fallen off, and the fragments were in the muck around the carving and around and adjacent, but not connected, to the large tenon that will be described. The pigment could not be kept in place and dried to a crumbly white substance, although the pieces kept their cylindrical form well. Most unexpectedly, the pigment—the only pigment known at the site—contained large quantities of maize pollen (chap. 8), quantities such that it must have been added deliberately to the lime-based pigment.

Carvings in this class have a distinct, usually somewhat conoidal, tenon for a base instead of a long cylindrical or square base made to reach to, and presumably into, the base of the pond. These tenons, or at least the smaller ones such as B and D in figure 4.7, fitted sockets that had been worked into the tops of long poles.

The carefully carved poles were squared at the top (fig. 4.8), and a socket was carved into the 6-to-10-inch-square segment. Below the squared portion, the timber was reduced somewhat to a round cross section 4 to 5 inches in diameter. Measurements were recorded in the

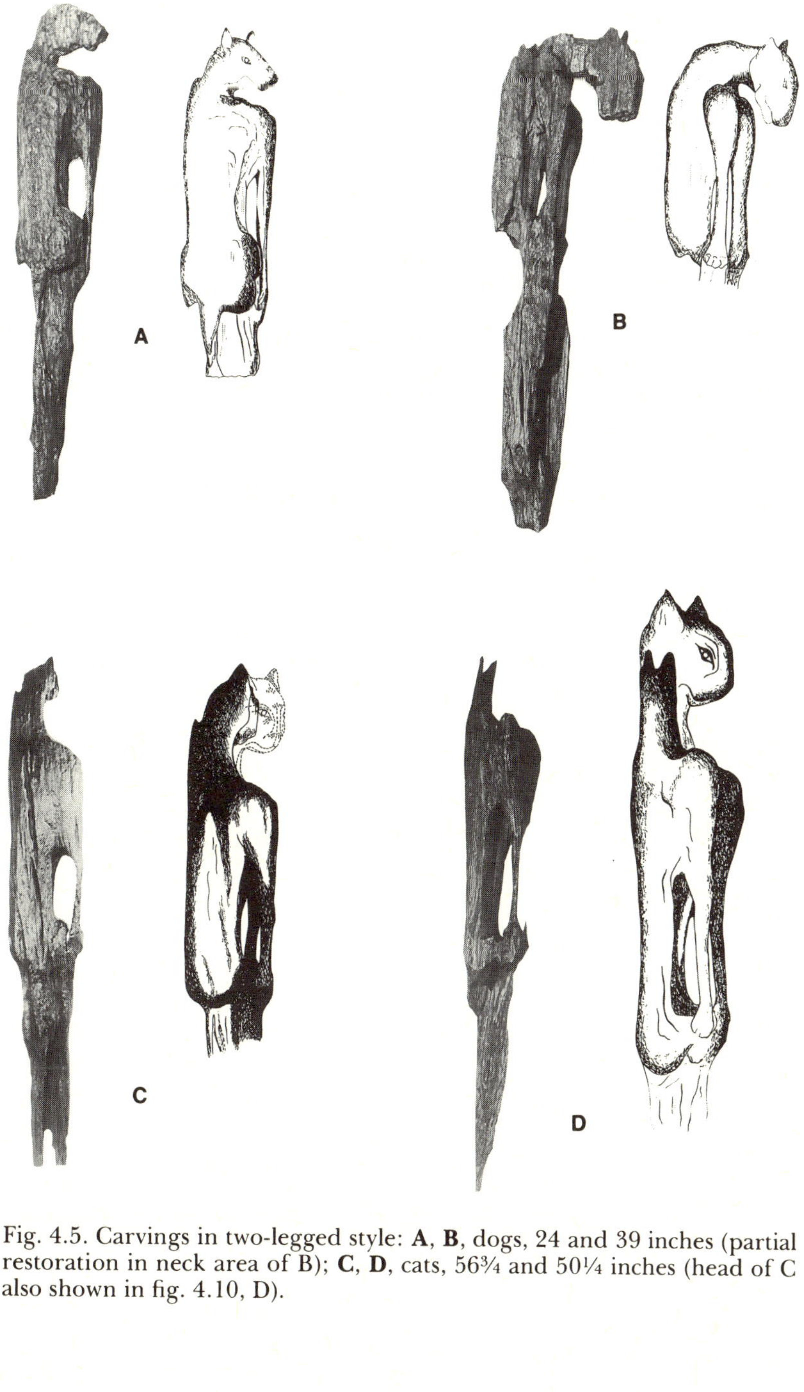

Fig. 4.5. Carvings in two-legged style: **A**, **B**, dogs, 24 and 39 inches (partial restoration in neck area of B); **C**, **D**, cats, 56¾ and 50¼ inches (head of C also shown in fig. 4.10, D).

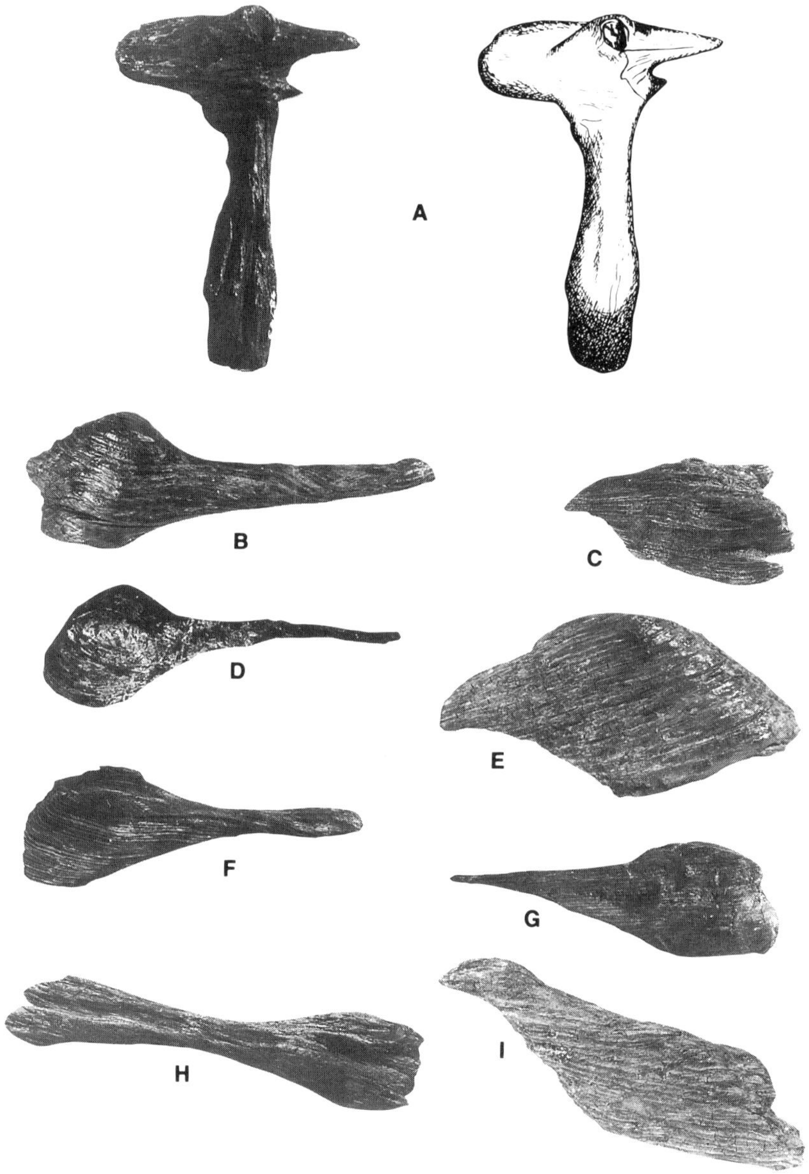

Fig. 4.6. Bird heads, probably from tenoned or miscellaneous style specimens: **A**, "Woody Woodpecker," tenon or plug base, 7¼ inches; **B**, wood duck, 11 inches; **C**, owl, 4¾ inches; **D**, ibis, 9¼ inches; **E**, eagle, 7¼ inches; **F**, spoonbill, 7¼ inches; **G**, heron, 6¾ inches; **H**, spoonbill, 8¾ inches; **I**, unknown bird, 8¾ inches.

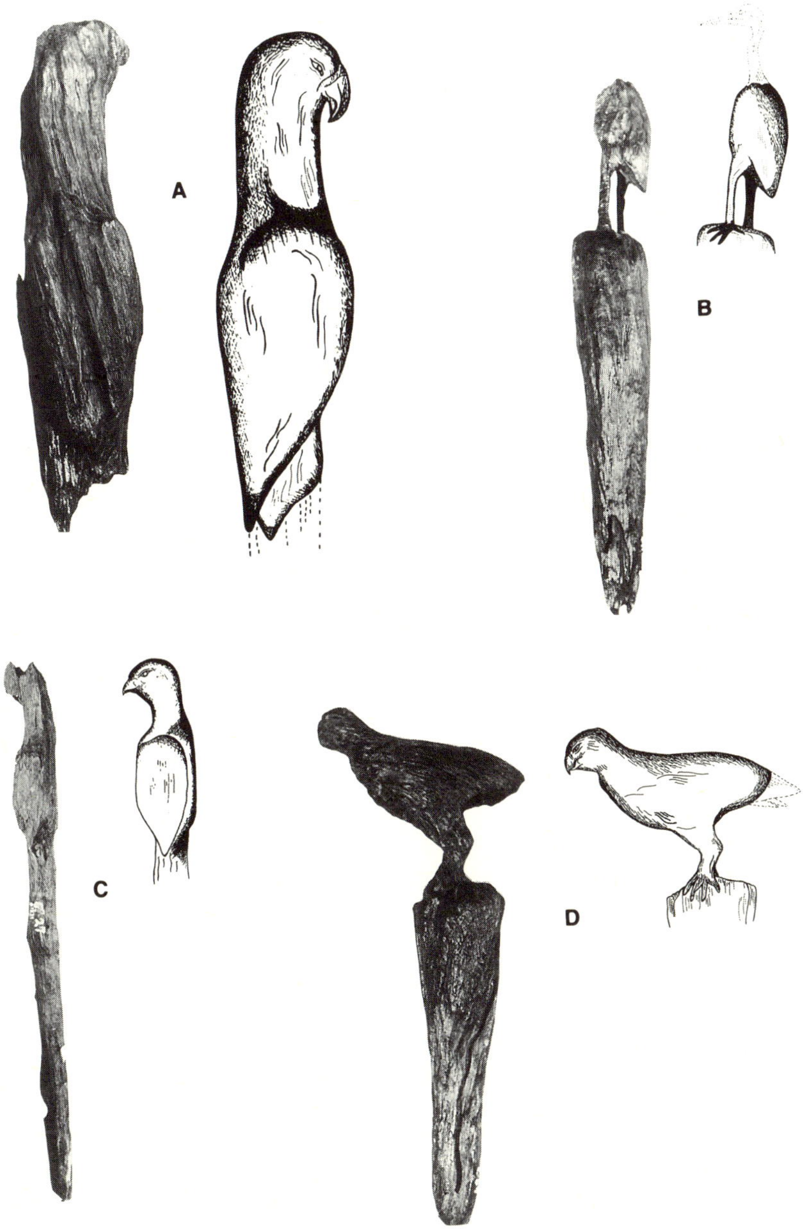

Fig. 4.7. Tenoned and unclassified style bird carvings: **A**, osprey, 19 inches (unclassified); **B**, egret, 29½ inches (tenoned); **C**, raptorial bird, 50¼ inches (unclassified); **D**, hawk, 22 inches (tenoned).

field for the 10 poles recognized, all located at the north end of the deposit. These fragments, with one or both ends missing, were 6 to 7 feet long except for one that was 15 feet. Except for the last, the lengths of the poles are compatible with base lengths for one-piece types.

One group of carvings, all shown in figure 4.9, appears to have been made with the large conoidal bases illustrated in figure 4.8. These, and one other somewhat battered specimen in the collection, are 30 to 36 inches long and up to 12 inches in diameter. The carvings—ducks, long-legged water birds, and a hawk or eagle—are in the same size range as the carvings with more reasonably sized tenons. Obviously, the outsized conical bases were made for some special application. They may have been worked into the center of inverted root masses from the fair-sized trees that were used in platform construction. In this environment, several species of oaks grow mats of surface and near-surface roots. When the trees blow down or fall into the creek from erosion, the exposed mat has a nearly flat underside, as much as 10 or 15 feet across. At least two of these were used in platform construction; one, at the north end of the platform, was charred by the same fire that charred the large bear and other wood specimens and calcined some human bone, demonstrating that the root mass was inverted at the time of the fire.

Besides the several carvings of the tenon variant discussed, waterbird heads in figure 4.3, A and B, and figure 4.6, B, D, F, and G, probably belong in this class. There are a few other poorly preserved heads that may also belong here.

Why one set of figures was made in a tenon and socket style, hence portable, is unanswered. These figures and the poles for them were clustered at the north end of the platform. Possibly this positioning is related in some way to the fact that almost all remains of children found were in this northern end of the platform. (The late Audrey Sublett, physical anthropologist from Florida Atlantic University, carried out an in situ analysis of the charnel pond's human remains.) Portability also suggests part-time use elsewhere, such as in a temple.

Miscellaneous

Several carved birds do not fall readily into any of the styles listed, and they are tagged unclassifiable in figure 4.7, A and C. They are not described further here.

Five carved wooden specimens are completely unlike any of those described but are clearly not utilitarian objects. All of them came from

Fig. 4.8. Tenons and sockets: **A**, **B**, large tenons, 41 and 48 inches; **C**, **D**, squared timbers with mortise (socket) interiors, 26¾ and 24½ inches; **E**, portion of squared timber, 19¼ inches.

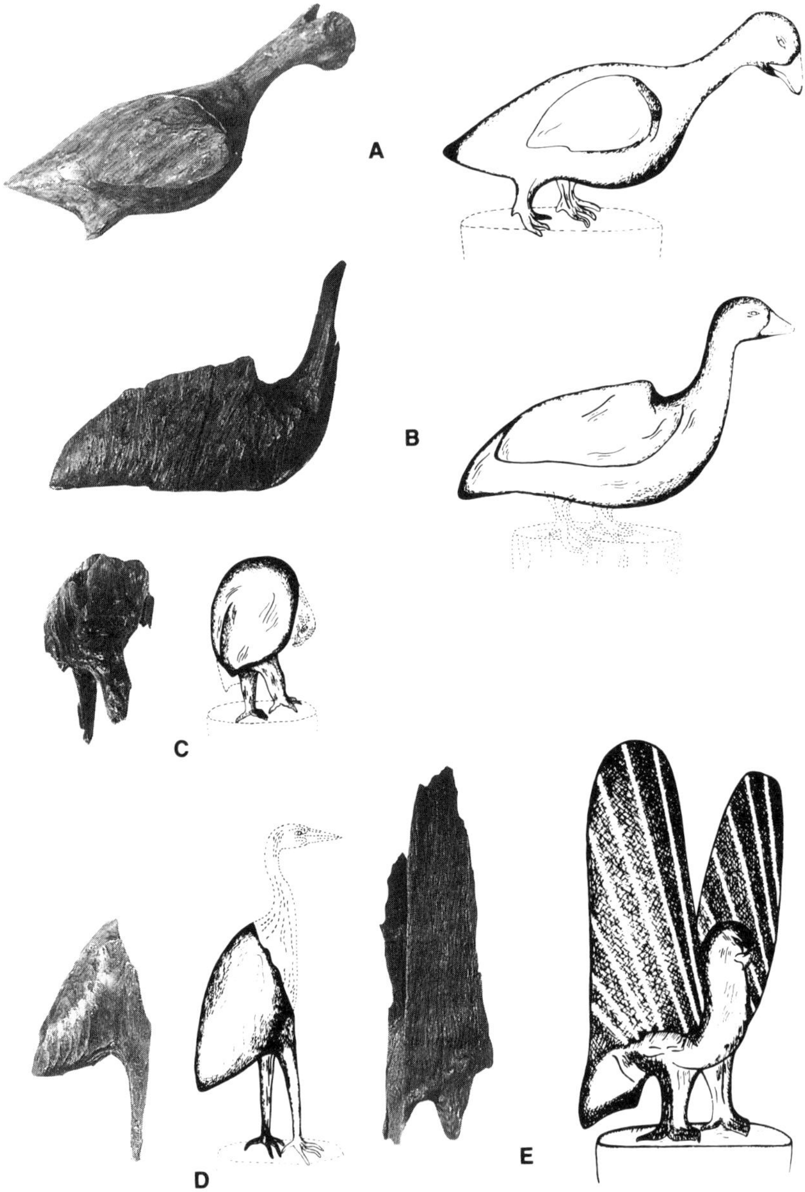

Fig. 4.9. Carved birds with large tenon mounts: **A**, duck, 15¾ inches long; **B**, duck, 16¾ inches; **C**, bird, 11½ inches; **D**, heron, 6½ inches; **E**, eagle with white pigment stripes, 22¼ inches.

the northern part of the deposit, the area otherwise characterized by the tenoned specimens and child remains.

One of these five specimens is a beautifully carved otter (fig. 4.10, B). Nearly identical to a much more poorly preserved one from the Belle Glade site (Willey 1949b: pl. 13, I), it is a realistic specimen, using, as the Belle Glade specimen does, natural twists in the wood to help portray a suggestion of the sinuous motion of an otter. The otter is clearly holding something in its mouth, but preservation of detail is not good enough to identify it. Near the middle of the side opposite that photographed, a handle 1¼ inches in diameter has been carved, standing out at an abrupt angle from the body. The grain runs at right angles to the body of the otter, across the handle, showing that the original piece of wood from which the otter was made was much thicker. The handle, a short rod 4 inches long that slants back toward the tail, has a clean break across the grain at its end. Its original length could have been much greater. If not a handle, the rod might have served to mount the otter on something with a socket. Another wood fragment (fig. 4.10, A) seems also to be the remains of an otter.

A pair of wooden deer antlers (fig. 4.3, G), one complete, the other with a tine broken off, are even more ambiguous than the otter's handle. The bases are neatly finished, so they did not break off from a complete wooden deer head. They could have been part of a composite carving, or they could have been made to attach to a headdress. The oddity here is that there were great numbers of real deer antlers available, many having been found in deposits in the pond.

Another specimen meant for use as part of something else is "Woody Woodpecker" (fig. 4.6, A). The junction of the limb and tree trunk as well as one knot were used to produce this character and to give it strength. The base is definitely shaped, rounded and slightly tapered, to form a plug or tenon for insertion into a socket.

The last of the miscellaneous specimens, a running panther (fig. 4.10, C), seems to be just that, a carving in full round, made from an oddly grained piece of wood, of a panther moving at high speed. There are no features of any kind that seem meant for attachment.

Utilitarian carvings

There are only three, possibly four, objects in this category. One expects that more would have been thrown into the water with the midden material from Mound A and thus have been preserved. But if ob-

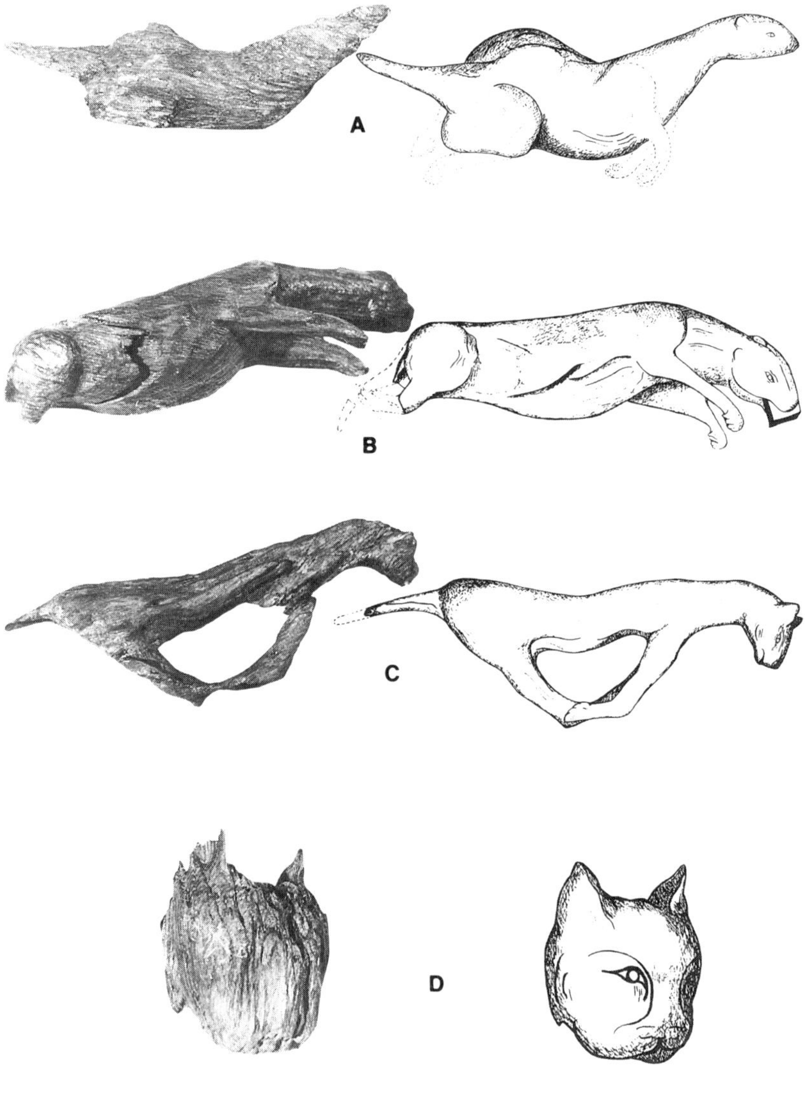

Fig. 4.10. Miscellaneous style carvings: **A**, **B**, otters, 15¾ and 15¼ inches long; **C**, running panther, 15½ inches; **D**, cat head (shown on body in fig. 4.5, C), 4 inches between ear tips.

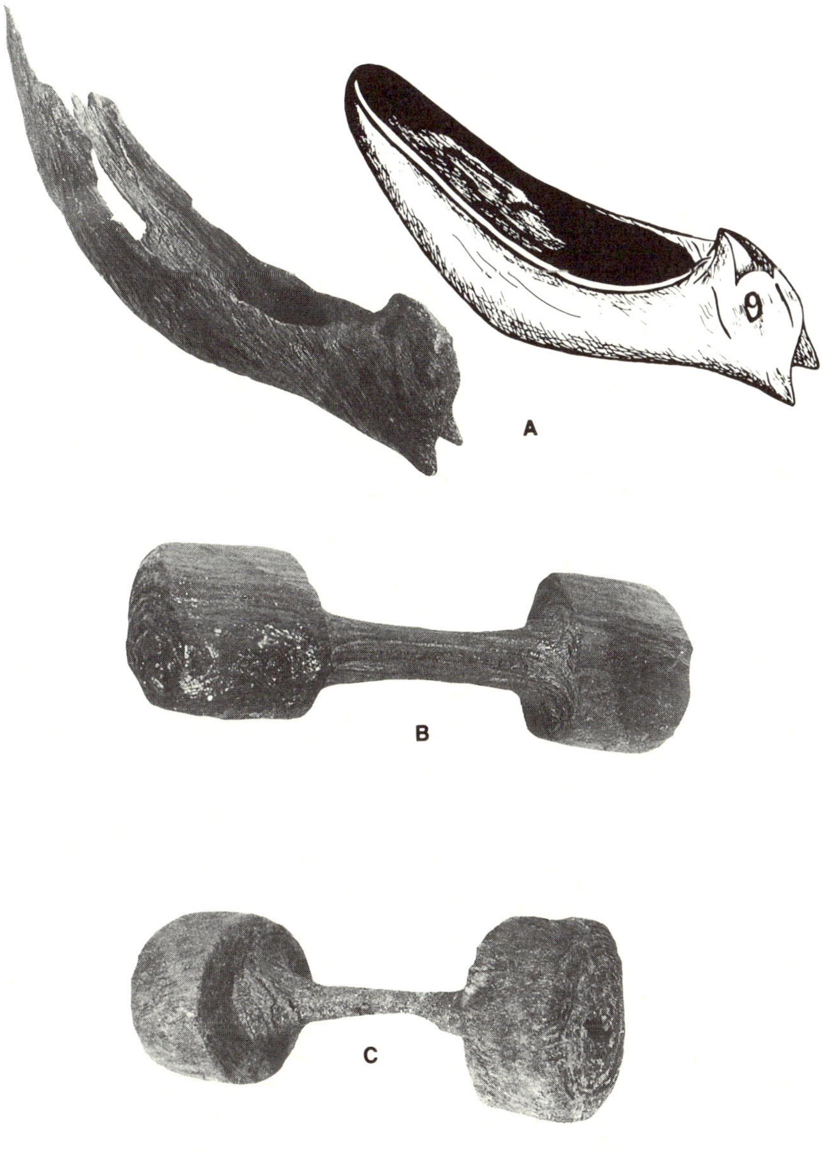

Fig. 4.11. Utilitarian wooden objects: **A**, bowl with owl head, 9¾ inches; **B**, **C**, pestles carved from lignum vitae, 10¾ and 9¾ inches.

jects were thrown in, they must have floated, drifted into weeds at the water's edge, and rotted in the normal way.

Double-ended pestles

Two double-ended pestles (fig. 4.11, B and C) were found, both at the southwest end of the pond. Their preservation can be attributed in some part to their fabrication from lignum vitae, one of the hardest and most durable woods known, so heavy that it sinks. It is native to South Florida and the Florida Keys. Sharks' tooth cutting and scraping marks are visible on the pestles. A virtually identical specimen came from the Belle Glade site (Willey 1949b: pl. 13, G).

Elongate bowl with owl head

Only one such object was recovered (fig. 4.11, A). The bowl, well made, is carved from pine, and it has thin sides.

Mortar fragment

One probably flat-base, cylindrical mortar fragment, 3½ inches in diameter, came from the pond. The remaining height is about 3 inches. The object could also be the remains of an oddly charred and rotted pine fence post. It was found near the surface of the pond in a wash deposit that covered the big bear at the south end of the pond.

Summary

Most of the carved wooden specimens found were parts of the wooden structure built in the artificial pond. Others, particularly the tenoned specimens, could have been in some sense structural parts of the platform, or they served some other functions on it. The total structure, approximately reconstructed (fig. 9.14) with the incomplete data we have, served as a charnel platform, a repository for the dead of the community and part of a ceremonial complex that included a low platform mound, a densely occupied living area, a large oval pit, and a low earthen wall enclosing the platforms, the pond, and some additional space.

I do not see, in carving style or function, any real resemblance or relationship to the wooden objects from Key Marco, but I think that the choice of creatures represented and their apparent use do have similarities to other prehistoric North American Indian art. We can compare style and motifs with others that existed at the same time.

5

Historic Period Artifacts

An amateur organization calling itself "The Florida Archaeological Society" secured from Lykes Brothers, Inc., in 1961 permission to "survey" the Fort Center site. It became apparent, after some time, that the survey involved extensive digging in the large mound, and permission to work at the site and to have access to it was canceled. Steps were taken to recover artifacts in the possession of the society, and, some time later, I was asked to survey and evaluate the site.

On my first visit, the top of Mound B appeared to have been shelled by a battery of 105-mm howitzers. The soil was churned, and craters 4 to 5 feet deep could be seen over the entire top half of the mound. Scattered sherds, handmade nails, and fragments of human bone could be seen. Obviously the digging, both horizontal and vertical, had had no system of control imposed. It was improbable that there was any dependable record of associations. Careful study of a copy of a report made available by a member of the society suggests that some of the group were at least well intentioned, if misguided. Others, according to a number of eyewitnesses, were simply hunting treasure.

The collection of artifacts recovered from the society has been made available for study by Lykes Bros., Inc., who keep it safely locked up. Several visits, the last with Roy Craven of the University of Florida, who photographed every specimen in black and white and in color, enabled me to produce the descriptions that follow.

It is apparent that the metal specimens were made from metal of Spanish origin, reworked in most cases into Indian forms. Some objects in Indian form have been cast, and some of the smoothing was done with coarse files, suggesting certainly that Spaniards, captive or not, were following Indian directions as they melted and cast silver objects. A few artifacts retain their original, but not Florida Indian, forms.

Symbol badges

Three symbol badges, representative of a widespread class in South Florida, are illustrated in figure 5.1, A (front) and B (back). I regard the design on the front as an Olmec style jaguar wearing a headdress with a four-direction symbol (Sears 1977b: 9). Michael Coe concurs, but neither of us can explain its occurrence at this place or time. John Griffin (1946) has suggested that it is a spider. The design on the back of all three, scratched so lightly as to be barely visible on one, has vertical bars quartered with crescent moons. This design occurs on other badges known in South Florida, and it is reminiscent of a European coat of arms more than anything else.

The three objects differ slightly in design and execution and in the fact that one lacks a perforation for suspension. All three, $3\frac{1}{4}$, $3\frac{1}{8}$, and $3\frac{5}{8}$ inches in maximum vertical dimension, are larger than others known, which are all much closer to 2 inches. Those from Fort Center are also heavier than others. They were made from heavy slabs of silver, $\frac{1}{16}$ inch thick, suggesting cutting from an available slab. Most of the other silver specimens are made from thin hammered silver.

Perforated disc-shaped ornaments with central button

Thirty-eight perforated disc-shaped ornaments with central button were recovered from Mound B. All have large central perforations and are made of gold, silver, or copper (fig. 5.2), and they are undecorated. The central section of each is usually depressed. The main part of the body is elevated on a gentle curve from the rim to the midpoint of a line to center, then curves downward to the central depression. Each had a button of wood or leather covered with metal fitted over the perforation. A thong or cord coming from the back of the ornament, through the central perforation, the button loop, and then back out through the central perforation, held the ornament in place. The back of one of the buttons is shown (fig. 5.2, M).

These ornaments are clearly related to many Mississippian period copper "ear" ornaments. Mississippian peoples also used objects, such

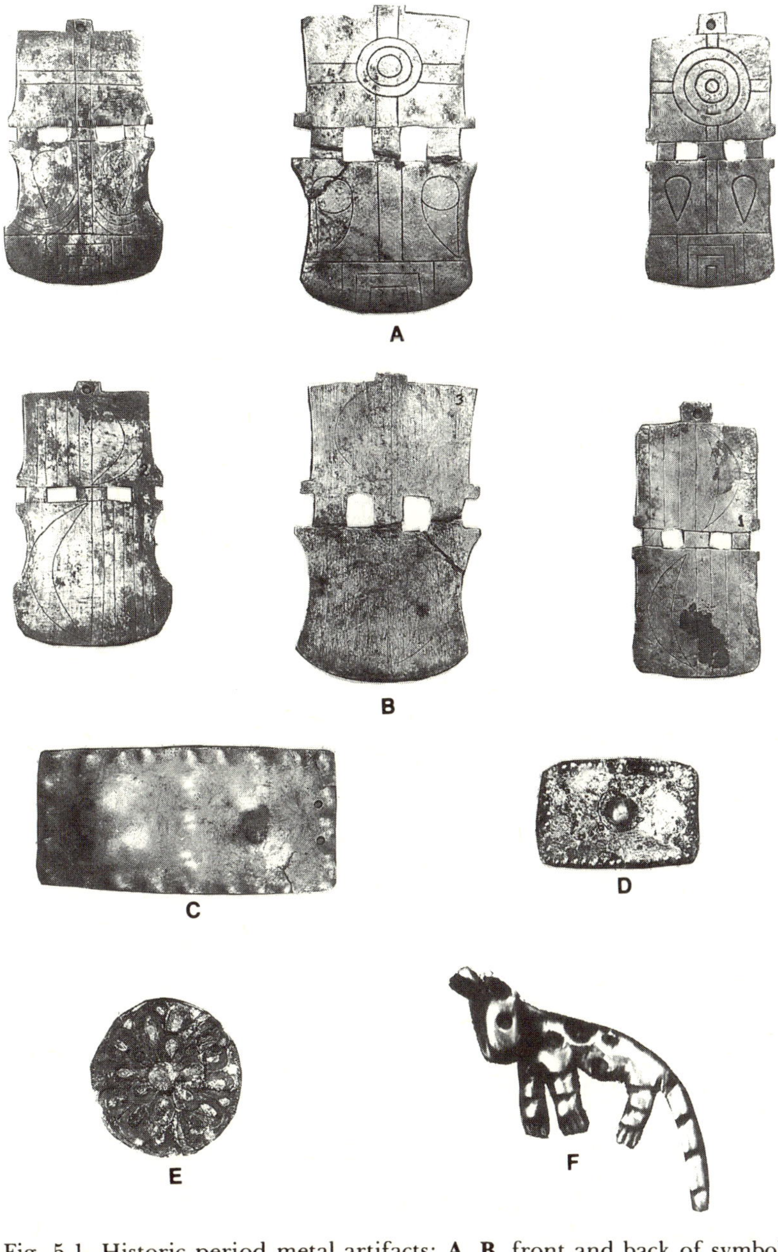

Fig. 5.1. Historic period metal artifacts: **A**, **B**, front and back of symbol badges; **C**, **D**, rectangular silver plates; **E**, composite disc; **F**, gold jaguar; all described in text.

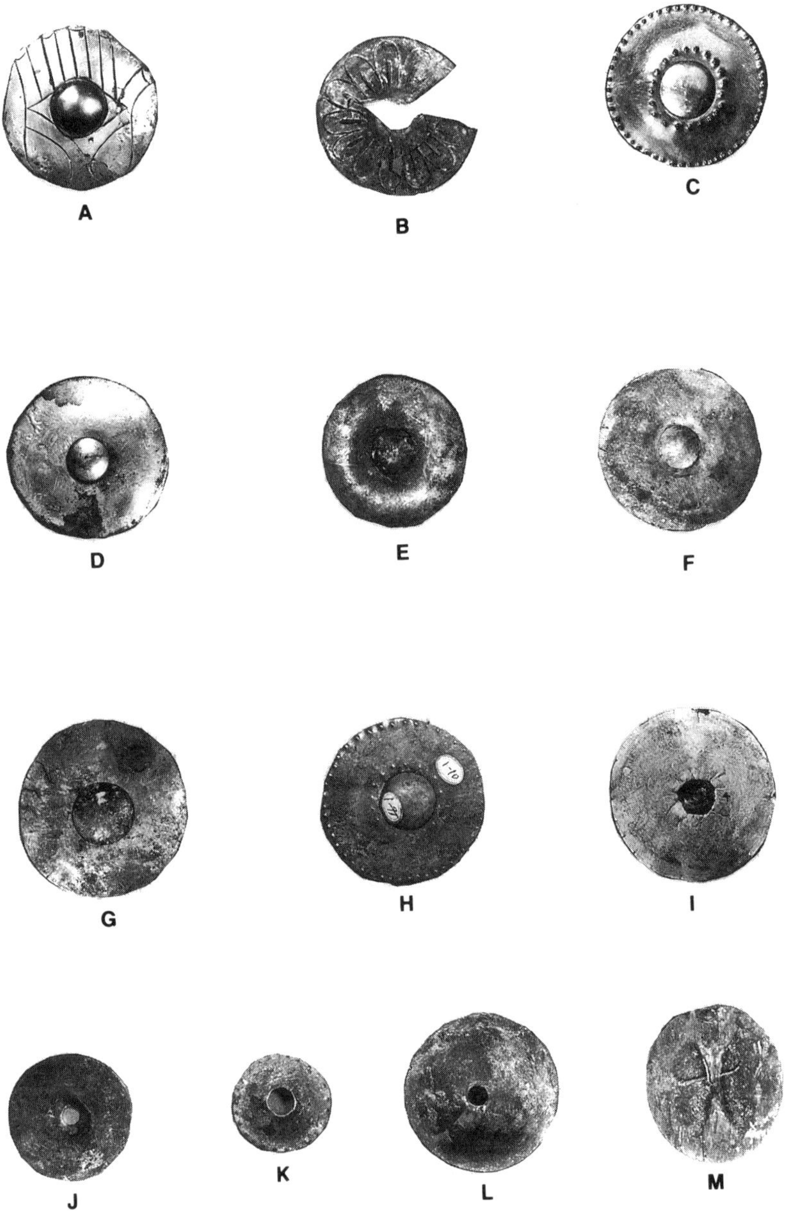

Fig. 5.2. Historic period metal disc-shaped ornaments.

Table 5.1. Metal discs

Method of manufacture	Gold	Silver	Copper	Total
Hammered	4	9	12	25
Cast	—	6	—	6
Uncertain manufacturing	—	5	2[a]	7
Total	4	20	14	38

a. These two were possibly plated with other metal.

as perforated pearls, on the outside of a smaller central perforation to secure the complete ornament.

These discs range from 1¼ to 3¾ inches in diameter; most of them are between 2½ and 3 inches. All of them are circular except one, which has a flange. In table 5.1 the discs are listed by method of manufacture, either cast or hammered, and by metal used. A gold and a silver specimen made by hammering are shown (fig. 5.2, I and G, respectively), as are two silver, cast discs (figure 5.2, E and F).

I cannot be certain of the association of any of the recovered buttons with any particular disc. Not only had all of the buttons been excavated before I saw them, but most of them had been cleaned and some polished. A few specimens had the same number placed on disc and button by a society member, and several had been glued together after cleaning and polishing.

As far as can be told, most of the buttons were made of wood, although some could have been made from thick leather. The covering metal was always thin and neatly applied and showed no obvious hammer marks.

Most of the copper buttons were heavily corroded. On a few pieces, only the green stain remains. There appears to have been a tendency, when assembling an ornament, to use metals of contrasting colors, for example, a silver disc with a copper button, and the reverse.

Embossed, perforated, and engraved discs

In addition to the 38 undecorated discs, there are 7 other specimens, all either cast or hammered and made of silver or gold, which had been decorated in some fashion.

One gold disc (fig. 5.2, C) has small perforations encircling both the rim and the central area. Two silver specimens are embossed around the edge and one silver disc around both the outer edge and the central area (fig. 5.2, H). One silver-plated disc has an incised circle inside the rim on the reverse side.

Two silver discs are incised. One, which was broken (fig. 5.2, B), has an incised floral design. The object is thick and heavy with casting, and file marks are evident on the reverse. The other (fig. 5.2, A) is engraved with a hand and eye motif. It is also heavy and was almost certainly cast, but cloth glued on the back makes examination difficult. The accompanying button is copper covered.

Conchas

Ten flattened conical conchas were recovered, two of silver, one of gold, and seven that seem to be gilded brass or alloy. They appear to be, or to be copies of, ornaments used on belts, horse trappings, and similar leather objects in the Spanish tradition (fig. 5.2, K and L). Sizes range from 1⅞ to 2⅞ inches in diameter; height is nearly ½ inch. Three of the gilded conchas have bosses around the edge and one has perforations. Central perforations appear to be proportionately a little larger than those in the discs.

At least one of the two silver conchas seems to be made in the same way as the hammered silver discs. The others, gold or gilded, are products of a different manufacturing technique, one which produced objects with uniform thickness and surfaces.

The gilded objects are completely European in origin, and they may not have come from the site at all. Corrosion is surprisingly minimal, even where gilding is absent. The silver specimens, and possibly the gold one, are probably of local manufacture.

Jaguar

An appealing little cast gold animal (fig. 5.1, F), 1⅝ inches long from tail tip to ears, is apparently a jaguar. It is, I believe, of South American Indian workmanship. The style appears to be pre-Columbian. Presumably, its appeal to Spaniards and Indians alike saved it from the melting pot.

Miscellaneous metal objects

A number of other silver, copper, or gold objects also apparently come from Mound B. They include various rectangular plates (both silver and copper), sharks' teeth effigies, gorgets, and plates. A unique composite disc and several fragments of gold complete the inventory of metal objects.

Rectangular silver plates

Two silver plates are both embossed. The smaller specimen, 1⅝ inches long, has a central boss surrounded by incised lines. Incised "rays" extend out to the four corners, and tiny bosses, impressed from the rear, extend around the edge (fig. 5.1, D). The second, larger specimen is 4⅝ inches across and has both two large central bosses and small edge bosses (fig. 5.1, C).

Copper plates

Two fragmentary copper plates were recovered. One appears to be similar to the larger silver rectangular plate described. The other retains only a line of small bosses along one end.

Some of these plates and several of the discs resemble those from the Grant Mound in Florida (Goggin 1952b: pl. 9). This resemblance may suggest the route for derivation of Mississippian influence.

Heavy silver objects

Two heavy silver objects are clearly in the form of sharks' teeth, perforated for suspension. They are over ⅛ inch thick, and the larger is 2⅝ inches long. There are file and cut marks on the back of the larger specimen.

Two elongated rectangles, each with two holes for suspension at one end and with rounded corners, probably should be called gorgets. The larger is 7⅛ inches long. Both show signs of casting and smoothing on the back.

Blade-shaped objects

There are two blade-shaped objects. The larger is copper, 10¼ inches long, with traces of embossed diagonal lines from the edge to the middle. The other specimen, plain, is silver.

Composite disc

The details of an elaborate composite disc are shown in figure 5.1, E. The disc appears to be made of wood. The reverse side is covered by a backing glued on by a society member. The design was incised, with symmetrical areas heavily excised, and it was then heavily coated with red pigment. The applied teardrop and oval pieces are copper. The disc is a unique specimen.

Fragments of gold

Some tiny gold objects, apparently found together, may have come from a single composite ornament. The pieces are thin and are square or rectangular in shape. The largest are about ⅛ inch in maximum dimension.

Beads

Since a number of society members presumably had beads from other sites in their private collections, there is more doubt about the associations of the beads than about most of the Mound B historic materials.

A few beads, such as the wooden, melon-shaped ones, are unique. Tiny shell beads, about the size and shape of white wampum from the eastern seaboard, were found in strings on cords of fine, untwisted fiber. We found a short string on an eroded dump pile left behind by the society. There is no copper stain, which makes it difficult to account for the preservation of the fiber. Lack of deep copper staining makes one wonder also about the wooden beads.

About 25 glass beads were examined; the exact number of the glass seed beads is difficult to ascertain because they have become fused. Other beads of shell, metal, or wood were found. Beads are listed in table 5.2.

Miscellaneous

The only other artifact included in the materials looted from Mound B is a quartz crystal plummet. It is similar to one recovered from the charnel pond.

Summary

Unfortunately, most collections comparable to the historic materials that were taken from the top of Mound B have also been dug up by pot hunters and are found in private collections and local museums. The top of almost every Belle Glade culture house or ceremonial mound has been pitted in the search for treasure, and an unfortunate amount has been found. One recent episode that almost produced criminal charges resulted in the information that the person had had three pairs of the symbol badges at one time.

Such looting has not produced records of associations, and even locations are dubious. One exception is the collection from the Good-

Table 5.2. Beads

Description	Number	Size
Glass		
Large chevron	1	
Large twisted chevron	1	
Large tubular		1/8–3/16 inch thick; 1/4–1 inch long
Blue	2	
Green	1	
Large spherical		
Blue	2	
Green	2	
Clear	2	
Large ovoid		1/2–3/4 inch in diameter; 1 inch long
Green	1	
Clear	1	
Seed		
Green, blue, and white	12+	
Other		
Shell, seed	4 strings; 10–20 per string	
Silver, round and oval	4	
Gold, rolled from thin sheet	2	
Wood, melon, dumbbell-shaped, some with slight copper stain	3–4 each	3/8–3/4 inch in diameter

now mound (Griffin and Smith 1948), north of Lake Okeechobee on the Kissimmee River, a site characterized by Belle Glade pottery. In the collection is a symbol badge like the three from Fort Center, although smaller and thinner. Also associated with burials were some beads similar to those from Fort Center and one or two similar metal ornaments.

Well to the north and west of Fort Center, from the Thomas Mound near Tampa Bay (Bullen 1952: fig. 4), the WPA excavated collections that include a silver symbol badge and a silver plate with a large central boss like the Fort Center specimen (fig. 5.1, C). There are also beads and other historic objects. A silver disc and odd ornaments from the Picnic Mound (Bullen 1952: fig. 22) are similar to Fort Center specimens, as is the gold disc with central button from the Buck Island Mound (Bullen 1952: fig. 24).

6

Other Nonceramic Artifacts

Karl T. Steinen

THE nonceramic artifacts from Fort Center were analyzed in two stages over a ten-year period. Those from the complex of Mounds A and B and the pond were analyzed at Florida Atlantic University in 1970–71 and those from the remainder of the site at West Georgia College in 1980–81.

The earlier analysis, conducted before a chronology for the site had been fully developed, was an attempt to reconstruct the tool kit of the inhabitants of the mound-pond complex. A series of artifact classes was established and interpreted as tool types. Conclusions of that exercise have been detailed elsewhere (Steinen 1971). The report here draws extensively on that earlier work for the description of artifacts.

In the second analysis artifacts from areas of the site other than the mound-pond complex were classified in the established categories. When that step was completed, all the artifacts were sorted by provenience into the four time periods that were developed by seriation of the ceramics from the site (see chapter 7), a process that allowed the materials to be sorted by time and space dimensions. Control of the spatial and temporal variables permitted the recognition of differences in artifact distribution thought to result from differential use of different areas of the site.

In the first analysis, all materials were sorted into five categories: lithics, bone, sharks' teeth, shell, and metal. After this preliminary sorting, the items in each category were placed into morphologically similar groups. Then each item was inspected under a variable power stereo microscope to detect any striation or wear patterns that could be attributed to the use of the artifact. Items within each morphological category that demonstrated similar use-wear characteristics were grouped. In most instances, these groupings were assigned names that corresponded to their reconstructed use, such as bone fid, shark-tooth knife, shell and stone abrader.

There has been no experiment to reproduce and use the defined tool types. The tool categories were defined through a deductive and comparative process based on observations. After these deductive inferences were drawn and hypothetical categories established, the categories were confirmed by comparing them to modern tools. Thus, a bone fid had a form and set of use-wear patterns similar to those of modern fids.

The description and discussion here are divided into several sections. The first has detailed descriptions of the artifacts from the mound-pond complex (sharks' teeth, lithic artifacts, stone and shell plummets, other shell tools, and marked bone, antler, and turtle shell). A single galena hemi-cone, recovered from Mound A, is the only metal item (other than the historic period items described in chapter 5) that was recovered from the charnel complex (fig. 6.1, M). The morphology and use-wear indicators are described as well as the deduced uses. In another section interpretation of these identifiable artifact complexes is followed by a discussion of the tool complexes from the whole site. In the final section we place the nonceramic technology of the Fort Center site in cultural perspective.

Sharks' teeth, mound-pond complex

We analyzed 197 sharks' teeth, divided into eight morphological categories, and set up a ninth category consisting of 14 broken, unanalyzable fragments.

Uniformity of wear-modification patterns became apparent upon initial observation. In some cases it was difficult to determine if a tooth had been used as a tool or not. Evidence of use consisted of cusp wear and breakage; battering of the tip; chipping of enamel on the tip, mesial and distal surfaces (mesial, toward mouth front, distal, toward back of the mouth); and striations. Blunting or removal of the gumline cusps, perforations, and notching and breakage of root tips indicated hafting. Teeth without any of these characteristics were classed as not used.

Particular attention was given to wear patterns and mode of hafting. If these could be established, the manner of use could be more accurately determined. When it was observable, the manner of hafting showed a uniform pattern within each of the separate categories to be described. Most evidence of hafting consisted of obvious blunting of the sharp areas of the teeth adjacent to the gumline as well as occasional perforations. Hafting perforations were drilled from both sides and were tapered toward the middle.

Category I

Teeth in Category I (79 examples; fig. 6.1, A), identified as *Galeocerdo cuvieri* or tiger shark, exhibit a fairly uniform wear pattern consisting of both mesial and distal wear of the cusps in the tip area. Although bilateral wear is present in most cases, it is generally heavier mesially. The manner in which the occlusal (biting) surface is affected is also patterned, with rounding most prevalent. However, the more heavily abraded specimens have a beveled form; the mesial edge is more worn than the distal. Chips are commonly missing from the buccal (toward cheek) and lingual (toward tongue) sides of the occlusal area. A pattern of striations is evident. Grooves barely penetrating the surface of the enamel occur in a mesial-distal plane. Angular and random striation patterns were also observed but are not as prevalent as the parallel pattern.

Evidence for hafting of sharks' teeth is common. Perforations, notching, and blunting or removal of gumline enamel of the tooth demonstrate this process. These modifications of the enamel reflect the hafting process because they appear to be produced by pressure on the tooth from the binding that held the tooth in the handle. No indications were found of a glue or cement (cf. Martin, Quimby, and Collier 1947:395) or of the grinding of the tooth roots (cf. Willey 1949b:45).

The evidence suggests two possible methods of hafting. In one, the tooth was placed in a groove at the end of a horizontal handle. This groove was deep enough to accept the roots of the tooth, which were lashed on using the gumline enamel and perforations. Such a tool would be used primarily with a pushing motion and secondarily with a pulling motion, thus accounting for the wear and striation patterns mentioned, particularly the beveling of the mesial surface.

A second possibility is that the tooth was lashed to a short vertical handle (for an example from Key Marco, see Willey 1949b: pl. 15). The manner of use would be much the same as that in the first method.

The use of these teeth in composite tools such as swords (Willey

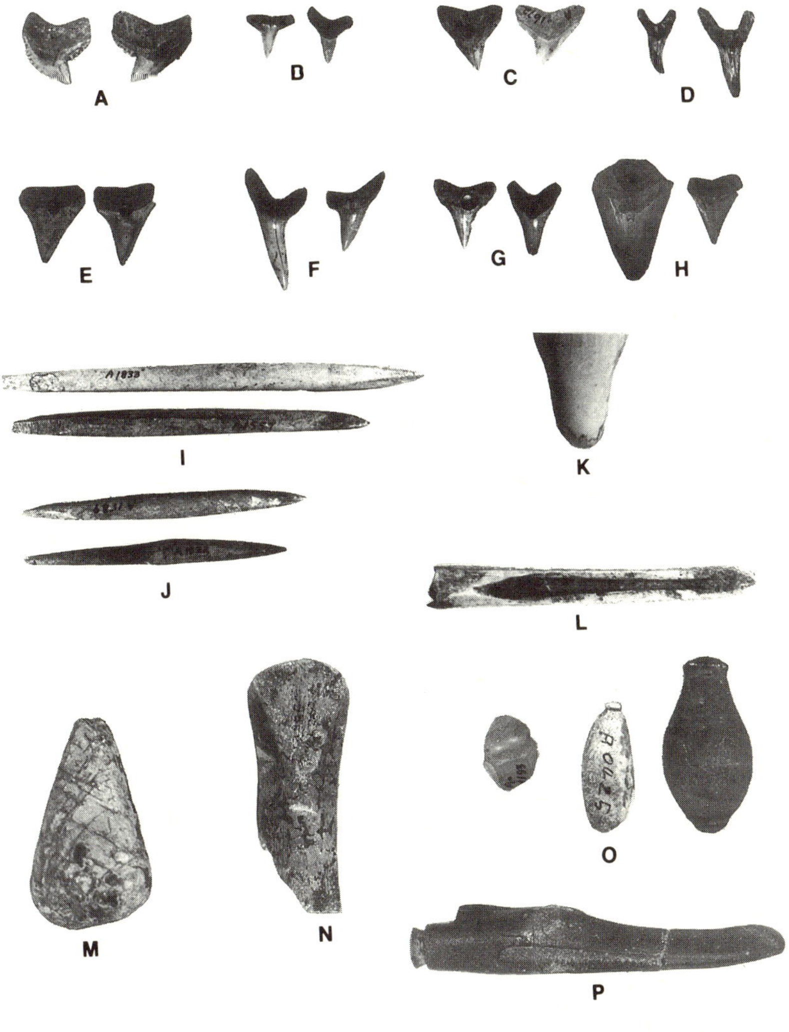

Fig. 6.1. Selected shark tooth tools (by category), bone implements, plummets, and stone artifacts: **A**, shark teeth (I); **B**, shark teeth (II); **C**, shark teeth (III); **D**, shark teeth (IV); **E**, shark teeth (V); **F**, shark teeth (VI); **G**, shark teeth (VIII); **H**, shark teeth (VII); **I**, bone fids (Category I); **J**, bone fids (Category II); **K**, close-up of Category II shark tooth showing edge wear; **L**, bone dagger (Category IV); **M**, galena hemi-cone; **N**, bone adze socket; **O**, plummets (left to right, quartz, shell, granite); **P**, duck effigy plummet; **A–G**, **I–K**, **M**, **N**, Mound A; **H**, **L**, **P**, pond; **O**, both Mound A and pond.

1949b:45; Martin, Quimby, and Collier 1947:395–96), sickles, harpoons, and fishhooks is possible, but the wear patterns do not support this supposition. Use of multiple teeth in hypothetical tools is possible as well as practical.

Category II

Category II teeth (43 examples; fig. 6.1, B, K), numerically second most important in the collection, have been identified as *Negaprion brevirostris* or lemon shark. However, this type may in fact include two species, since 32 of the specimens show serrated distal and mesial edges and 11 no serrations. But aside from these differences, the teeth are morphologically the same. The 11 without serrations have uneven, thin mesial and distal edges, perhaps indicating a purposeful, functional removal of the cusps.

The wear pattern is predominantly bilateral with, generally, a slightly heavier use of one side. In 10 instances the occlusal tips are battered and broken. The remaining 33 teeth range from possibly unused, through moderate cusp wear, to the absence of cusps due to wear. Striation patterns are at best difficult to detect and usually nonexistent. Of the 13 cases that show striations, 6 are in a mesial-distal direction angled from the tip to the gumline, 3 have horizontal mesial-distal striations, and 2 have undifferentiated striations going at all angles. One tooth shows vertical striations, and another shows angled mesial-distal parallel striations around the tip and horizontal mesial-distal markings on the main portion of the enamel.

Indications of hafting are generally the same as for Category I teeth, but there are no instances of drilled teeth. Nineteen specimens show blunting of the gumline cusps, 15 have at least part of the gumline enamel removed, 8 show no modifications, and one tooth has bilateral notching accompanied by cusp blunting.

The 11 nonserrated teeth have extremely thin edges, and close inspection shows them to have undulating surfaces and small chips removed from the lingual and buccal sides. This feature could indicate a deliberate attempt to remove the cusps and produce sharp edges.

The hafting process suggested would be similar to that reconstructed for Category I, that is, that the tooth was lashed into a groove in a stick or handle. But the extreme morphological differences between the two categories makes the same use impossible. Category I teeth are asymmetrical in shape and show a corresponding asymmetrical wear pattern. Category II teeth are symmetrical but do not show a symmetrical wear pattern. The shape of the tooth and subsequent tool makes use as a rasp or any similar tool unlikely. The best assumption seems to be use as a cutting or graving tool. The point that exists naturally would be ideal for detailed work on small items. The 11 teeth with the possible ground edges and secondary enamel chippage from use could have been employed either as woodworking tools or as small knives.

Category III

Identified as *Hemipristis serra* (no common name), Category III teeth (20 examples; fig. 6.1, C) have many similarities to those in Category I. Both types are asymmetrical and have much the same wear, striation, and hafting patterns. One difference that should be noted is the inclusion of an angled mesial-distal striation pattern on three Category III examples. They are generally smaller and less robust than their Category I counterparts. The use and hafting interpretations presented for Category I evidently are also true for these.

Category IV

Identified as sand shark (*Odontaspis tarus*), Category IV teeth (7 examples; fig. 6.1, D) represent only 3.6 percent of the sample. These are nonserrated and symmetrical with marked eversion. Five examples have either broken or highly battered occlusal surfaces; the remaining two show only minor tip wear. No striation pattern was detected. In four cases slight blunting of the gumline enamel was noted, possibly an indication of hafting.

A proposed use for this category is difficult to formulate, since the sample is too small and the key indicators of use are not present. We can safely say only that the activity in which they were used placed great stress on the tip of the tooth, demonstrated by the traumatic loss of the tip end and much of the enamel on most of the teeth.

Category V

Identified as *Carcharodon carcharias*, white shark, the specimens of Category V teeth (7 examples; fig. 6.1, E) comprise less than 4 percent of the sample. Six of the seven are perforated; four specimens exhibit distal-mesial horizontal striations, one has distal-mesial angled striations, one has a broken tip and partially absent enamel, and the seventh has no observable striation patterns. The wear pattern generally follows that established for Category I; it is confined to the occlusal region, bilateral, and slightly more pronounced on one side.

Aside from the six perforated teeth, only three of the seven teeth show indications of hafting. One has a blunted gumline and is not perforated. The other two have a grayish-white patina and exhibit corner notching.

As in Categories I and III, evidence indicates that these teeth were incorporated in tools that were used to work dense materials. The motion used was back and forth, and the cusps of the tooth probably aided in the use of the tool.

Category VI

Category VI, identified as *Isurus oxyrinchus* (6 examples; fig. 6.1, F), an extinct variety of mako shark, bears similarities to Categories II and IV. The teeth are asymmetrical, and they have narrow enamel sections and no cusps. The wear pattern is centered around the occlusal area. Striation patterns are not uniform in nature and range from small, horizontal mesial-distal markings, restricted to the mesial and distal edges, to random striations. Edges tend to have small chips of enamel missing, and the tip of one specimen showed beveling. As in Categories II and IV, it appears that these teeth were used in a manner that placed a premium on a sharp edge for slicing and detail work rather than on a large cusped surface with a sawlike effect.

Category VII

Category VII teeth, identified as *Carchardon meglodon* (6 examples; fig. 6.1, H), a fossil shark with no common name, are much larger than the other varieties; the two almost complete examples are 40 mm and 70 mm in length. Two complete teeth were recovered from the charnel house pond and four fragmented examples from Mound A. One of the teeth from the pond shows either a perforation or the beginning of one; another is corner-notched, and a third has a broken root tip. No striation patterns can be seen on any of the six teeth. The generally battered condition of all the specimens could be the product of their Pleistocene origin and not an indication of use.

It is difficult to suggest a use for these teeth. The specimens from the pond are probably burial inclusions (suggesting that they were sociotechnic); Mound A specimens could be either sociotechnic or technomic (Binford 1962) in origin. Battering on the teeth could indicate use, but it probably does not since it is similar to that present on the same kinds of teeth recovered from Pleistocene fossil deposits.

Category VIII

Category VIII teeth (6 examples; fig. 6.1, G) are from an unidentified species and combine morphological features of the categories already described. Specimens are symmetrical and fairly narrow, with highly tapered enamel sections and serration. Three of the teeth have either broken or heavily chipped occlusal surfaces, and two are perforated. Striation patterns range from horizontal mesial-distal to angled mesial-distal to random, but in all cases these patterns are restricted to the tip area. Hafting evidence consists of the usual gumline enamel cusp blunting and perforations.

Lithic artifacts, mound-pond complex

The lithic materials were divided into three morphological-classificatory categories: chipped stone, ground stone, and raw materials–debris. These are described by class and provenience within the mound-pond charnel complex.

Chipped stone

Forty-six chipped stone artifacts were recovered, 17 from Mound A, 11 from the pond, and 18 from Mound B. Raw materials for the chipped stone implements have been identified as probably from chert deposits in northern sections of Florida.

Chipped stone artifacts from each provenience unit were examined separately. Analysis showed indications of blunting, striation patterns, secondary chipping, and condition of the tip and basal treatment, as well as the morphology of the artifact. These aspects of the tools seemed to be the best indicators of use. Frison (1968:49) writes: "Stone tools become dull rather quickly, but are surprisingly effective if they are kept sharp and if their structural limitations are kept in mind. Tools such as side scrapers, knives, and drills are continually modified throughout their lifetime of functional utility, and at the time when they were discarded or became non-functional, they were usually quite different than when originally completed." He states, in effect, that through differential use and resharpening, culturally determined types may lose their group integrity. Thus, the history of use of an artifact makes a difference in its classification.

Mound A

By far the most common of the 17 stone artifacts from Mound A (fig. 6.2, A), 8 of 17, is a broad, stemmed "projectile point" with weak shoulders that resembles Bullen's (1968:23) Alachua point type. Examination fails to reveal many striation patterns on the chert surfaces. Wear, indicated by blunting and smoothing of the edges, is restricted to the upper one-third to one-half of the blades. There is no indica-

Fig. 6.2. Stone tools from the Mounds A–B/pond complex: **A**, **C–E**, chipped stone points or knives; **B**, celt; **F**, limestone grinding stone; **G**, grooved hone; **H**, petrified wood object; **A**, **F**, **G**, Mound A; **B–D**, pond; **E**, **H**, Mound B.

tion of resharpening. Edge-dulling in the area just above the shoulders is thought to be an indication of hafting. The blunting of the upper edges was accompanied by the removal of small chips in a steplike pattern. One example shows extensive polishing on the edges. All irregularities of the edge have been removed and a polished surface left. Only faint striations are discernible, and these are parallel to the edges of the blade, indicating a back-and-forth sawing motion. Armistead (1949:47) found a similar point at the Safety Harbor site, Pinellas County, Florida, and thought it to be a saw used in the modification of conch shells.

Another possibility is that these points were used as wood saws. However, Witthoft (1967) thinks that flint blades make poor wood saws: "Used against wood, it [the flint blade] serves as a fire saw, evolving heat from friction through intense rubbing" (p. 386). Whatever its function, it is obvious that this flint tool was used until it could no longer cut and was then discarded.

Two of the Alachua-like implements have broken distal ends. Both either were used after breaking or were being reworked. One shows step-like chips removed from the broken distal end, which may indicate use as an end scraper. The other shows repointing after breakage and polishing on one edge. The remaining nine chipped stone specimens do not cluster into a group as do the others. One, a broad-bladed, side-notched tool with a ground base and a beveled tang, is made from brown chert and still has some limestone attached to the surface of the tang. There are a few small chips removed from the edge, and one side is slightly sharper than the other. The second is a broad, contracting-stemmed, asymmetrical tool of the Marion type (Bullen 1968:29). The stem has been deliberately resharpened on both the sides and the base. Small chips have been removed intermittently from the edges, probably through use, and the broken point shows grinding and polishing.

Another contracting-stemmed artifact is of the Levy type (Bullen 1968:29). It is made of white chert; base and edges show deliberate thinning and sharpening, but there was no indication of use. Another stemmed artifact is made from mottled brown chert and has a snapped-off base. No special edge modifications can be seen on the small specimen, which is only 33 mm in length.

One small (33 by 11 by 4 mm), serrated, triangular artifact, made from a tan-colored chert, is unifacially worked and has a beveled base. The absence of blunting and serrations near the base indicates that it was hafted. The tip has been broken, and, aside from the serrations, no special edge modifications can be noted.

Another specimen is either an asymmetrically made blade or a blank that was being worked into one of the large stemmed points. It is made from brown chert, and the chipping along the edges shows only minor use. The area around the tip lacks the sharpness of the remainder of the edges.

A long, thin, triangular "point" with basal notching is of the Hernando type (Bullen 1968:23) but has dulled or polished edges near the base, indicating that it was hafted. The edges of the point are moderately sharp, and no striations are discernible.

The remaining two chipped stone artifacts are pieces of broken blades made from mottled gray-white chert. The larger of the two, the distal end of a fairly large blade with irregular and sharp edges, is bifacially worked, and one of the edges is extremely beveled. The other is small and is possibly a broken stem. Both edges are dull, and the blade has an oval cross section.

Mound B

Mound B produced 18 chipped stone artifacts (fig. 6.2, E), which show little difference stylistically from those from Mound A. The main exception is the absence of the large, wide-bladed, stemmed artifacts found on Mound A. The Mound B chipped stone artifacts tend to be smaller, thinner, and more delicately made. Seven triangular "points" are represented in the sample; three are Pinellas points, three Hernando points, and one highly reminiscent of an unserrated Tallahassee point (Bullen 1968:12, 23, 45).

The three Pinellas points range in length from 66 to 45 mm and in width from 24 to 17 mm. They are made from a gray-white chert, a translucent tan chert, and a reddish granular chert. Two have bifacially beveled bases, and the third had a broken base. Tip wear is minimal, and no striation patterns can be detected. Two points show dulled edges.

Two of the basally notched Hernando points were probably hafted, as evidenced by the dulling of the edges near the base. None of their blades exhibits polishing of the edges, and both show only intermittent minor edge chipping. The third example is a broken base.

A fourth triangular point is unclassified. It is long (74 mm) and narrow (12 mm) and has a deeply concave base. The edges to either side of the base are duller than the distal end, indicating that this implement was hafted at one time. The sharp edges are regular in outline, as is the base. No striations are evident, and the point is intact.

Three small, pinkish-red, irregularly shaped, stemmed points were also found. Bearing only slight resemblance to each other, they are set off from the other Mound B implements by their color and small size. Blades are equilateral triangles, and the stems contract. One has a broken tip and another an intentionally manufactured blunt tip. Striation patterns are not detected. The bases have been all bifacially beveled.

Two broken lanceolate blades were recovered. Both are finely chipped along the edges and base and show no striation patterns or dulling.

The remaining seven artifacts have no attributes in common and are described separately.

A contracting-stemmed point with convex edges and an irregular tip, which is asymmetrical in form, has intermittent step-like chips removed through use. Its shape is reminiscent of the Perkiomen Broad defined by Ritchie (1961:42–43) and a point of the Dallas component of Hiwassee Island (Lewis and Kneberg 1946: pl. 66b). The stem of the point, which is made from a mottled light tan material, is narrow and contracting.

A crudely made point with a small, rounded stem was made from a flake of translucent gray-brown chert, which has been worked just enough to give it edges and a stem. The edges are not sharp but are blunt and rounded, indicating a sawing motion. The stem is relatively thick and is not bifacially beveled, unlike nearly all of the other tools. Striation patterns are not discernible.

A Hillsborough point made from a multicolored chert, well made and with delicate chipping, resembles others of this type. The only observable bluntness on this specimen is near the tip, where impurities in the chert prevented delicate chipping. As with most of the other stemmed points, the stem is bifacially beveled and sharp.

A broken, broad-bladed, stemmed point has the end flaked away and the stem snapped off. It is made of reddish-brown chert and is bifacially worked; the blade edges are quite sharp and have only a few obvious use-wear chips.

A stemmed, triangular-bladed point has the stem and tip snapped off. The point is made of a reddish-brown chert and is bifacially worked. Blade edges are sharp with only a few obvious use-wear chips toward the stem.

A thick (12 mm) fragment of a poorly shaped point was made from a granular chert. The irregularity of the edges and the materials from which it was made make identification of any use-wear patterns impossible.

A large, triangular-shaped blade, poorly made, is thick (11 mm) and shows no evidence of ever having been used as a tool. Probably it is a blank that was in the process of being worked.

Charnel house pond

The 13 chipped stone points from the charnel house pond came from four contexts, two clusters and two finds of single specimens. The first cluster of points consists of a tip broken from a point and two intact, large, broad-bladed and stemmed points made from green-gray or blue and white banded chert. The two complete points (fig. 6.2, D) are of interest because of their size and fineness of manufacture. One has a contracting stem and delicate chipping, with finely formed stem and base. The distinctive aspect of the green and white point is the edge treatment: Both edges and the adjacent faces of the body have been ground smooth. Faint striations were observable parallel to the blade edges. The tip is battered and was probably as smooth and uniform as the remainder of the blade before it was altered, since the polishing effect is abruptly terminated where the battering begins. The only possible deduction is that this polishing effect was deliberately produced and was not caused through use.

The second broad-based implement, made from a gray-blue banded chert, has a parallel-sided, round-based stem, delicate chipping, and no indication of edge polishing. It is much longer than the other specimen (125 mm compared to 91 mm) and shows no indication of having been used as a tool.

The third specimen from this cache is a broken point of brown and white chert. Its dull tip appears blunted through use.

The second cache of points has eight specimens, of which seven are stemmed and the eighth a piece of worked chert with no specific shape (fig. 6.2, C). One example from this group is made from a gray and white chert and has a broken corner. The contracting stem is well formed and the chipping delicate. Edges are not polished but do show some nicks that are not the result of the manufacturing process.

Another specimen from this cache is similar in shape to the first specimen described from Mound A. It is much longer (62 mm compared to 46 mm) and thicker (14 mm compared to 8 mm), and the stem differs by flaring at the base. Edges are irregular in shape and dull near the point. The latter trait is a product of manufacturing, not use. There are small step-like chip scars near the tip on one side, which may be indicative of use.

A third specimen is very crudely reworked chert flake. A short, thick stem has been formed by chipping, but no other modifications were noted. Another specimen is an unclassified point with shallow flaking on its surface and a deep notch on the side.

The fifth is a Culbreath point made from brownish chert and having a straight stem, finely made barbs, and definite secondary chipping to form the edges. The base is deliberately wedge shaped and the tip is broken; edges show no indication of having been used. Another stemmed point, made from a mottled gray chert, has a deliberately shaped edge and stem like the Culbreath point.

The seventh artifact from the second cache is made from brown chert. Its stem and lower section are finished, but the tip appears not to have been worked. The last one is an orange-brown chert point with a bifacially beveled stem, one broken barb, and edges that show some intermittent chip scars.

Two serrated triangular points were recovered apart from the two caches. One, made from a grayish-brown chert, is bifacially worked. The base is bifacially beveled, and the serrations directly adjacent to it have been blunted—an indication of hafting. No striations are present. The second serrated point, made from a dark brown chert, has a sharp base and blunted adjacent serrations. In contrast to the other serrated triangular points from the mound-pond complex, which all have straight sides, this specimen has concave sides.

Ground stone from the mound-pond complex

The ground stone artifacts from the charnel area consisted of celts, hones, and grinding stones. Plummets are described in a separate section.

Celt

A single ground-stone celt was recovered from the bone and wood layer of the charnel house pond (fig. 6.2, B). Made from a fine-grained granite, a material alien to the Okeechobee Basin, the celt shows small nicks on the bit and extra polishing adjacent to it. The flattened butt is roughened, either the remnant of the pecking process or from having been struck by a hard object after manufacture.

Hones

There were 12 examples of hones recovered from Mound A. These specimens show special shaping, through either use or manufacture, that enables them to sharpen the cutting edge of tools. This shaping is manifested in two ways. The first kind, similar to modern hones, are long and fit into the hand and were used with a rotary or pushing motion (fig. 6.2, G). The second type have short, beveled edges formed on medium-to-small stones (locally available sandy limestone) and a use motion resembling that of the long variety.

Wear patterns are difficult to detect. The sandy limestone specimens show no striation patterns because of the deterioration of the rock while in the ground. The surface softened, and the marks were lost either while it was in the midden or during the postexcavation processing.

Grinding stones

Grinding stones are defined as slab-like stones that appear to have been abraded over large portions of their surface (fig. 6.2, F). Thirty-five specimens have smooth or ground surfaces, and in each case this modification seems to be the only one present. These stones range from large limestone slabs (200 × 200 mm) to small, highly worn examples with only small patches of recognizable ground surfaces.

Four specimens have marked grooves on their surfaces. Three of them are made of dark gray sandy limestone, and none of the four displays any purposeful shaping. The grooving is the only apparent modification to these stones. Although no striation patterns can be detected, it is possible that these stones were used in the manufacture of the shell and bone tools. Their coarse surfaces would be ideal for the grinding involved in shaping bits of conch tools and long, slender bone splinters.

Of particular interest in this collection is the largest sandy limestone slab. It was found in association with a lime deposit that Sears feels was used in the preparation of maize. While it is recognized that physical association in a midden does not necessarily mean that the artifacts or features are functionally correlated, this association may be meaningful. This particular grinding stone is concave and may well have been used for grinding maize or other vegetable products.

Chert and quartz debitage

A large quantity of quartz and chert debris was recovered and is described for Mounds A and B and the pond.

Mound A

Most of the quartz and chert materials from Mound A are chert nodules and chips. Of the 270 specimens recovered, 189 are unworked chips and 81 nodules. The debitage is mostly the gray, white, and brown chert from which the majority of the Mound A points were made. Nodules, although water-rolled, are still covered with a limestone patina. One cache of 52 nodules and 15 percussion chips was recovered. Of the 52 nodules, 31 are broken or chipped in such a way as to expose their interiors, suggesting that the knappers were concerned with the nature of the chert. Only 11 chips and a nodule differ from the usual range of colors; these include one fragment of quartz and one piece of quartzite.

The number of unworked chert nodules from Mound A suggests that the mound was a locus for chipping activities. Unfortunately, no concentrations of chips or partially completed points were recovered to support this conclusion. The absence of raw materials corresponding to the finished points from Mound B and the charnel house pond may be explained by any of three alternatives: the points were made on Mound A but in a different and unexcavated place; the points were brought to the area already made; the points were manufactured on Mound B. This last possibility is supported by the materials recovered from Mound B.

Mound B

As expected from the ceremonial nature of Mound B, few materials were recovered. Thirty-two unworked chips and one broken chert nodule were recovered along with a shaped, flat-sided, oblique spheroid made from partially mineralized wood (fig. 6.2, H), a smoothed piece of sandstone, and two pieces of limonite with hematite. Pieces of the same type of material from which the oblique spheroid object was manufactured were recovered from Mound A and from under the human bone layer of the charnel pond, indicating perhaps that the object was manufactured on Mound A from imported raw materials.

The unworked chips, for the most part, are materials not found on Mound A, including pink, red, and white chert chips and a pink chert blade-like object that was struck from a core. No reworking or use-wear patterns are noted.

The correspondence in color between the chipping debris from Mound B and the points recovered from Mound B and the pond indicates that Mound B was the center of production of most of the points that were recovered from sacred associations.

Charnel house pond

The recovery of lithic materials from the human bone layer of the pond was limited. A few nondiagnostic chips were recovered from the base of the midden as well as 118 limestone, sandstone, and hematite rocks. These were probably in the bone layer purely by accident and represent a mechanical mixture of materials that were transported from Mound A.

Shell and stone plummets, mound-pond complex

Eight stone and 8 shell plummets were recovered from the charnel complex (fig. 6.1, O), 12 from Mound A and 4 from the charnel house pond. Of the Mound A plummets, 5 are of stone and 7 of shell. Of the pond specimens, 3 are stone and one shell. The 16 can be divided into groups on the basis of shape: the *classic teardrop*, with grooves at one or both ends; the *expanded center* variety, with grooves at both ends; a single *duck head* effigy of stone from the pond (fig. 6.1, P). The teardrop and expanded center forms are made from both stone and shell.

The plummets, without exception, are made from stone and shell materials that are alien to the Okeechobee Basin, including granite, crystalline quartz, granodiorite, gneiss, diorite, rhyolite-granite, quartz crystal (one specimen), and conch (*Busycon*) columellas. The most exotic plummets are the duck head effigy and the one of broken quartz crystal. These two differ markedly in both form and materials from the other specimens. Both were recovered from the human bone layer of the charnel house pond.

Other shell artifacts, mound-pond complex

A total of 441 shells, shell tools, and shell fragments was recovered. In addition, the stains of decomposed conch shells and a few partial shells were recorded during the excavation of Mound B.

The shell tools represent one of the largest samples from a single site in the eastern United States. They are divisible roughly into two categories, those made from the lip of the conch and those made from whole conch shells.

Terminology for the classification of shell tools is taken from modern definitions of cutting tools. An ax is a bifacially beveled, grooved, or perforated tool whose cutting edge is set parallel to the haft. A celt is a bifacially beveled cutting tool lacking grooving or perforations, whose cutting edge is set parallel to the haft. An adze is a unifacially beveled cutting tool whose cutting edge is set at right angles to the haft. A gouge is a cutting tool whose cutting edge is curved and hollow.

Blade tools

Sixteen shell adze or celt blades were recovered from Mound A (fig. 6.3, A). Mound B produced no shell celts or adze blades, and only one came from the pond. These blades are all highly weathered, and no use-wear indicators can be observed. The shapes correspond closely to those usually attributed to a tool of this kind: The cutting edge is broad, and the body of the tool tapers to the butt end. In all instances the tools have weathered to such an extent that indicators of bifacial

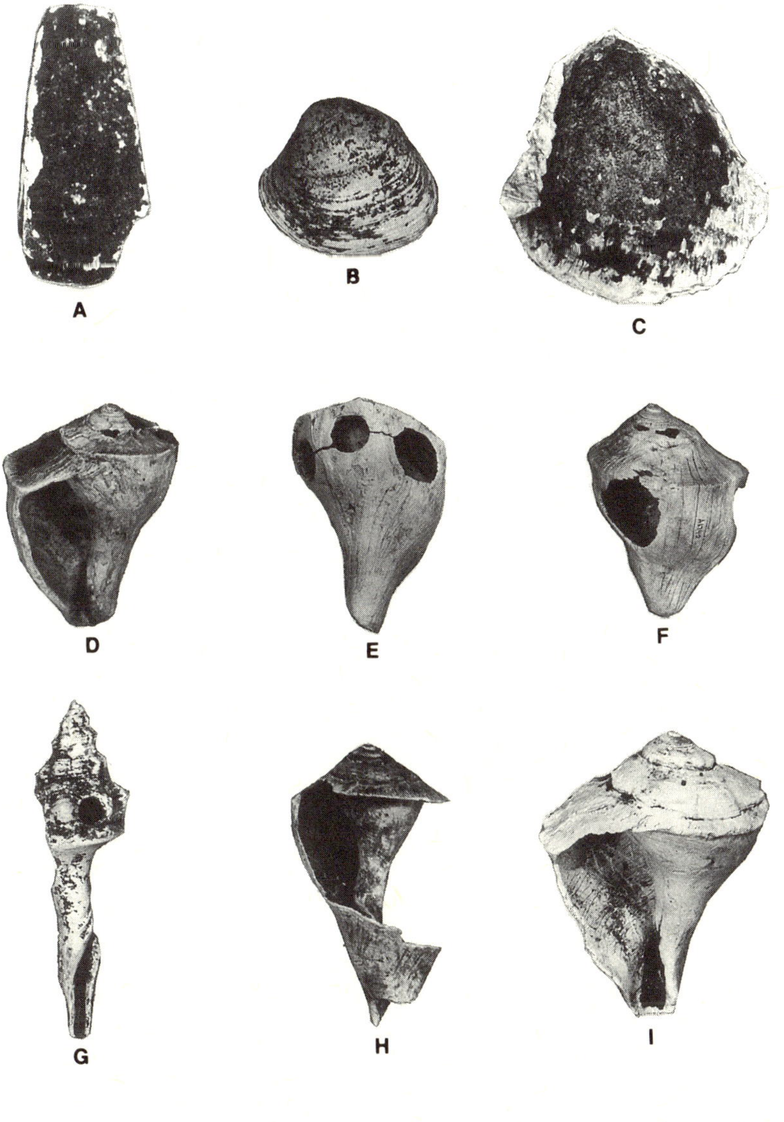

Fig. 6.3. Mound A shell tools: **A**, celt–adze blade; **B**, *Venus* shell; **C**, conch cup; **D**, one-hole conch adze; **E**, three-holed conch adze; **F**, one-holed conch tool showing lip notch and whorl perforation; **G**, *Pleuroploca* gouge; **H**, conch "pick"; **I**, conch gouge.

or unifacial beveling have been obliterated and hafting particulars cannot be determined.

Whole-shell tools

Whole-shell tools were made from *Busycon perversum*, *Pleuroploca gigantea*, and possibly *Strombus gigas* and *Marginella* shells. To be classified as an artifact, the shell or fragment in question had to demonstrate intentional shaping or modification. In the case of the conch shells, grinding, notching, pecked holes, and the removal of the columella indicate modification.

Hafting of a shell was accomplished by wedging a wooden shaft through pecked holes in the whorl of the shell or through a notch in the lip and a hole in the whorl. Further strength for the haft could be obtained by lashing the shell to the handle. Examples of hafted shells were uncovered by Cushing at Key Marco and are illustrated by Willey (1949b: pl. 15c) and Martin, Quimby, and Collier (1947 : 396). Presumably, the Fort Center specimens were similarly hafted for use.

The whole-shell tools are divided into three morphological types, all variations on the same basic theme: adzes and one- and three-holed celts. The differences among these types are in the manner in which the beak and anterior canal were modified and in the angle of the haft. The celts and adzes are characterized by having the beaks of the shells ground at an angle to form a bevel, with little or no modification of the anterior canal. To make gouges, the beak is removed leaving a large, open, sharpened anterior canal. In addition, some conchs have been modified into cups or dippers.

The celts can be further divided into two categories, one-holed (fig. 6.3, D, F) and three-holed (fig. 6.3, E). The differences in the number of holes in the shell wall can represent different methods of hafting. The four one-holed celts recovered from the site were hafted by using the notched lip and a whorl perforation. The beak was then ground so that the bevel was set at right angles to the haft.

For the three-holed tools, Moore (1901 : 384) suggests that two holes were used for the haft and the third served to help to lash the shell to the shaft. Another explanation is that the shell tool was hafted by placing the handle against the notched lip and through a single hole, securing it with a thong passed through the other two perforations of the whorl. If the three-holed tools were hafted in either of these two ways, they would have been celts because the cutting edge was parallel to the haft.

Six gouges were recovered (fig. 6.3, I), two with broken beaks. The four whole specimens are strikingly different. The only example of a tool made from a *Pleuroploca gigantea* shell is a gouge with a narrow bit (fig. 6.3, G). Most of the whorl was removed, and the spiral is perforated in two places. The pecked hafting holes are placed in such a manner as to point the working edge toward the worker.

There is a single two-holed gouge, which also has a notched lip and a well-formed working surface and has had a portion of the body removed. The large size of the working edge and the robustness of the shell indicate that this tool was designed for heavy, large-area work. The single one-holed *Busycon* gouge recovered has a notched lip. As with the *Pleuroploca* specimen, the working edge points toward the worker. There is also a single three- or four-holed *Busycon* gouge; breaking of the whorl in the area of the perforation prevents an accurate determination of the number of holes. Again, these multiple perforations could indicate lashing, multiple hafting angles, or a broken haft.

Three *Busycon* shells were recovered that had part of their whorls removed so that a pointed surface was left. These implements fit the definition of what are generally considered "picks" (fig. 6.3, H). All implements have two pecked holes in their whorls and notched lips indicating that they were hafted.

Other artifacts made from whole shells include two dippers or cups (fig. 6.3, C), eight *Venus mercenaria* shells, all of which were the same side or valve (fig. 6.3, B), and two problematical *Marginella* shell beads. The remainder of the shells recovered are fragments of conch shell, clam shell, or oyster shell.

Bone, antler, and turtle shell, mound-pond complex

Bone, antler, and turtle shell materials are divided into categories mainly on the basis of morphological characteristics and use-wear indicators. Except when indicated, these materials were all recovered from Mound A.

Bone artifacts

Bone tools are divided into six categories.

Category I

Category I tools (fig. 6.1, I) are made from bone splinters that have been made, in cross section, with a round distal end. Each tool can be divided into three sections: distal and proximal ends and the area between them, referred to as the body. Of the 36 examples, 10 are complete, 17 are broken distal ends, and the remaining 9 are body sections with broken distal and proximal ends.

The only evidence of wear is the varying amounts of sheen on the distal ends. No striation patterns can be discerned on any of these ends. Careful examination reveals that the tips are uneven and irregular in nature, a characteristic attributable to manufacturing processes, not wear. If the tips had been worn down through use, they would be sharp and much more regular in form.

The more bone is handled, rubbed, or used, the more sheen or luster it acquires. The foremost example of this is arthritic eburnation where the bones of a joint take on a highly polished ivory look. Complete examples of this tool type show a continuum of use with surfaces ranging from highly polished to rough, the lower end of the scale represented by specimens that do not have a shiny surface.

Proximal ends of the tools demonstrate the use of a uniform manufacturing-hafting technique. Unlike the distal ends, this portion of the implement does not have a finished appearance. It is angular and rough from manufacture and shows distinct parallel cut marks on the flat surfaces. The extreme proximal ends of the implements were shaped to either a point or a wedge, and in a few instances this portion was broken off. In eight of the ten complete examples the proximal end is darker in color than the distal end; this staining may be the result of a hafting process.

There is an abrupt change in the body area, marked by a cessation of cut marks and staining. Breaks in the bone occur in this region, indicating that leverage was applied to these tools and the body was the weakest point of the implement. Use-wear evidence and the position of the breaks are all consistent with the tools' use as fids.

Category II

The 87 specimens in Category II (fig. 6.1, J) have distal ends that are angular in cross section. All are made from bone splinters. Proximal ends are morphologically the same as the proximal ends of the Category I tools. Since there is no way to differentiate the proximal ends of the different categories from each other, all broken examples were arbitrarily placed in this group.

In addition to the differences in cross section, there are two other distinctive differences: This category does not have the full range of "sheen" evident on the Category I fids, and Category I implements, with their round cross sections, avoid using the medullary canal of the bone. Category II tools incorporate the medullary canal and achieve a comparatively flatter profile and possibly greater structural strength.

The tips tend to be longer than those of Category I and show a noticeable lack of abrasion from use.

As with Category I tools, the body between proximal and distal ends is abrupt and marked. The proximal end demonstrates the same flat-sided and beveled or pointed characteristics that Category I implements show, as well as the short parallel cut marks on the flat surfaces.

An examination of the broken proximal ends shows that the break usually occurred at or just distal to the body, indicating that the distal end was subjected to enough pressure to snap it at or just above the body. Again, these tools were probably used as fids.

Category III

Category III bone tools, manufactured from splinters, all have flat cross sections, but the 11 artifacts in this group have few other similarities. Only two examples are complete, and none demonstrates any observable use-wear indicators.

Category IV

There were three examples of Category IV tools, generally referred to as daggers (fig. 6.1, L). Two are complete and one is a tip fragment. The two complete examples are morphologically similar: Both have bilaterally beveled points, exposed medullary cavities, and sockets on the proximal ends. Edges are markedly dull, probably intentionally. Points, while not blunt, cannot accurately be described as sharp. Again, this appears to be intentional. The socket on the proximal end seems to indicate that these "daggers" were hafted.

Category V

Category V is a "catch-all" for materials that do not fit into the other groupings. Two are stingray spines, one broken both distally and proximally, the other only on one end. The more complete example has been worked with a resulting contraction of the body. Both examples have an induced sheen on one side.

One other Mound A tool is a carved long bone with two sockets, one on each end (fig. 6.1, N). It closely resembles adze holders illustrated by Cushing from Key Marco (1897). One socket would have been for a small shell adze blade and the other for the tool handle.

Category VI

Category VI bone artifacts were recovered from the human bone layer of the charnel house pond and are treated separately because of the nature of the deposit. The quantity of materials recovered is not as great as that from Mound A, but there is a distinct difference in the nature of the items.

The worked bone includes one splinter tool with typical parallel cut marks on the proximal ends, one highly polished bird bone, one animal long bone with a drilled hole, two elaborately carved bones that show the remnants of a highly polished surface, and two highly polished pins with expanded carved heads. A highly polished dark brown splinter tool with a reworked surface was also recovered from the pond, the reworking in the nature of beveling. As with the other bone artifacts, no striation patterns can be discerned.

Turtle shell and antler

Artifacts manufactured from turtle shell and antler were very few in number. From the pond only fragments of worked turtle shells were recovered; they had been modified by drilling and rounding the edges. A deer antler was recovered that had an intentional groove made in it along its interior margin.

Interpretation of the mound-pond tool complexes

Sharks' teeth

Shark-teeth tools can be divided into two classes based on morphology and wear patterns. The first, composed of triangular-shaped, asymmetrical, serrated teeth, has wear patterning that is bilateral, with the mesial surface usually showing slightly greater wear. The second is composed of tapering teeth, usually symmetrical in nature, without cusps or having had the cusps ground off. Both classes of teeth were hafted in the same manner, either through the use of perforations and blunted enamel-cusps or just blunted cusps.

Three categories described on the basis of the mound-pond sample (I, II, and III) account for 77 percent of the sharks' teeth recovered (both worked and unworked); the remaining five categories represent only 15 percent. Worked teeth (both classes together) represent over 80 percent of the total sample. These figures suggest a specialized shark-tooth tool kit. Limited variance within the morphological categories and between the two classes tends to support this conclusion. A more generalized tool kit would show greater variations in wear and striation patterns and in tool morphology than those that occur at Fort Center.

Before questions about the use of the shark-teeth tools can be answered, the rest of the material culture at the site must be examined. The extensive bone and wood industries reflect manufacturing processes that can be attributed to the hypothetical shark-tooth tools. The bone splinter tools show fine-line parallel cut marks on their proximal ends, and several of the wood carvings exhibit similar markings. These markings could have only been made by small, sharp cutting tools. Shark-tooth tools would have been ideal for this task of wood and bone carving.

Chipped stone

An interesting pattern is discernible in the chipped stone assemblage. The Mound A point collection can be divided roughly into two major groups: the large, broad-bladed, stemmed, and side-notched specimens; and the smaller and lighter points, the basally notched triangular point (Hernando) and the serrated, triangular specimens.

The Mound B sample is different: The points tend to be smaller and lighter. Any overlap in typology seems to be restricted to the Hernando points. The seven stemmed points from Mound A are not similar to Mound B specimens, and the large, straight-stemmed point so common to Mound A is completely absent in Mound B. The small, pink, stemmed points from Mound B are small for the site and are the only ones made from this color material. Serrated triangular points are absent from Mound B, and refinement of manufacturing technique ranges from crude to delicate.

The pond materials are a combination of the Mounds A and B types. In the same stratigraphic layer in the pond are found large, delicately chipped, polished points and serrated triangular points. These stemmed points are morphologically unique. The pond materials could have come from two sources, burial contexts (representing intentional inclusions) and midden material that was transported from the midden on Mound A. The Mound A midden was stratigraphically below the level from which the two lots of points described were recovered.

Although there is little typological overlap among Mounds A and B and the pond, there is even less overlap in the basic materials from which the chipped stone implements were manufactured. The largest points from the pond are the only ones made from a green and gray banded chert; Mound B has the only representative of pink or red chert; and the pond has the only implements made from orange chert.

This difference in morphology of the points and their materials is significant and suggests that the roles that the three areas played were quite different. The charnel nature of the pond could explain the uniqueness of the chipped stone implements that were recovered from it.

The assemblage of chert artifacts from Mound A consists only partially of projectile points. The large stemmed and side-notched artifacts are probably knives, as indicated by the wear patterns: general dulling and blunting of the edges confined to the upper one-half to one-third of the blade. Dulling of the edges adjacent to the stem is thought to indicate hafting. Wear such as that noted for these implements cannot be attributed to projectile points and most closely matches that found on knives and saws.

The two small, stemmed points, one serrated triangular point and the Hernando point from Mound A, may or may not have been projectiles. Nance (1971:361–66) argues that such small "points" may well be knives if striation patterns are observed. Unfortunately, only one specimen from Mound A demonstrates any striation patterns; this is the highly polished "stemmed knife." These smaller implements did not show any significant use-wear indicators.

The Mound B points are unique at the site. There are no "stemmed knives" like those from Mound A. The artifact inventory of Mound A suggests that the area was the center for the manufacture and maintenance of items like the specialized wood carvings. Absence of the "stemmed knives" from both Mound B and the pond indicates that they were special tools and were not related to charnel activities. Mound B points could have been projectiles, which would indicate that the occupants of Mound B were involved in procurement activities for at least part of the time, or the points could have been some form of sociotechnic item. The unique materials and morphology tend to support the latter interpretation.

The two roughly square, chipped stone "points" from the pond are of special interest. Their fine workmanship, probable large size when intact, and thickness make them unlikely candidates for projectile points. A complete lack of any use-wear evidence suggests that they had a ceremonial use and were not utilitarian.

Analysis of the use-wear indicators on the large stemmed "points" indicates that they were used as knives and were apparently not resharpened when they became dull. The specimens exhibit a wide range of edge treatment, from almost pristine to smooth through abrasion. There are no indications that any of them was sharpened at all, suggesting that the form of the tool was extremely important.

Since any attempt to resharpen them would have modified shape and size to such an extent that they would no longer fit the culturally determined concept of the implement, they would have been discarded when they could no longer be used properly.

The use of the other chipped stone artifacts could not be definitely identified. The materials from Mound B and the pond were likely sociotechnic items and were not used as tools. The smaller implements from Mound A could have functioned as projectile points, although there is no evidence to support this interpretation.

Ground stone

Numerically, the most important stone objects are the grinding and sharpening stones. Made of locally available sandy limestone, the abrasiveness of each was determined by the amount of sand it contained. The large, flat sandy limestone slabs are probably grinding stones for modifying and sharpening the conch shell tools.

A reconstructed grooved hone is illustrated by Semenov (1964: 140–41), who shows them being used to sharpen tools similar to the Category I bone fids. He writes: "Unexpectedly the abrasive instruments wore very slowly, almost imperceptibly. This was evidently due to the fact that almost the whole surface of the rod made contact with the enclosing face of the groove" (p. 141).

Adze and celt blades

To be classified as a tool a piece of broken conch shell had to exhibit worked surfaces from manufacturing or use. As explained by MacLaury (1968:33), mere shape is not sufficient; accidentally broken conch shell can assume the shape of a defined tool.

The amount of curvature of the blade does not seem to be significant; it appears to be a product of the original conch shell.

There was no evidence of hafting techniques for the shell blades. The bone adze socket recovered from the site suggests that at least some of these blades were used in compound tools. Lashing to wood handles, a common technique in tropical areas, is probable.

The blade tools were probably used for woodworking. Their small size indicates that they were used for the shaping of medium-sized wood objects. They would have been useful for work on structural and decorative members of the charnel platform.

Whole-shell tools

The whole-shell tools have been divided into four types: adzes, celts or axes, gouges, and cups or dippers. Usually they are made from whole

Busycon perversum shells that have been modified by grinding the beak and by pecking holes and notches in the whorl and lip. They are hafted by wedging a shaft through the holes or notched lip and against the columella. Further strength can be obtained by lashing through additional holes or removed sections of the spiral.

There is evidence for multiple-angled tools. The three-holed celts can be mounted in two ways: using the notched lip and a whorl hole or using two pecked holes. The choice does not alter the apparent function of the tool but does change the angle of the working surface to the craftsman. The one-holed specimens with a notched lip can be divided into celts and adzes depending upon the orientation of the ground beak to the haft.

Gouges were made from *Busycon perversum* and *Pleuroploca gigantea* shells. The *Busycon* varieties gave the craftsman a moderately wide gouge; the *Pleuroploca* gouge was narrow. The tool type tentatively identified as a "pick" has the whorl of the *Busycon* removed from around the beak, leaving a pointed projection.

These shell tools were all recovered from the Mound A midden. It is possible that they were used in the manufacture of wood objects, especially the wood carvings associated with the charnel platform. They could have been used in all stages of the woodworking process needed to produce both the structural members of the platform and the carvings.

The eight *Venus mercenaria* shells that were recovered may be of some significance; they were all from the same side or valve, evidence that there was some kind of cultural selection in operation. The *Venus* shells recovered by Cushing from Key Marco also demonstrate this one-sidedness. The use of these shells has not been determined.

The large amounts of broken conch shell indicate that the shells were available in large quantities. Because of the great variety of tools and other objects made from their shell, the conchs must have been of great importance to the community as a whole. The other shell remains are both marine and freshwater. The two problematical shell beads show that there was some concern with decoration of the body or dress.

Plummets

Distribution of the plummets is the best indication of their function. No debitage from the manufacture of igneous rock artifacts was recovered from the site. From this it can be concluded that the stone plummets were not manufactured at Fort Center but were imported as finished items. The closest possible source for the stone is the piedmont of Georgia and Alabama. Raw materials would have been available there as would populations to participate in an exchange network.

There are obvious similarities in form between the stone and shell plummets. The teardrop plummet and the expanding-center plummet forms are represented in both shell and stone. Except for the retention of part of the shell whorl on two examples, the similarity of the stone and shell plummets is remarkable.

An exception to this similarity in design is the duck effigy plummet. It has no shell counterpart at the site, but it does bear a close resemblance to a stone plummet from the Indian River area of East Florida (Rouse 1951: pl. 4). With the exception of minor differences around the eye and beak, these two could be considered an identical pair. The single quartz crystal plummet that was recovered, while broken, bears a close resemblance to one recovered from the Belle Glade site by Willey (1949b:36).

Bone

Morphological differences between the Categories I and II bone-splinter tools are not sufficient to warrant designating them as separate types. Differences between these categories and the remaining ones, especially Category IV, are significant. Unfortunately, the lack of wear patterns makes it impossible to classify the remaining categories into functional types.

Categories I and II tools were subjected to use over their entire distal ends. They seem to have been hafted in a handle that served as the female member of a compound tool. They were not used in association with hard or abrasive materials; striation patterns on the surfaces are light, indicating wear from only slightly abrasive material. Lack of heavy wear on the tips supports this deduction. A few show old breaks that had been smoothed over through use, indicating a lot of light wear over a long period. Their use as projectile points is doubtful, and it is difficult to imagine that a point could be used enough to acquire the sheen that these implements have and still remain intact. The same can be said for their use as leister points or gorges. Compound fishhooks are a possibility, but size and sheen make this improbable.

The most probable reconstruction is that Categories I and II implements were part of compound fids used in the production of textiles and basketry. The abrasion of the grass, bast yarn, or basket fibers on the exposed bone during manufacturing would account for the overall sheen and lack of abrasion on the tip. The torsional pressures that would have to be applied to the distal end of a fid to pry apart the warp and weft of the textiles or baskets would account for the breaks at the bodies of the tools.

The bone materials from the pond are rather distinctive in that they have a high gloss, carving, or indications of both, suggesting that great care was used in the production of these objects as grave goods. The amount of time needed to manufacture these implements would be considerable; they are of high quality. Their association with ceremonial activities is without question.

The worked turtle shell fragments from the pond may have been portions of rattles, but this use cannot be positively determined. The deer antlers could have been part of compound headdresses, as has been suggested for other specimens recovered from Hopewellian associations (Dragoo 1964).

Metal

The only metal recovered from the mound-pond complex (other than historic artifacts) was a small galena hemi-cone. It represents the importation of an extremely rare and exotic type of material into the site.

Nonceramic technology by temporal periods

The nonceramic technological complex for Fort Center can be classified by temporal periods. These periods were developed by ceramic seriation and the use of radiocarbon dates (chap. 7). Furthermore, the site can be divided into two distinct types of areas, ceremonial and habitational. The mound-pond complex was ceremonial. Even though Mound A was primarily a living area, it functioned as an adjunct to the ceremonial Mound B and the charnel pond. As such, the total complex functioned as an integrated area. The outlying midden areas and the habitation mounds were "normal" living areas. They did not function directly as part of the complex ceremonial site. This division is clearly demonstrated in the nonceramic technology to be discussed. The various structures (mounds, ponds, middens) are described in chapter 9.

Period I (before 450 B.C.–A.D. 200)

Evidence for the nonceramic technology of the earliest inhabitants of the Fort Center site comes from midden deposits on the western and central portions of the site (see table 6.1). Midden B had a material

Table 6.1. Period I tools

Type	Midden B	Mound 12	Mound 13
Stone	15 flint debris	1 Alachua PP	1 small Alachua-like PP
	1 piece coral		
	4 small flint bifaces		
	1 Hernando PP		
	1 distal end PP		
	24 grams mica		
Bone	1 fragment unclassified worked bone		
Sharks' teeth	1 Category V		
Shell	3 fragments shell		
	1 *Busycon* beak		
	1 *Strombus* celt blade		

PP: projectile point.

culture that relied heavily on imported resources. Of the 27 items that were recovered from dated contexts, 20 are of nonlocal stone, 5 of marine shell, and one a broken Category V sharks' tooth. The only tool fragment made from a local resource is the single fragment of worked bone. Mound 12 and Mound 13 produced only a single Alachua point each, but excavations were limited.

The nature of the artifacts from these areas indicates that the outlying middens were part of the adaptive system of the Fort Center occupants. The stone tools, points, and two unifacially worked flint pieces are implements for such activities. The single sharks' tooth did not show any wear, and its use cannot be determined with certainty. However, like those from the mound-pond complex, this tooth was probably used in the manufacture of bone and wood artifacts.

Period II (ca. A.D. 200–ca. A.D. 600–800)

Period II is represented in two distinct areas of the site, in the mound-pond complex and in Middens A and B, Mound 3, and the University of Florida Mound, all domiciliary areas spatially separated from the ceremonial area. Mound A, technically a habitation area, must be considered functionally different from the other domiciliary areas, because of its proximity to and cultural relationship with the pond and Mound B. Artifacts from these various contexts are listed in table 6.2.

The Period II artifact inventory can be divided into three groups based on function. The first is the adaptive tool kit, which consists of the various projectile points, bone tools, shark-tooth tools, and shell

Table 6.2. Period II tools

Type	Mound A	Mound B	Pond	Midden A	Midden B	Mound 3	University of Florida Mound
Stone	17 abrader fragments 4 hones 1 teardrop plummet 1 Hernando PP 1 serrated Pinellas PP 1 flint uniface 7 pieces porous petrified wood 2 pieces igneous rock	1 broken flint blade 1 Hernando PP 1 untyped stemmed PP 1 PP tip 2 abrader fragments	1 triangular PP 2 Alachua PP 1 Culbreath PP 1 small stemmed PP 1 untyped stemmed PP 1 PP tip 2 large, abraded stemmed PP 4 abrader fragments	71 flint debris 1 untyped PP base 1 PP tip	1 Alachua PP	2 flint debris 1 piece red ochre	1 flint nodule
Bone	18 Category I fids 33 Category II fids 4 Category III implements 2 Category IV implements	1 turtle shell	1 grooved deer antler 1 piece deer antler 2 unclassified worked bone	5 unclassified worked bone	5 Category II fids 1 unclassified worked bone 4 reworked bone tools	5 unclassified worked bone 1 fishhook	

(Continued)

Table 6.2.—*Continued*

	10 Category VI implements 2 antler pieces 13 pieces unclassified worked bone		1 grooved deer cannon bone 2 stingray spines 1 Category VI implement 1 deer bone with engraved ring			
Sharks' teeth	20 Category I 21 Category II 8 Category III 1 Category IV 4 Category V 1 Category VI 4 Category VIII	1 Category IV 1 Category VII	1 Category VII	1 Category V	1 Category I	1 Category I
Shell	1 expanded center plummet 6 *Strombus* celt blades 20 shell fragments	2 *Strombus* shells 4 pieces *Strombus* dippers (?) 1 turtle shell with hole	1 unclassified conch tool			

PP: projectile point.

tools. All of these could have been used in everyday life to procure food and process raw materials for clothing, basketry, shell or wood tools, structures, and wood utensils.

The second tool complex contains those implements that were used in the production of the wood carvings and includes the shell tools used for the rough and large-area work and the shark-tooth tools and stone knives used for the fine carving. This second tool complex obviously overlaps the adaptive complex. Differences between the two are conceptual in nature and are not discernible from the use-wear indicators on the tools. Production of the sacred items, such as the wood carvings, has a different cultural meaning than the production of everyday items. These cultural differences make recognition of a second tool complex useful in understanding the complexity of the site's artifactual system. Without it the functional nature of the Mound A materials would be difficult to ascertain.

The third artifact complex has those implements that were used for nonadaptive and nonproductive purposes: the plummets, the two large polished stemmed points, the celts from the pond, daggers and carved bone pins, and the stingray spines. All of these are rare, are made from exotic materials, or are from burial contexts.

The materials from Middens A and B, Mound 3, and the University of Florida Mound are classifiable as parts of an adaptive technology. The tools are in the normal range of adaptive implements recognized at the site, except the shell cutting tools are not present, suggesting that the heavy woodworking industry was centered at the mound-pond complex.

Period III (A.D. 600–800–A.D. 1200–1400)

The Period III artifact complexes are similar to those from Period II (table 6.3), and all three are still present at the mound-pond complex. During Period III, however, they are restricted to Mound A. There is a noticeable decrease in the number of stone abraders, but the other tool types appear to remain constant in number.

The presence of a single bone fishhook suggests a shift in fishing technology during this period, since Period I and II inventories had none. The evidence is scant, however.

In Midden A there is a dramatic increase in the number of points and a decrease in the amount of flint debris, a reflection of increased habitation and concomitant increased food procurement activities. The larger number of artifacts at Midden B would also indicate more activities away from the charnel-ceremonial complex.

Table 6.3. Period III tools

Type	Mound A	Midden A	Midden B	University of Florida Mound
Shell	2 flint debris 2 stemmed knives 1 broken blade 1 limestone hone 1 limestone abrader 1 teardrop plummet	1 Columbia PP 9 Hernando PP 4 untyped PP fragments 13 flint debris	1 corner-notched PP base 1 untyped PP fragment 2 limestone hones 3 limestone abraders 1 quartz fragment 7 flint debris	1 flint debris 1 limestone abrader
Bone	1 bone fishhook 7 Category I fids 22 Category II fids 2 Category III implements 5 Category VI implements 29 pieces unclassified worked bone	3 Category I fids 1 Category II fid 1 engraved animal bone 10 pieces unclassified worked bone	2 Category II fids 8 unclassified pieces worked bone	
Sharks' teeth	21 Category I 6 Category II 12 Category III 2 Category IV 2 Category VI 1 Category VII 3 Category VIII	1 Category I		
Shell	2 *Strombus* celt blades 1 2-holed whole-shell celt 1 teardrop plummet 9 fragments shell	9 shell fragments 1 piece drilled turtle shell	1 1-holed whole-shell celt 4 fragments shell	

PP: projectile point.

Period IV (A.D. 1200–1400–A.D. 1700)

The final period of occupation at the Fort Center site is marked by a complete lack of use of the mound-pond complex except for placing burials in the top of Mound B and placing the cache of historic objects in the mound. Activities at the site are concentrated at Middens A and B and Mound 3 (table 6.4). Mound 1 had only two nonceramic artifacts in it. Artifact types cluster around those associated with adaptive technology. Noticeably absent, with one exception, is the full range of shell cutting tools, indicating that the woodworking industry had declined significantly. The small number of shark-tooth tools that were recovered further supports this contention. Smaller triangular points were more popular; the single Duval point is an exception, although the basic form of this smallish point is triangular.

There are six intrusive artifacts listed in table 6.4 that represent a much later occupation of the site. The single gunflint may be an artifact of the occupation of the site in the Second Seminole War. The items made from lead are later in time. Two identifiable 54-caliber minié bullets were recovered from Mound 3. These were introduced during the 1860s and were still in use in the twentieth century. Examination by the Georgia Bureau of Investigation's Crime Laboratory disclosed that they were fired from weapons of the same manufacture, but there was too much erosion of the rifling marks to determine if they were fired from the same weapon.

Period IV is notable because of the complete lack of nonadaptive technology. The extensive inventories from the four units did not include any nonutilitarian artifacts, but there were objects that were used to mark social status and rank included with the historic burials. These were described in chapter 5.

Cultural perspective interpreted

The nonceramic artifacts from Fort Center can be interpreted in at least two ways. The first, and most obvious, is their behavioral aspect—how they functioned in a cultural system. The second way of viewing tools is in terms of patterns of adaptation and origin. With the exception of the bone tools and abraders, all of the nonceramic artifacts recovered were manufactured from exotic materials. The Okeechobee Basin, while rich in subsistence resources, is poorly equipped to supply raw materials to a sophisticated technological system. The Belle Glade people were forced to operate their adaptive systems as well as their elaborate ceremonialism with imported mate-

Table 6.4. Period IV tools

Type	Midden A	Midden B	Mound 1	Mound 3
Stone	5 flint debris 2 distal ends PP	11 flint debris 1 unfinished Duval PP 1 Pinellas PP with serrations 1 heavy triangular PP 1 archaic stemmed PP 1 flint uniface 2 fragments greenstone		1 Pinellas PP 1 untyped PP fragment 1 small flint uniface 1 gunflint (intrusive)
Bone	12 pieces unclassified worked bone 2 fragments antler	6 pieces unclassified worked bone 5 Category II fids 2 unclassified bone tools 1 turtle shell with drilled holes	1 piece unclassified worked bone	1 Category I fid 1 fragment unclassified worked bone 1 fragment antler 1 bone fishhook
Sharks' teeth		1 Category I 1 Category II 1 Category VII		2 Category I 1 Category VI
Shell	1 fragment scallop shell		1 *Strombus* celt or adze (beak only)	
Metal	1 deformed lead projectile 1 fragment lead waste			2 54-calibre minié balls 1 fragment lead waste

PP: projectile points.

rials and finished products. Both of the interpretations will be examined in an effort to understand the cultural system of the Fort Center site's inhabitants.

Following Lewis Binford (1962), the Fort Center materials can be divided into three conceptual groupings: technomic, sociotechnic, and ideotechnic. Binford designated these systems in an effort to define more clearly the behavioral aspects of different classes of material culture. If we are to understand past cultural groups from their material culture, we must first determine how the artifacts that we observe functioned in the subsystems of a total cultural system.

Technomic

The technomic system consists of those items that are used by a population to adapt to the natural environment (Binford 1962:219). In essence, this system consists of the tools of a society. We normally think of adaptive technology as that used by people to procure food and materials, build houses, make canoes, and weave—in short, activities that maintain life. Much of the Fort Center material falls into that category, but there are implements that were made and used that go beyond this concept. Many of the artifacts that have been interpreted as tools for wood and bone working were used not for life-maintaining activities but for the manufacture and maintenance of sociotechnic and ideotechnic items. This differentiation separates some of the Mound A artifacts from other technomic implements. Technomic artifacts at Fort Center are bone tools; conch shell adzes, celts, and gouges; shark-tooth tools; stone abraders; and chipped stone implements recovered from midden contexts. These all functioned in some form of production or procurement activities.

Sociotechnic

Sociotechnic artifacts are the implements that function primarily in the social subsystem of the total cultural system. This subsystem functions as the extrasomatic means of articulating individuals with one another into cohesive groups capable of efficiently maintaining themselves and of manipulating the technology (Binford 1962:219). In essence, the sociotechnic system is that system that expresses rank or status of individuals in a society. Sociotechnic artifacts are generally those items that are qualitatively and quantitatively different from the technomic items and are often spatially separated from them. They are often made from exotic materials and represent high-energy expenditures, and they may be of exotic form. In archaeological contexts sociotechnic items are most easily identifiable in mortuary contexts, where it has been demonstrated that an individual's status in life can be reflected in the burial (see Brown 1971 for a complete discussion).

The sociotechnic items from Fort Center are artifacts that are generally not assignable to the technomic system. These include the large abraded stone implements from the pond, the plummets (especially the duck effigy and quartz crystal specimens), the bone daggers, the elaborately carved and polished bone implements from the pond, the shell and stone celts from the pond, the galena hemi-conc, and possibly the pink and red points from Mound B. All of these items have a limited availability in the society, are made of nonnative materials, or were recovered from burial contexts. The materials from the pond were probably burial inclusions. While exact contexts cannot be determined, we do know that they were not associated with the basal midden, a technomic context. They were recovered from the human bone layer of the pond, demonstrably ceremonial in nature.

The clearest examples of these exotic items are the duck effigy and quartz crystal plummets. These are items that require an immense energy expenditure in production as well as in the movement of the items into the Okeechobee Basin. The occurrence of virtual twins at the Turkey Creek site in Brevard County, Florida (Rouse 1951: 166–67; Moore 1899: figs. 23–28), and the Belle Glade site (Willey 1949b) strongly suggests that they were status markers over a large region.

The interpretation that plummets are sociotechnic items and not technomic can be supported from comparative sources. Plummets are never found in great numbers at any site and are frequently encountered in mortuary situations. In the Southeast, plummets have been recovered from post-Archaic sites, both villages and burial mounds. Bullen, Partridge, and Harris (1970: 117–18) write: "The most common non-ceramic artifacts at the Stafford Mound were plummets, all seemingly well made. The continued occurrence of these objects in burial mounds and their virtual absence in middens surely indicates their use as personal adornments and not as weights for fishing." Outside of Florida, the plummets also have a similar occurrence: "In the eastern United States plummets are rare in late Archaic sites but were apparently used with maximum frequency in Burial Mound I and Burial Mound II stages" (Ford, Phillips, and Haag 1955: 125). This pattern of distribution and the general scarcity of plummets indicate that they were items of limited availability throughout the Southeast. The workmanship of the plummets and the nature of the materials they were made from (often imported and always time-consuming to work with) indicate that they were "expensive" items in terms of energy expenditure. These factors would mark plummets as valued items in a society.

Ideotechnic

The third grouping of artifacts at Fort Center is ideotechnic. These artifacts "have their primary functional context in the ideological component of the social system. These are the items which signify and symbolize the ideological rationalizations for the social system and further provide the symbolic milieu in which individuals are enculturated, a necessity if they are to take their place as functional participants in the social system. Such items as figures of deities, clan systems, symbols of natural agencies, etc., fall into this general category" (Binford 1962 : 219–20).

Identifiable ideotechnic items from Fort Center are, primarily, the wood carvings described in chapter 4. Of the materials described in this chapter, the most obvious ideotechnic items are those observed and recorded from the first sand cap on the Mound B primary platform mound. These are the conch shell dippers, the other conch shells, and the spheroid object made from petrified wood. These can be classified as ideotechnic because they came from an exclusively ceremonial context and would therefore be representative of the supernatural component of the social system. When Mound B was closed (by its builders or users), the dippers, conch shells, petrified wood object, and human remains were intentionally and carefully arranged on the mound surface. This deliberate placement of these items in a ceremonial context excludes them from the technomic and sociotechnic systems and identifies them as ideotechnic in nature.

The origin of the nonceramic technology at Fort Center must be considered. The people of Fort Center were forced to rely on outside sources for both raw materials and finished goods to support their social system. The Belle Glade culture may have been self-sufficient in terms of subsistence and social organization, but it was heavily dependent on external sources for the material goods needed to support these systems.

The technomic system utilized both native and exotic materials. Bone fids and other bone implements were made from locally available deer bone, but materials for most of the other tools had to be imported. Flint sources closest to the Okeechobee Basin are in north-central Florida. Abrading slabs could have been made from limestone available throughout peninsular Florida. Some of the slabs were coquina limestone, indicating a coastal origin. The shark teeth, conch shells and *Venus* shells are, obviously, of marine origin.

The question of where the sharks' teeth were obtained can be answered by looking at the relative availability of the teeth in midden deposits outside of the Okeechobee Basin. Sharks' teeth are found in abundance in middens on the Atlantic coast south of Palm Beach, Florida (see Furey 1972). They are found only occasionally in Gulf coast sites and sites north of Palm Beach. This pattern of distribution of sharks' teeth in middens indicates that the Fort Center specimens were probably obtained from the southeastern coast of Florida. While sharks and sharks' teeth are resources that are available to all coastal dwellers and were exploited to some extent throughout the circum-Caribbean area and along the Gulf Coast, there was a definite cultural selection for their extensive use in southeast Florida and the Okeechobee Basin (Larson 1980). Elizabeth Wing (1977) has discussed the use of sharks as a resource in pre-Columbian cultures. She notes that on Florida coastal sites shark remains constitute between 6 and 14 percent of recovered materials, representing an adequate potential supply for inland sites. Her conclusion is that lack of shark remains inland would be due to the absence of distribution networks and not to their unavailability on the coast.

The sociotechnic system was based on materials and artifacts imported from the coast and the north. Lithic resources and perhaps the complete artifacts were available from areas outside of the Okeechobee Basin. Stone for plummets and chipped stone implements, galena, and shell for plummets and dippers are not native to the interior of southern Florida. Perhaps the only resources that were available and used in the sociotechnic system were the large fossil sharks' teeth and the long bones from deer. These teeth could conceivably have been obtained from Pleistocene strata in the basin, and the bones were readily available.

This reliance on exotic materials to support the social ranking system suggests that the system had its origins outside of the Okeechobee Basin. The lack of any data to support a conclusion that the sociotechnic system developed in the Okeechobee Basin further indicates that it was added onto an in situ developing culture. If the sociotechnic system had developed in the Belle Glade culture area, it would seem that most of the sociotechnic items might be made of locally available materials. Because the system used exotic materials and styles and because it is found only at the mound-pond complex, it must have been added to the existing culture and have been tied directly to the ceremonial practices at the charnel complex.

The complete absence of sociotechnic and ideotechnic artifacts from site portions not part of the mound-pond complex during Periods II and III also suggests that the social ranking system and the ideological system were intimately tied to the ceremonialism at the complex. However, only a fraction of the material culture of the Belle Glade inhabitants was recovered. Tropical peoples use large quantities of perishable materials for artifacts associated with religion, rank, and status; these may have been present in the outlying areas of the site as well as in the charnel complex. If present at Fort Center, these perishable items have been lost to the archaeological record.

Dynamics of development of the ideotechnic system are much the same as for the sociotechnic system. The absence of identifiable ideotechnic items in areas other than the mound-pond complex suggests that this system also did not develop at Fort Center and ceased to function when the ceremonial complex was closed out.

If the overall technological system did not develop in the Okeechobee Basin, its origin can be determined by comparing the Belle Glade area materials to those of adjacent areas. We know little about the cultures in the lake area directly north of the Okeechobee Basin. From the reports that are available (Bullen, Jahn, and Brooks 1974), the technological systems seem to be adapted to the lacustrine environment. Bone splinter tools and chipped flint implements predominate, and there are few items of marine origin. Further to the north, in north-central Florida, the same pattern predominates. The clearest examples of the nonceramic technological systems that functioned in this area are in the Alachua tradition. These cultures used bone-splinter tools, chipped flint points, and knives, and only rarely items that had their origins in the sea (Milanich 1971:37–41; Milanich and Fairbanks 1980:169–80).

The Gulf Coast is an area that would be able to supply the needed materials such as conch shells, limestone, and shark teeth. But there is little correspondence between the technomic, sociotechnic, and ideotechnic systems of the Gulf Coast and those of the Okeechobee Basin. The technomic systems of the Gulf coastal sites generally lack sharks' teeth and apparently do not have the same variety of conch-shell tools that are found in the Okeechobee Basin. Collections from Key Marco (Cushing 1897), Weeden Island (Fewkes 1924, Sears 1971b), Garden Patch (Kohler 1975), Tucker (Sears 1963), and other reported sites on the Gulf Coast (see Willey 1949a) support this lack of resemblance between the Gulf Coast and Fort Center. A comparison of the Fort Center nonceramic materials with those from Crystal River and the Yent complex (Moore 1903, 1907, 1918, Bullen 1953, Sears 1962) demonstrates that there is little correspondence.

To the northeast in the St. Johns area and adjacent areas of the Georgia coast, the technological systems have little similarity to those at Fort Center. These two areas are remarkably deficient in nonceramic technology. The few conch-shell tools that are found are small and crude in nature. Sharks' teeth are generally absent, as are bone splinter tools and plummets. Ground stone and chipped stone artifacts are present but not in the same concentration or variety as at Fort Center.

The area that has the closest resemblance to the Okeechobee Basin's technological systems is the Indian River area of southeastern Florida (Rouse 1951). Rouse illustrates bone, shell, and lithic artifacts that are morphologically the same as the bulk of the Fort Center materials. His illustrations show great variability in plummet forms and in carved bone splinter implements. At the same time there is less variability in the whole-shell tools illustrated than was observed at Fort Center, and there were few sharks' teeth or bone tools described or illustrated. These last two tool classes, however, have a direct correspondence to the Fort Center materials.

Of particular interest are the three plummets from the Turkey Creek site in Brevard County, a site that has been thoroughly disturbed by construction through the years. Rouse concludes that the collections represent materials from several different time periods. He illustrates two duck effigy plummets, one made from igneous rock and the other from shell, and a bird-head plummet made from conch shell. As noted, the stone duck plummet (Rouse 1951: pl. 4) from Turkey Creek resembles closely the one from the Fort Center pond. The execution of this basic design in shell at Turkey Creek is further evidence of the pattern of having plummet designs executed in both stone and shell. The bird-head effigy appears to be similar in design to some of the carved wood birds from the Fort Center pond, suggesting a similarity in choice of basic subjects for sociotechnic and ideotechnic items.

The Belle Glade culture could have drawn from or donated to numerous outside areas. The presence of similar duck effigy plummets representing the sociotechnic subsystems from both the Belle Glade and Indian River areas suggests that they were in cultural contact. The similarities in the technomic systems between these areas also indicate that there was a strong connection between them. Ties with southeastern Florida are indicated by the common presence of shark-teeth tools and conch-shell tools. Other areas of Florida seemingly had less contact with the Belle Glade area.

The widespread presence of teardrop and expanded-center plummets throughout the Southeast indicates that they were sociotechnic implements that functioned over a large area. Their presence may be tied directly to Hopewellian cultural systems or their descendants.

Whatever the nature of the similarity with other areas of Florida or the Southeast, it is evident that the peoples of Fort Center and the entire Okeechobee Basin participated in extensive networks of exchange with other areas. These exchange systems functioned to maintain the adaptive system in an environment relatively poor in resources (raw materials) as well as to maintain social and religious systems that were dependent on exotic materials for their existence and continuation.

7

Chronology

RELATIVE dating of structures and artifacts at Fort Center was achieved by a seriation of potsherd frequencies from a large variety of contexts at the site, with full recognition that no two samples are of precisely the same "length" in time. Nevertheless, relative dating seemed to offer a finer-grained assessment of the relations of various structures and deposits to each other than could be achieved by "exact" C-14 radiocarbon dating.

The basic seriation chart for the site (fig. 7.1) includes the relative frequencies of rim forms, the sequence of which is tied to the chronology. In the late periods, the relative popularity of rim-lip forms is more sensitive to time than the relative frequencies of the major ceramic types or classes. The chart was readjusted for late periods in accordance with the temporal distribution of rim forms.

The seriation has followed in all respects the principles of stylistic change expounded by James A. Ford for many years and presented by him in "A Quantitative Method for Deriving Cultural Chronology" (1962). There has been discussion about seriation methods, even of the approximation of the results to reality, but the basic premises of style initiation, popularity peak, and decline have been tested empirically, especially by James Deetz.

The seriation chart was produced by the unsophisticated, mechanically simple, cut-and-fit method. We had at this site more than the usual need for a relative time scale. Having only a few sequences was not helpful, since it was apparent early that there were 2,000 years or

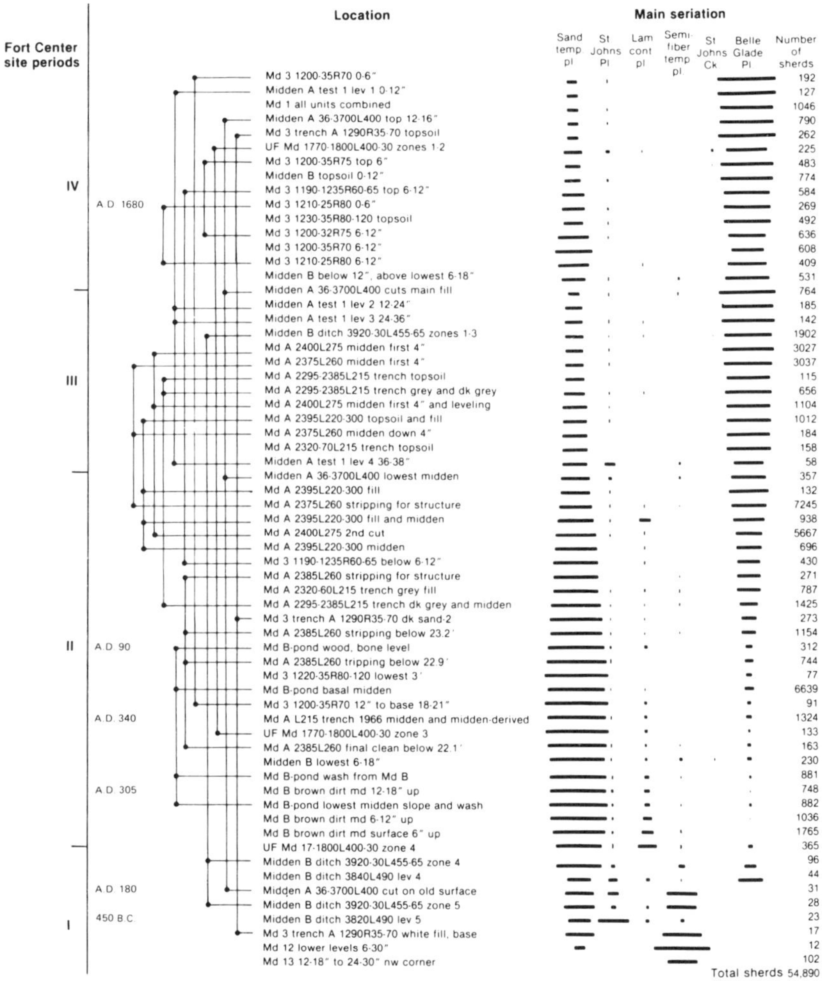

Fig. 7.1. Seriation chart with rim changes. Radiocarbon dates are beside unit that provided sample (see table 7.1). The A.D. 1680 sample is actually from an adjacent unit (1210–35, R70 0–6″); the sherd sample from that unit was too small to seriate.

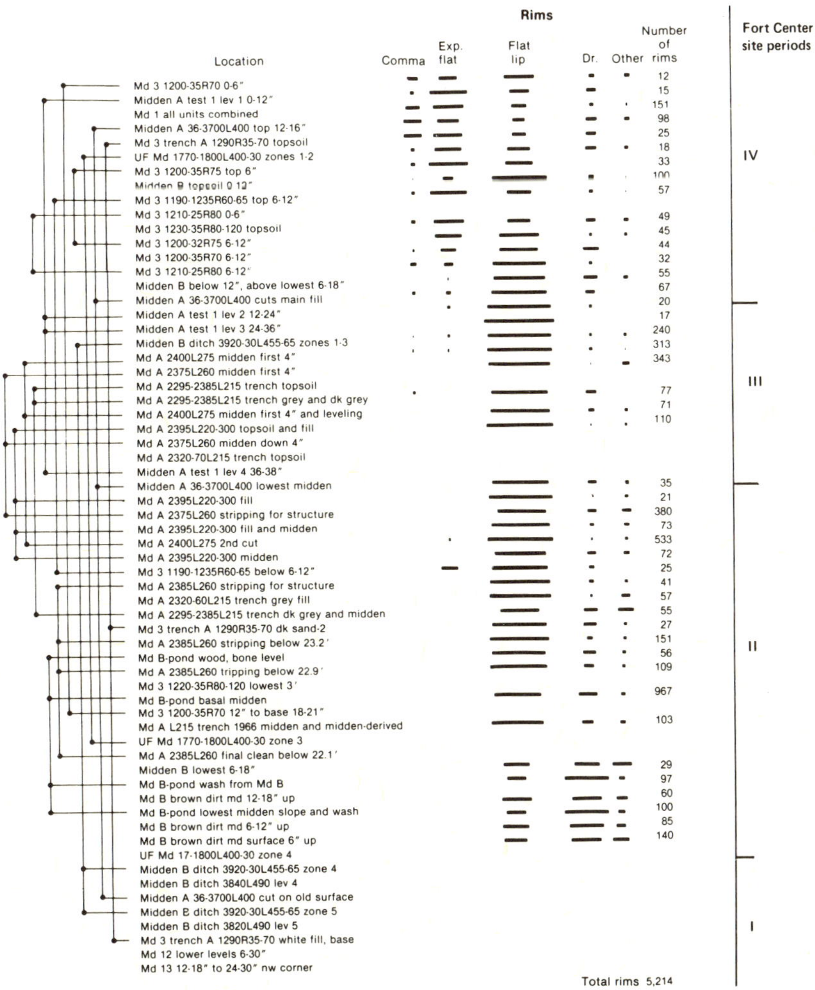

Rims
Location
Comma
Exp. flat
Flat lip
Dr.
Other
Number of rims
Fort Center site periods
Md 3 1200-35R70 0-6"
Midden A test 1 lev 1 0-12"
Md 1 all units combined
Midden A 36-3700L400 top 12-16"
Md 3 trench A 1290R35-70 topsoil
UF Md 1770-1800L400-30 zones 1-2
Md 3 1200-35R75 top 6"
Midden B topsoil 0-12"
Md 3 1190-1235R60-65 top 6-12"
Md 3 1210-25R80 0-6"
Md 3 1230-35R80-120 topsoil
Md 3 1200-32R75 6-12"
Md 3 1200-35R70 6-12"
Md 3 1210-25R80 6-12"
Midden B below 12", above lowest 6-18"
Midden A 36-3700L400 cuts main fill
Midden A test 1 lev 2 12-24"
Midden A test 1 lev 3 24-36"
Midden B ditch 3920-30L455-65 zones 1-3
Md A 2400L275 midden first 4"
Md A 2375L260 midden first 4"
Md A 2295-2385L215 trench topsoil
Md A 2295-2385L215 trench grey and dk grey
Md A 2400L275 midden first 4" and leveling
Md A 2395L220-300 topsoil and fill
Md A 2375L260 midden down 4"
Md A 2320-70L215 trench topsoil
Midden A test 1 lev 4 36-38"
Midden A 36-3700L400 lowest midden
Md A 2395L220-300 fill
Md A 2375L260 stripping for structure
Md A 2395L220-300 fill and midden
Md A 2400L275 2nd cut
Md A 2395L220-300 midden
Md 3 1190-1235R60-65 below 6-12"
Md A 2385L260 stripping for structure
Md A 2320-60L215 trench grey fill
Md A 2295-2385L215 trench dk grey and midden
Md 3 trench A 1290R35-70 dk sand-2
Md A 2385L260 stripping below 23.2'
Md B-pond wood, bone level
Md A 2385L260 tripping below 22.9'
Md 3 1220-35R80-120 lowest 3'
Md B-pond basal midden
Md 3 1200-35R70 12" to base 18-21"
Md A L215 trench 1966 midden and midden-derived
UF Md 1770-1800L400-30 zone 3
Md A 2385L260 final clean below 22.1'
Midden B lowest 6-18"
Md B-pond wash from Md B
Md B brown dirt md 12-18" up
Md B-pond lowest midden slope and wash
Md B brown dirt md 6-12" up
Md B brown dirt md surface 6" up
UF Md 17-1800L400-30 zone 4
Midden B ditch 3920-30L455-65 zone 4
Midden B ditch 3840L490 lev 4
Midden A 36-3700L400 cut on old surface
Midden B ditch 3920-30L455-65 zone 5
Midden B ditch 3820L490 lev 5
Md 3 trench A 1290R35-70 white fill, base
Md 12 lower levels 6-30"
Md 13 12-18" to 24-30" nw corner
12
15
151
98
25
18
33
100
57
49
45
44
32
55
67
20
17
240
313
343
77
71
110
35
21
380
73
533
72
25
41
57
55
27
151
56
109
967
103
29
97
60
100
85
140
Total rims 5,214
IV
III
II
I

more of occupation registered in a series of discrete locations within the site. It would not be possible to work out environmental preferences, settlement patterns, ceremonial complexes, or anything else much until fine-grained temporal control could be achieved.

We did not adapt excavation techniques to the particular requirements of chronological control, however, except in Midden A. In most units, particularly in the mound-pond complex, achieving understanding of the complex construction-use-destruction phenomena had to take preference, and chronological information was derived secondarily. Description, explanation, even justification of the methods used will be found in the sections on the various units (chapter 9). The point here is that the units on the chart represent everything from single excavation units with completely arbitrary vertical and horizontal dimensions to combinations of such units, up to and including the entire artifact-bearing layer of a mound or a stratum in a midden deposit.

Data used to effect valid combinations included field notes, drawings, photographs, and analysis results. For example, at a certain stage in the process, these results sometimes made it clear that a stratum observed in the field had actually accumulated over a long period. Such a stratum was not comparable to most of those used and was not useful for our purposes, so a fair number of such units were dropped from further consideration in the analytical process. While we could not control the actions of Indians who dropped a potsherd a century ago, we were not under any compulsion to use these sherds or "samples" in our pursuit of temporal order. The purist will find the specimens neatly numbered, boxed, and stored and the relevant field notes and photographs filed.

Radiocarbon dates have been entered in the margins of the chart. The dates support the seriation on the whole, and they place those points on the continuum. Interpolation of absolute dates is rather simple and even reasonably accurate.

Trade wares were not used in chart development, nor are most of them listed on the chart. Because they are too few in quantity to be considered in a method relying on popularity, they are presented in a separate tabulation (table 3.1). They, too, strongly support the seriation in terms of their places in other sequences and in the range of absolute dates available for them elsewhere. There has been some discussion of these points and of the significance of trade ware (chapter 3); further discussion will be found (where appropriate in chapters 9 and 10), since the significance of trade wares is considerably more than calendrical or chronological.

Radiocarbon (C-14) "absolute" dating

The years I have spent in the practice of archaeology nearly coincide with the availability of "exact" C-14 dates. For just about as long, it has been apparent that a lot of dates, or the one sigma ranges (one standard deviation), were wrong. Regardless of advances in knowledge about fluctuation in carbon in the atmospheric reservoir, isotope fractionation, and so on, dates that invert repeatedly demonstrated stratigraphic sequences cannot be correct, although efforts have been made to show that they are.

After some thought about how apparent error in radiocarbon dating was related to temperature and moisture, factors directly related to movements of hydrocarbons and carbonates of various origins through the soil, it seemed reasonable to infer that inadequate chemical cleaning of the charcoal that had absorbed these substances could be an error-causing factor. This proposition was substantiated by Cook (1964) in an article in *American Antiquity*, though it does not appear that many archaeologists have read it. The removal of carbonates by acid is simple and apparently has been reasonably effective. Removal of various carbohydrates—no matter whether called "humic acids," a wastebasket term for dissolved hydrocarbons of unknown origin—is not so simple.

Questions addressed to many labs produced some testy responses that proper procedures called for an alkali wash, which was done routinely. Yet archaeologists were still concerned with rootlet removal and the prevention of mold formation, neither of which should have been of any consequence since the alkali should remove them and their products completely. Obviously something was wrong. Elsie Sears discovered that a single "wash," no matter how it was done, removed only a fraction of the soluble compounds. Eventually, multiple treatments with alkali, each involving treatment, centrifuging, and washing, were required to remove all of the soluble materials and to leave pure carbon. The materials so removed ran up to 55 percent of the weight of the charcoal. The dates that follow are based on carbon treated by Elsie Sears. In all cases but one (M-1601), we submitted dry, clean, powdered charcoal to the laboratory.

We still have errors, and some of the determinations are not useful. But, with contamination error eliminated, the remaining errors are clearly those of sampling. I do not play the game of why some dates are "better" than others, which really means how well they fit a preconceived scheme. The dates and sample locations are listed in table 7.1; three sampling errors follow.

Table 7.1. Radiocarbon dates

Sample #	Date	Location	Comment
I-3552	A.D 305±115	Midden on surface of low platform mound under Mound B	—
I-3553	A.D. 304±110	Midden Mound A	—
I-3554	A.D. 260±100	Mound B fill	Sampling error
I-3555	A.D. 180±100	Midden B	—
I-3556	450 B.C. ±105	Fill and midden from circle junctions near river; Great Circle built before this date	—
M-1601	A.D. 80±100	Midden on base of charnel pond	Not properly cleaned; caution
I-11,301	A.D. 1680±75	Midden, Mound 3, 0–6 inches	—
I-11,302	A.D. 635±85	Midden, Mound 3, 6–12 inches	Sampling error

(1) A specimen (I-3554) of solid wood charcoal (section of a small branch) came from gray sand fill of Mound B. In the wall profile from which it was collected, the sample had a white ring around it, representing the material the charcoal had absorbed from the gray sand. But the specimen is related to some event in the borrow pit from which the sand came, not to the time of construction of the mound.

(2) The sample M-1601 was not thoroughly alkali cleaned. The stratigraphic context, the midden at the base of the charnel pond, is the same as that for dates I-3552 and I-3553.

(3) Mound 3 was rebuilt and added to a number of times. The sample I-11, 302, from the 6–12-inch level, apparently relates to an early event.

Inspection of radiocarbon dates on the seriation chart, inserted after construction of the chart, shows that the dates used there fall in proper positions in an appropriate sequence. It is also important that they relate to units or segments of the continuum that have demonstrable relationships with cultures and complexes elsewhere (based on trade wares or artifact styles) that are dated in the same time ranges. Some of our units have check- and simple-stamped sherds identical to those classified as Turner Check and Simple Stamped in Hopewell contexts in Ohio (Prufer 1968a: 7–11). These sherds enter both Fort Center and Ohio Hopewell complexes from a third source. The check-stamped specimens resemble some from Illinois, again from a third source. The clay platform pipes from the Fort Center units resemble those from Marksville. Our dates of A.D. 305 and 340 are acceptable in any of these other complexes. I find this situation far more satisfactory than having dates that conflict with those from cultures known from artifactual evidence to be in contact.

A number of dates recently published for complexes in the Florida area have this problem of conflict, and in some instances the conflict can be resolved only by reversal of established sequences when all dates are accounted for. I have commented on this situation at some length (Sears 1977a:178–81).

On the other hand, in a final note of despair, I have seen dates from thoroughly cleaned and carefully chosen charcoal specimens that still leave one with only the choice of who is wrong. For example, a Georgia complex with trade sherds from Louisiana should not be dated 500 years earlier than the Louisiana complex. Perhaps offering alternative time scales as Phillips (1970:965–72) has done is the best solution. This approach suggests that there are only two possibilities instead of an infinite number. Someone will figure it out eventually, and until then one ought to mistrust any and all "exact" radiocarbon dates.

8

Pollen Analysis

Elsie O'R. Sears

ANALYSIS of pollen from the Fort Center site had three objectives: to obtain evidence of agriculture, if any; to determine what, if any, environmental changes had taken place during the period of occupation; and to obtain information about the inhabitants' diet. Samples analyzed for pollen included soil samples, coprolites, and white pigment found on one of the charnel pond wood carvings. Soil samples, taken from cleaned excavation profiles with a clean trowel and sealed in plastic bags, were thoroughly mixed before analysis. Coprolites, collected from the deposit at the bottom of the charnel pond, were washed with distilled water, scraped to remove any surface contamination, and ground in a mortar. White pigment, associated with a wood carving of a raptorial bird (fig. 4.9, E) found at the bottom of the pond, was pulverized and thoroughly mixed.

About 5 grams of each mixed sample were treated with potassium hydroxide, heated on a boiling water bath for four hours, and strained through a fine wire mesh. The filtrate was centrifuged, the supernatant discarded, and the residue washed several times with distilled water. Wash water was removed by centrifuging and decantation. The residue was treated with hydrochloric acid to remove carbonates and with hydrofloric acid to remove sand and silicates, washed with hydrochloric acid and then with water, and dehydrated with glacial acetic acid. The residue was further broken down by acetolysis, i.e., heating with a mixture of acetic anhydride and concentrated sulfuric acid, and washing, first with glacial acetic acid, then with distilled water. A small amount of the residue was mounted on glass slides in prestained glycerine jelly; a safranin stain was used. The remainder of the material was stored in glycerine.

All samples were treated with all reagents so that the pollen recovered would have complete comparability. Occasionally it was necessary to repeat treatment with one or more reagents.

Slides were scanned for cultigens (maize, manioc, squash, sweet potato) at × 100 magnifications. Large Gramineae grains were examined under the phase contrast microscope at × 600 magnifications. Measurements were made using an eyepiece micrometer calibrated against a micro disc (Bausch and Lomb) graduated in 0.1 and 0.01 mm units. The microscope used was a Bausch and Lomb Balplan microscope equipped for phase contrast microscopy. Photographs were made with 35-mm Kodak Panatomic X film.

Since the main objective of pollen analysis at the Fort Center site was to determine whether the occupants practiced agriculture, several hundred slides of pollen grains were examined for pollen of maize, manioc, sweet potato and squash. Only maize pollen was found.

Zea (maize) pollen

Size

Large Gramineae grains were identified as maize pollen on the basis of size, i.e., length of the long axis of the grain, and of exine pattern. According to Irwin and Barghoorn (1965 : 40), *Tripsacum* and teosinte are "the only New World grains so far investigated which cannot be distinguished from maize by a simple measurement, i.e. greater than 45 microns for the long axis and greater than 5.7 for the pore-axis ratio." Since teosinte is not a native Florida grass (Irwin and Barghoorn 1965 : 44), Gramineae pollen grains larger than 45 microns found at the Fort Center site could be only maize or *Tripsacum*.

The extremes in size of *Tripsacum* pollen grains are reported by Barghoorn (Barghoorn, Wolfe, and Clisby 1954 : 231) to be 33–64 microns. A specimen of *Tripsacum dactyloides* from the herbarium of Dr. Daniel Austin, Department of Botany, Florida Atlantic University, was found to have pollen grains with extreme measurements of 45–70 microns, with a mean of 54 microns (Sears and Sears 1976 : 54).

In order to determine the mean value of the long axis measurement of the maize pollen from Fort Center, four samples were studied (Sears and Sears 1976 : 54). Gramineae pollen grains larger than 50 microns in length with exines appearing regularly punctate under the phase contrast microscope were identified as maize pollen. The mean values of long axis measurements of maize pollen from these four samples ranged from 61.8 to 63.5 microns. A herbarium sample of *Tripsacum dactyloides* was prepared by the same method as the study samples and was also mounted in glycerine jelly. Mean value of the long axis measurement of this *Tripsacum* pollen sample was 54.3 microns. Whitehead and Langham report the mean value of the long axis measurement of Chapalote pollen to be about 69 microns, slightly larger than the mean for the Fort Center corn pollen (Whitehead and Langham 1965 : 13).

Exine pattern

The exine of *Tripsacum* pollen is verrucate with considerable clumping of the columnellae (Whitehead and Langham 1965 : 17). The grain has an irregular edge and a mottled appearance when viewed under the phase contrast microscope. Maize pollen has an essentially psilate exine. The columnellae are distinct and show little clumping. Under the phase contrast microscope, maize pollen grains have a fairly smooth edge and appear regularly punctate (Whitehead and Langham 1965 : 18). Differences in exine patterns are illustrated in figure 8.1, E, F.

Results

Maize pollen was found in the white pigment samples, in three of the coprolite samples, and in soil samples from the Great Circle, the single linear mound between Mounds 8 and 9, and the Mound 1 linear mound. Table 8.1 shows the number of maize pollen grains found in each sample, the length of the long axis of the largest grain found in each sample, and, for the soil samples, the location from which the sample was taken. Typical grains are illustrated in figure 8.1.

Environmental changes

The second objective of the pollen analysis was to determine what, if any, environmental changes had taken place on the site during the period of occupation. Fort Center now includes three types of environment: river meander belt, savannah, and oak hammock. A series of soil samples was taken from each of the current environmental zones, representing each time period for which material was available. After preparation of the pollen as described, pollen grains were identified and counted at × 600 magnifications, using the Bausch and Lomb mi-

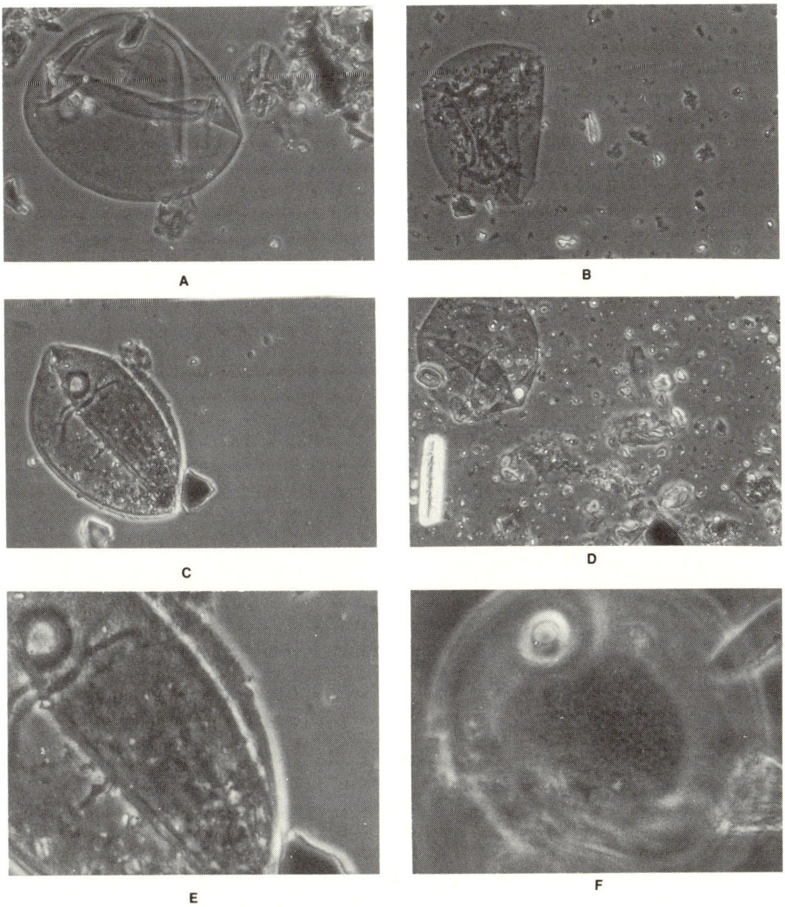

Fig. 8.1. Typical *Zea* (maize) pollen grains: **A–D**, samples P-294, 182, 47, and 81; **E**, enlargement of exine of C; **F**, enlargement of exine of *Tripsacum* grain from herbarium specimen.

croscope equipped for phase contrast microscopy. A minimum of 200 pollen grains from each sample was counted, since this has been shown to be a reliable basis for analysis (Barkley 1934:283). Identifications were made by comparing specimens with reference slides of known origin. Some typical grains from the soil samples analyzed are shown in figure 8.2.

Plants occurring on the site were grouped into two main categories:

Table 8.1. Maize pollen grains

Origin of sample and sample number	No. of maize pollen grains	Length of long axis of largest grain (mm)
White pigment associated with wood carving, Mound B		
P 294	101	95
P 257	8	95
P 295	2	88
P 296	3	75
Coprolite		
P 157	20	80
P 182	24	85
P 165	1	92
Great Circle, modern topsoil		
P 116	43	83
Great Circle, topsoil under modern surface		
P 267	2	65
P 301	1	63
Great Circle ditch, 3935 L 525		
P 47, zone 4	25	85
P 51, level 13	2	65
P 52, level 14	14	70
Great Circle ditch, 3701 L 914 layer 3		
P 68	1	62
Great Circle ditch, 3925 L 525 zone 3		
P 69	2	60
Single linear mound between Mounds 8 and 9		
P 79	3	74
P 80	1	60
P 81	6	65
Mound 1 linear mound		
P 99	1	71
P 100	1	65

the hydric or wetland plants and the grassland plants. Pollen of Palmae (cabbage palm, palmetto), *Quercus* (oak), pine, and cheno-am (goosefoot and pigweed) were considered separately.

Hydric plants

Included in hydric plants are Cyperaceae (sedge), *Lycopodium* (club moss), Liliaceae (lily), Iridaceae (iris), Typha (cattail), *Sagittaria* (water plantain), *Potamogeton* (pond weed), *Utricularia* (bladderwort), and Nymphaea (water lily) (McPherson 1974:11; Goodrick 1974:48; Gleason 1963).

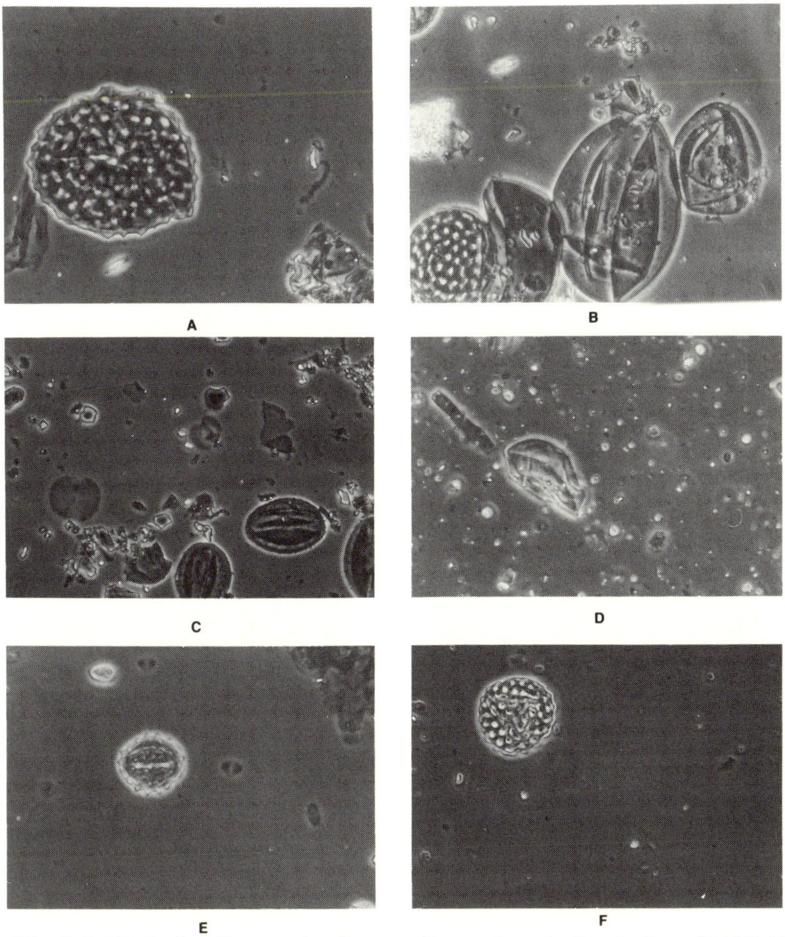

Fig. 8.2. Typical pollen grains from soil samples: **A**, *Lycopodium*, P-105; **B**, *Zea* with *Chenopodium* and Gramineae, P-47; **C**, *Quercus*, P-264; **D**, Cyperaceae, P-92; **E**, Compositae, P-105; **F**, *Chenopodium*, P-105.

Grassland plants

Placed in grassland plants are Gramineae (grasses) and the flowering plants and shrubs, including Compositae (sunflower family), Rosaceae (rose family), *Smilax*, Leguminosae (legume family), Phytolaccaceae (pokeweed), Plantaginaceae (plantain), Ericaceae (heath family), Primulaceae (primrose family), Caryophyllaceae (pink family), *Cephalanthus* (buttonbush), Ranunculaceae (buttercup family), Cucurbitaceae (squash family), and Apocynaceae (dogbane family) (McPherson 1974: 11; Gleason 1963; Long and Lakela 1971).

Results of the analysis are shown in table 8.2 and figure 8.3. In the river meander belt zone, samples from the three periods of site occupation were analyzed. Period I is represented by two samples, one each from Mound 12 and Mound 3, Period II by one sample from Mound 3, and Period III by two samples from Mound 3. All samples from this zone have more pollen of the hydric plants and less pollen of grassland plants than had any of the samples from the present-day savannah or hammock areas. This difference suggests that there has been no significant environmental change in the river meander belt zone at Fort Center from the earliest Period I occupation to the present time.

The only period represented by samples from the savannah is Period IV. Four soil samples were analyzed, from the Mound 1 linear mound, the Mound 2 linear mound, the Mound 5 linear mound, and the Mound 1 south parallel causeway. All samples have lower percentages of pollen of hydric plants and much higher percentages of grassland plant pollen than had the samples from the river meander belt.

During Period IV the modern savannah area apparently was a prairie with scattered cabbage palm and palmetto, as it is today. All four samples contain a few grains of oak pollen, indicating the presence of oak trees in the vicinity.

Ten soil samples were taken from the area that is hammock today. Period I is not represented. Period II is represented by three samples, one each from Midden B, the University of Florida Mound, and Mound A; Period III by three samples, two from Midden B and one from Mound A; Period IV by two samples, one each from the University of Florida Mound causeway and Midden A. The modern period is represented by two samples, one from the top inch of topsoil and one from the topsoil under the modern surface, both in the Great Circle.

All soil samples from the hammock area contain high percentages of grassland pollen and low percentages of hydric pollen. Palmae pollen is present, as it is in the savannah samples. Except for two samples, only small amounts of oak pollen were found, about the same percentages as in the savannah samples. In two samples, however, one from Period III and one from the modern period, large amounts of oak pollen were present, suggesting that in the past oak trees were present on the site in the vicinity of these samples. The low percentages of oak pollen in the other hammock samples indicate that only scattered oaks were present on the hammock site during the prehistoric occupation period, compared to the rather thick oak hammock growth existing today.

We can conclude that the river meander zone, then, is essentially unchanged from the earliest period of occupation to the present time. The savannah zone during the latest period of occupation was similar to the savannah today, a prairie of grass, composites, and other flowering weeds and shrubs, with scattered cabbage palms and palmettos. No data are available for earlier periods. The hammock area could have contained a few scattered oaks during Period II, although the amount of oak pollen found for that period could have resulted from air transport from another area (Faegri and Iverson 1964:118). Some oak trees were growing on the site during Period III, a conclusion we draw because the high percentage of oak pollen in one sample from Midden B probably resulted from local conditions (Faegri and Iverson 1964:104). However, the thick oak hammock growth on the site today must have developed after the last occupation. This sequence of prairie to hammock growth is typical of South Florida, where the hammock is the climax community (Alexander and Crook 1974:66). The hammock area, then, was similar to the savannah zone from Period II through Period IV, differing only in that scattered oak trees occurred in the hammock area, at least from Period III on.

Pollen in coprolites

Slides of pollen from 100 coprolites recovered from the bottom of the charnel house pond were scanned at × 100 magnifications for evidence of cultigens. Maize pollen was found in three samples. Table 8.1 shows the number of maize pollen grains found in each sample and the length of the long axis of the largest grain. A typical maize pollen grain from a coprolite sample is illustrated (fig. 8.1, B).

For each of 50 coprolite samples, a minimum of 200 pollen grains was counted. Counting and identification were done at × 600 magnifications. Cheno-am pollen was found in all samples, comprising from 11.5 to 51.0 percent of the total, with a mean of 30.2 percent. Since the soil samples examined contained only 2.0 to 11.0 percent of cheno-am pollen, it seems likely that pigweed-goosefoot plants formed part of the diet. One sample contained 14.5 percent of Caprifoliaceae pollen, indicating possible ingestion of elderberry.

Table 8.2. Percentage diagram of pollen samples from three environmental zones

Locations

(1) Md. 3, 0–6″
(2) Md. 3, 0–6″
(3) Md. 3, 12–16″
(4) Md. 3, 30–36″
(5) Md. 12, 8–11″
(6) Md. 1 earthwork mound fill
(7) Md. 2 earthwork buried humus
(8) Md. 5 earthwork mucky layer
(9) Md. 1 south parallel causeway
(10) Great Circle, test 3 top 1′
(11) Great Circle, buried topsoil
(12) UF Mound causeway, white sand fill
(13) Midden A, layer 2, 3690L440–450
(14) Midden B, 3925L525, level 13
(15) Midden B, 3935L525, zone 6
(16) Md. A, fill on midden, 2376L260
(17) Midden B, 3840L490, level 4
(18) UF Mound, 1780L430, layer 3
(19) Md. A, black fill, 23″ down, 2400L260

	River meander belt					Savannah			
	(1)	(2)	(3)	(4)	(5)	(6)	(7)	(8)	(9)
Lycopodiaceae	18.0	17.0	18.0	20.5	22.5	3.0	2.5	5.5	2.0
Cyperaceae	20.0	30.0	20.5	24.0	20.0	8.0	8.5	6.0	12.0
Liliaceae	1.5	2.0	6.5	3.0	7.5	1.0	3.0		1.0
Iridaceae	6.0	5.5	1.5	4.0	8.0				2.0
Typhaceae	0.5		3.0	2.0					
Sagittaria	4.0	9.0	4.0	3.0	3.0				
Potamogeton		1.0	1.0		0.5				
Utricularia		4.0	1.5	2.0	0.5				
Nymphaeaceae	1.0	1.5	1.0	2.0	0.5				
Malvaceae									
Hydrophyllaceae	4.0								
Gramineae	7.5	6.0	7.5	9.0	7.0	31.0	26.0	45.0	32.0
Compositae	6.0	3.5	8.5	7.5	6.0	24.5	16.5	14.5	23.0
Rosaceae			1.0	1.0	1.5	3.5	5.0	5.5	2.5
Caprifoliaceae							0.5		2.0
Umbelliferae			1.0			1.0	3.5	1.0	
Smilax									
Leguminosae									1.0
Phytolaccaceae									
Ericaceae									
Primulaceae					1.0				
Caryophyllaceae		0.5		0.5					
Cephalanthus						2.5	3.5	0.5	
Cucurbitaceae									
Polygalaceae									
Apocynaceae									3.0
Ranunculaceae									1.0
Plantaginaceae					2.5			0.5	
Arecaceae	1.5		2.0			4.5	12.0	6.0	0.5
Cheno-am	16.0	9.0	8.5	7.5	3.5	11.5	5.5	6.0	7.0
Quercus						1.5	1.0	0.5	1.0
Tillandsia									

(*continued*)

Table 8.2.—*Continued*

	(1)	(2)	(3)	(4)	(5)	(6)	(7)	(8)	(9)
Orchidaceae									
Pinus						1.5	1.0	3.0	2.5
Salix							0.5		
Acer			1.0						
Fern spores	9.0	6.0	8.5	10.0	10.5	4.5	8.0	3.5	5.0
Zea									
Unknown	5.0	5.0	5.0	4.0	5.5	2.0	3.0	2.5	2.5
Total grains counted	200	200	200	200	200	200	200	200	234

	Hammock									
	(10)	(11)	(12)	(13)	(14)	(15)	(16)	(17)	(18)	(19)
Lycopodiaceae			4.5	0.5	1.5	3.0		3.5	5.5	2.0
Cyperaceae	1.0		5.5	3.5	1.5	4.5	8.5	8.5	11.0	8.0
Liliaceae		2.0		2.0	5.0	2.0	2.5	4.0	2.0	0.5
Iridaceae									1.5	
Typhaceae										
Sagittaria										
Potamogeton										
Utricularia										
Nymphaeaceae										
Malvaceae							1.0			
Hydrophyllaceae										
Gramineae	29.0	12.5	33.5	15.5	30.0	38.5	36.5	30.5	31.5	22.5
Compositae	20.0	10.5	13.0	29.0	11.0	19.0	17.5	24.5	14.5	23.5
Rosaceae	9.5		2.5	16.5	0.5	8.0	0.5	6.0	4.0	9.0
Caprifoliaceae	15.0	2.0		1.0	5.0	1.0				
Umbelliferae	6.0	1.0		1.0	2.0	1.0		0.5	0.5	1.5
Smilax		1.5	7.5	3.0		1.0			4.0	0.5
Leguminosae	2.0	0.5			0.5	1.5	0.5			
Phytolaccaceae					2.0					
Ericaceae			1.0			0.5	3.0	0.5	0.5	
Primulaceae										
Caryophyllaceae	1.5				0.5	0.5				
Cephalanthus										
Cucurbitaceae			0.5							
Polygalaceae									0.5	
Apocynaceae										
Ranunculaceae		0.5							0.5	
Plantaginaceae						0.5		4.5	5.5	0.5
Arecaceae	8.0	0.5	8.0	2.0	3.0	2.5	2.0			1.0
Cheno-am	2.0	5.0	11.0	12.0	6.5	5.0	8.5	6.0	4.5	21.5
Quercus	0.5	60.0	2.5	1.5	22.0	0.5	2.0	1.0	1.0	1.0
Tillandsia			1.0		0.5					
Orchidaceae		0.5		1.5					0.5	
Pinus					3.0	2.5	0.5			
Salix										
Acer										
Fern spores	3.0	2.0	5.0	8.0	3.5	4.0	13.0	6.5	4.5	6.0
Zea	1.0									
Unknown	1.5	2.0	4.5	3.5	2.0	4.5	4.0	4.0	8.0	2.5
Total grains counted	227	214	200	200	220	200	200	197	200	204

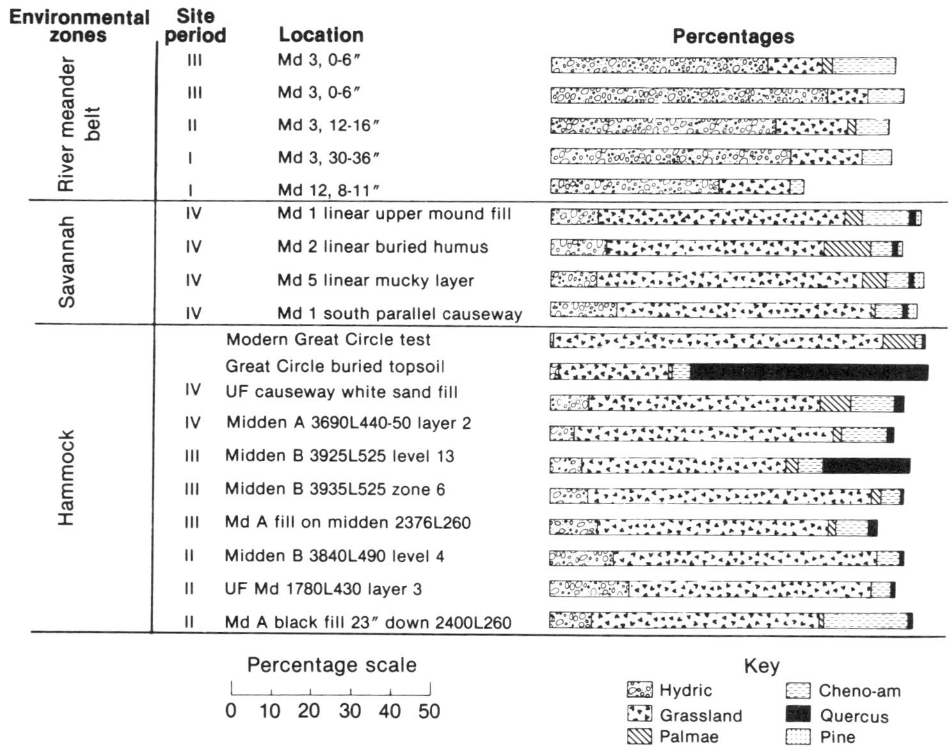

Fig. 8.3. Percentages of hydric and grassland pollen and percentages of certain pollens from site environmental zones.

Conclusion

Pollen analysis at the Fort Center site shows that maize was grown at the site, within the Great Circle and on at least two of the linear mounds. Analysis of coprolite samples confirms that corn was a part of the inhabitants' diet. Pollen evidence also indicates that the river meander belt is essentially unchanged from prehistoric times, that the savannah was the same during Period IV as it is today, and that the dense oak hammock growth present today is of fairly recent origin, probably moving in on an area that was savannah during the occupation of the site.

9

Structures and Deposits

A PHYSICAL description of each structure at the Fort Center site is followed by an account of its excavation. Reasons are noted for the combination or exclusion of artifact samples. Final accounts provide information on probable reconstruction, function, and history of the unit, including period or periods of use.

Usually, in North America, mounds on aboriginal sites that contain evidence of human occupation are artificial structures. In recognition of this fact, a few numbers were assigned to features on the site that, on closer inspection, were not human made, resulting in gaps in the sequence of mound numbers (fig. 1.1).

The use of house mounds is required in most places in the Lake Okeechobee Basin to raise house floors out of the way of frequent floods. At Fort Center there is only one naturally high area along the riverbank, an old natural levee, where this practice was not followed. Middens A and B both developed on this levee. On the other hand, not all of the earthworks constructed at the site were for occupation. Many of them served other environmentally or ceremonially defined purposes.

Mound 1 and abutting linear earthwork

Mound 1, the linear mound whose east end appears to touch Mound 1, and the encircling borrow pit and nearby linear mound to the north (fig. 9.1) are located in the open savannah. During the time that the mounds were used and until today, the ditch–borrow pit complex en-

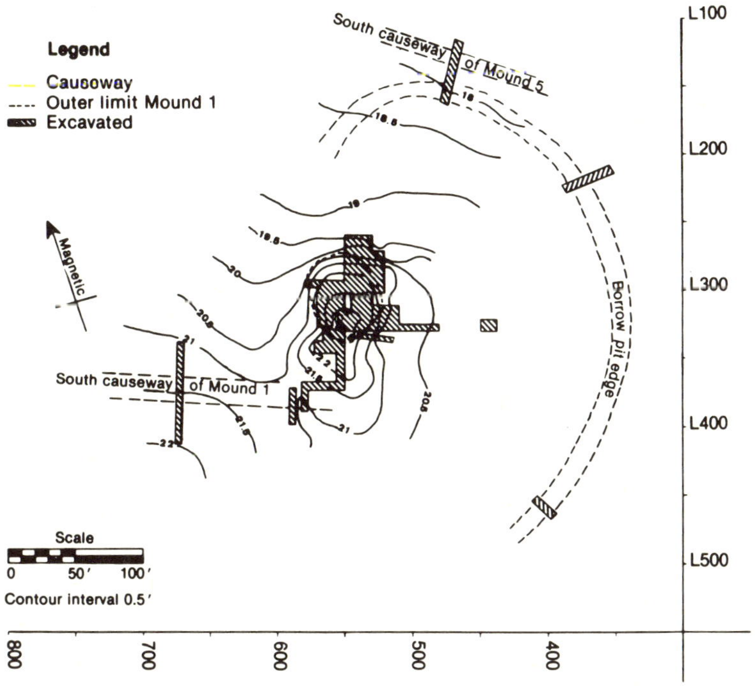

Fig. 9.1. Mound 1 with adjacent structures and excavated area.

circling the mound and the ditches on each side of the linear causeways were frequently—perhaps usually—filled with water (perhaps it would be more accurate to say filled with water, aquatic plants, and amphibious fauna).

Mound 1, built on land with an average elevation of 20 feet above sea level, was about 30 inches high and 35–40 feet in diameter when we started to excavate. The "borrow pit edge" designated in figure 9.1 is actually the outer edge of a borrow pit complex, which shows clearly in the aerial photograph (fig. 1.2) but is difficult to trace on the ground. This pit was the source of mound fill, some of which was thrown up away from the mound to form the distinct circular earthwork that shows in the photograph. This use of the pit suggests that it was kept wet and that there was value in so doing, but we have no idea what that might have been.

An associated linear earthwork runs in a westerly direction from Mound 1. Neither this earthwork, nor the others, are sets of parallel linear embankments as they appear to be in the aerial photograph. Their appearance in the photograph is a product of dry weather and erosion from cow hoofs. Instead, as shown on figure 1.1, this associated earthwork is a single structure with the present road on its north edge; it is about 100 feet wide and 450 feet long.

Using a tractor, I cut trenches across all linear earthworks on the site, long enough to include the flanking ditches, and profiled one side of each trench. The data gained from these cuts demonstrated that this linear earthwork and the others were indeed each a single structure and not two parallel ones.

This linear mound is not and never was attached to, nor did it ever touch, Mound 1 at its eastern end. Nor are the cow paths forming a vague arc at the western end, perceptible on the aerial photograph, prehistoric structures at all. They are traces of paths reflecting the presence of an unusually wet spot, a fence, and bovine psychology.

I put a trench into the western side of Mound 1 as part of the first stage testing program. Most of the excavation in Mound 1 and the linears shown in figure 9.1 was done by Colgate University. Excavation was by 5-foot squares and 6-inch arbitrary levels. Usually, a number of adjacent squares were open at the same time to the same level to make perception of minor soil changes or any other evidence of structures better visible.

Occupational debris was limited to the top foot of the central part of the mound. A reasonably uniform midden-humus, the two almost indistinguishable, contained fair quantities of living refuse. Some squares were occupied solidly by the root masses of cabbage palms and could not be excavated. A few charcoal concentrations were interpreted as fireplaces, and a few apparent post molds were recorded.

Essentially, the picture is one of a low sand mound built by throwing soil to the inside of a circular ditch. It was built to approximately its present height to support a single structure, which, considering the permeability of fine sand to trash (including sherds and garbage of various kinds), probably had a floor level close to the height of the present mound surface. Some debris, in aiding humus development, probably added a few inches to mound height.

As suggested by the relative thinness and uniformity of the topsoil-midden deposit, the artifact assemblage from this mound was uniform both vertically and horizontally (see the seriation chart, fig. 7.1). In every unit, most specimens were in the top 6 inches. Occasionally, and especially near the center of the mound, level 2 (6–12 inches) yielded almost as many specimens.

In view of the uniformity found, we have concluded that Mound 1 represents a single occupation and a single structure for a relatively short period of time in the late sixteenth or early seventeenth century. This relative temporal position is supported by five Pinellas Plain sherds.

The trenches cut by Colgate University and my tractor provided some information on the linear earthwork abutting Mound 1 on the west side. (Part of these data have been reported.) There were no associated artifacts in or on any part of the structure. Its original height was probably 2–3 feet, judging by the quantities of wash into the ditches. It was definitely built by excavating dirt from boundary ditches and moving it toward what would be the midline of the completed structure. Ditches appear to have gone down about 2 feet from the present surface and were 20 to 30 feet wide, with their bases solidly on the yellow-brown humite that underlies the savannah.

Mound 2 and abutting linear earthwork

Mound 2 was covered with heavy vegetation, including several large trees. It was not possible to measure it accurately, but it appears from the aerial photograph (fig. 1.2), supplemented by careful ground checks, that Mound 2 is similar to Mound 1 in height, diameter, presence of encircling borrow-ditch, and relationship with the abutting linear earthwork.

Excavation, late in the project, was limited to a single 5-by-5-foot test; the limitation was imposed by the vegetation as well as by time and funds. In the mound, the gray topsoil-humus was only 6 inches thick. Only 8 sherds were recovered: 6 sand-tempered plain, 1 St. Johns Plain, and 1 Belle Glade Plain rim sherd with a flat lip—not a diagnostic collection. The mound is assigned to Period IV on the basis of environmental location and the attached linear mound.

The linear earthwork was bisected near its midpoint by a tractor-cut trench, with one profile hand cleaned. Information acquired was about the same as that for the linear mound adjacent to Mound 1, but this mound is longer and narrower: 1,200 feet compared to 450, 75 feet instead of 100.

Mound 3

At a junction of a hammock–savannah–river meander, Mound 3's history differs from that of any other structure at the site. Not only is

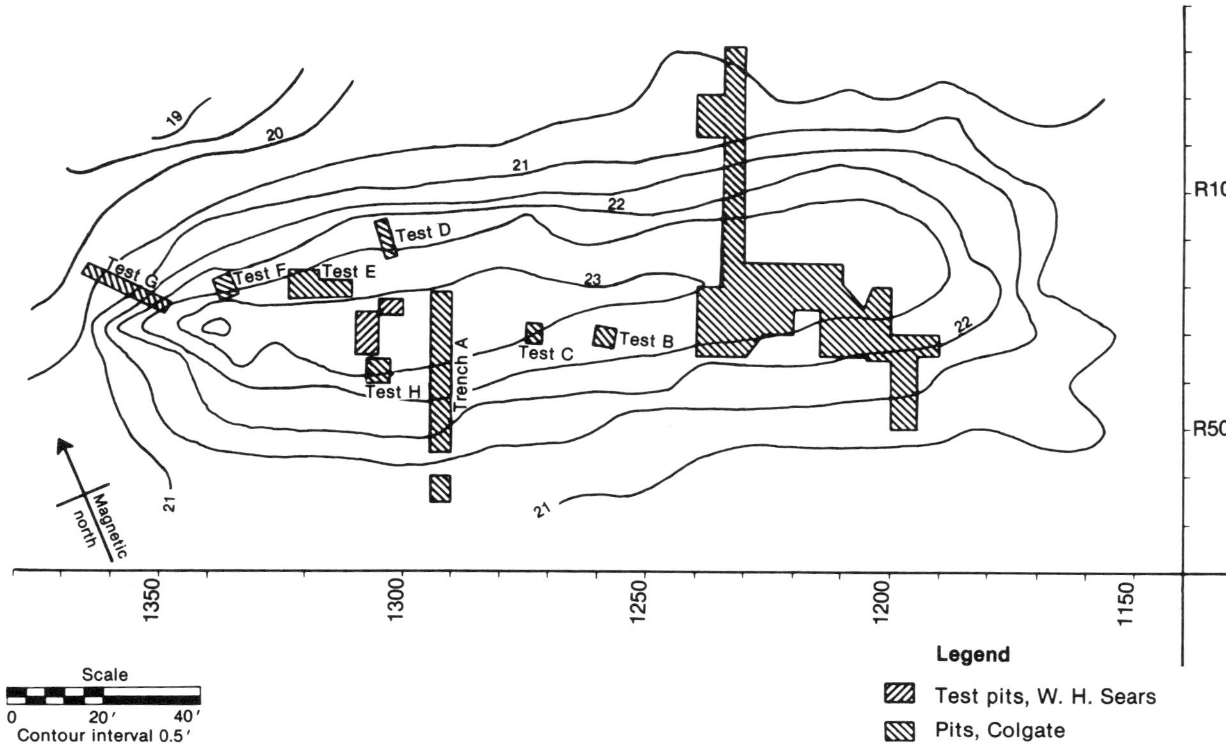

Fig. 9.2. Mound 3 excavation diagram.

it in a unique environmental situation, but its form, a long 200-by-60-foot oval (fig. 9.2), is different from that of other mounds. Final shape is the result of long-term natural and culturally determined processes. The mound has no apparent functional relationship to any other structures, although it is contemporaneous with several mounds and was occupied during three periods.

Except for two test pits that were parts of a Florida Atlantic University weekend project, a Colgate team of 12 students excavated the mound in 1968. The problem of sorting out natural zones and artificial structures was recognized early, and fieldwork was designed to interpret construction-deposition sequences and their relationship to artifact complexes.

The large area at the eastern end of the mound was excavated by 5-foot squares and 6-inch levels. Most of the area was opened and cleaned simultaneously at the 0–6- and 6–12-inch levels, which coincided with the artifact-bearing modern humus and the aboriginal midden deposit. Under these strata, at or near the original ground surface, the gray midden-humus gave way to a brown sand—an unusual occurrence at the site, since brown sand is normally related to a humite layer at a depth of 2 to 3 feet. However, a similar curiosity appeared in other structures in the river meander belt. It seems to be a product of percolation and precipitation in older structures that were wet more often and for longer periods than soils and structures in the hammock and savannah.

The brown surface contained some fire pits, each about 2 feet in diameter and 12 to 18 inches deep, which had in them bits of charcoal and burned bits of bone and pottery. The tops of these pits were not recognizable in the first foot of the structure—the humus-midden layer—and the period of origin cannot be determined.

Trench A into the western part of the mound revealed a more complex situation. It cut into a definitely artificial structure of nearly sterile white sand, a low mound with its top 12 to 18 inches above the surface upon which it was built. Midden was deposited on this mound. Tests C, D, E, F, and G were placed solely to locate its limits.

The data are ambiguous, in some part because of the presence of old natural strata and of some recent disturbance in mucky areas around the east end of the mound. It is my opinion that the white sand was one addition to a slight natural rise and that there was some midden material on the original ground surface before the white sand was added. The final product was the long, low mound that was utilized over a long period.

All artifact assemblages large enough to be significant have been studied and combined into three samples. One is from the major flat area just east of center (1220-35), one from the trench to the north, and a third from trench A. Areas where the 6 inches of midden seemed to include materials from two or three periods or, as in the case of parts of the two units I excavated, materials that were mishandled in laboratory processing produced samples that were too small to be used and that could not be rationally combined.

The seriation chart, figure 7.1, shows three temporally distinct, well-separated clusters of Mound 3 ceramic samples. One is late and is graphed as the latest sample on the site. It is followed by a temporal gap, to another cluster coeval with the main occupation of the mound-pond ceremonial complex. Finally, a single small but distinctive sample is the third oldest on the site.

Clustering shows three well-separated occupations of Mound 3. Early in the history of the site, there was occasional light occupation on this spot. Later, the area that was a natural hummock at the time was extended a bit with white sand from the periphery and was used while the ceremonial center functioned. Finally, its most intensive occupation left about a foot of midden over the entire mound; it contained several thousand sherds in the portions excavated.

I believe that Mound 3 was actually a variant of the riverbank Middens A and B and of the Platt site a mile upstream, excavated by Goggin (1952a): It was an occupation area on a spot that had a slight natural elevation. Early inhabitants of Mound 3, like those of Midden areas A and B, probably participated in the horticultural pursuits carried out in the Great Circle and its predecessors.

Mound 5 and abutting linear earthwork

When I first saw the site, Mound 5 had been destroyed by a road. The ruts in the soft sand of the mound were widened and deepened, as were those in the mucky borrow areas on each side, by vehicles that became stuck and spun their wheels. As this process continued, drivers cut over to get out of the ruts, trying to keep one wheel on the center crown. A truck with all four wheels spinning can move a lot of soft dirt.

My notes from this first visit refer to a perceptibly flat-topped elevation. A collection of a few sherds from the ruts includes St. Johns Check Stamped, which places the mound in the Periods III and IV, at least after A.D. 1,000. Unfortunately, the collection has been misplaced, but a mistake in identifying St. Johns Check Stamped is scarcely possible.

The abutting linear mound was tested in two places. Colgate University ran one cut from the edge of the Mound 1 borrow ditch right across the edge of the linear earthwork. I later bisected the structure at its midpoint with one tractor cut. Except for length, the earthwork seems identical in construction, probably in original height, and in ditch width and depth to the linear earthworks related to Mounds 1 and 2. Like them, it contained no artifacts either in the areas excavated, a reasonable sample, or in surface areas exposed in various ways.

The data we have suggest placing Mound 5 and its linear earthwork and borrow complex in a class with Mounds 1 and 2 and their linear earthworks. That is, Mound 5 was almost certainly a single-house platform, and the simplest hypothesis to account for the linear earthwork is that it, like the others, was a long, narrow garden plot, originally 24 to 30 inches high and about 75 feet wide.

Mound 8 and abutting linear earthwork

Mound 8 may not be an artificial structure. Its apparent size and shape are nearly identical to those of the other mounds with similar linear structures, and the linear earthwork extends in the proper direction. On the aerial photograph there are hints of a circular work around it. Its top and most of the slopes are occupied, possibly formed by, the interlaced mass of a large oak tree. Other trees cover the rest of the slopes and most of any encircling borrow ditch, making excavation impossible.

The short linear earthwork is definitely an artifact. It shows clearly on the aerial photograph and can be seen on the ground. A machine-cut trench across its center produced a profile with the usual evidence for a washed- and worn-down sand structure, and sand has again refilled most of the borrow ditches paralleling the work. Height was probably the usual 2 to 2½ feet. Width is less than average, perhaps 30 feet, so it shows as a single trace on the aerial photo.

Mound 10

Mound 10 is definitely an artificial structure, but, because of an oversight on my part, it was not excavated. The mound is definitely a round platform type, probably to be grouped with the mounds that follow as 11, 12, 13, and 14. This grouping is suggested by its meander belt location and the lack of any trace of a linear earthwork.

Mound 11

Mound 11 is one of a number of mounds 50 to 100 feet in diameter and 2 to 3 feet high located in the river meander zone. All of the mounds have hammock growth, particularly cabbage palms. They have all been cut into to some degree by the river, although they appear on the aerial photograph to be remnant natural levees. Possibly they are factors in the production of these levees.

Mound 11 has a definite circular form with an approximate 100-foot diameter. Its surface is occupied by several cabbage palms and a few other trees. Elevation above the surrounding terrain, where not disturbed by river cutting, seems to be 24–30 inches.

A Florida Atlantic University student excavated one 5-by-5-foot test pit near the center of the mound. Excavation in 6-inch levels was completed to a depth of 42 inches. The lower levels are clearly below those occupied or made by humans (fig. 9.3).

Topographic information, combined with the data from this profile, suggests deposition of 12 to 18 inches of soil to produce a low, artificial mound. The thick, old humus of the gray sand stratum suggests the presence of a hammock on the natural levee prior to construction of the upper mound. Possibly this accumulation is on an older mound surface, but, since we lack adequate vertical control, we cannot determine the point.

Aside from glass and metal scrap in the modern topsoil, along with one chert chip, the material found was limited to potsherds. Levels 1 and 2 produced 4 sand-tempered plain sherds and a Belle Glade Plain sherd. This accumulation is recent, probably Period III, but the old humus produced 44 sand-tempered plain sherds (42 of them from one large sherd broken in place). These sherds suggest a Period II occupation prior to building of the mound. Thus, the low mound appears to have been built early in Period III, with some possibility that it was added to an earlier, Period II structure.

Mound 12

Mound 12, well out in the meander belt and perched neatly on an obvious natural levee, looks much like Mound 11. Its diameter is approximately 100 feet and its height in the 24-inch range, with a variation of a foot either way.

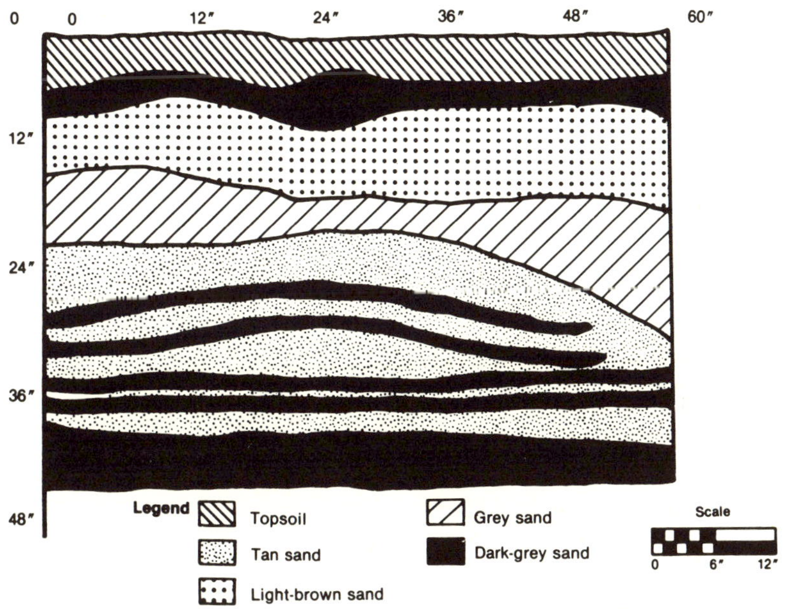

Fig. 9.3. Profile in Mound 11.

A 5-by-5-foot test pit was excavated in 6-inch levels near the mound's center by a Florida Atlantic University student. The profile (fig. 9.4) can best be interpreted as a foot of topsoil and midden developed on an artificial structure. A leached midden zone and a brown mottled and white sand zone represent the base of the mound structure. The mound rests on dark brown sand, probably an old topsoil, and it rests in turn on the normal white sand.

Sherds and other artifacts were recovered from all levels to 30 inches deep, through the old topsoil. One small projectile point came from the 24–30-inch level. Other than this point and some historic scrap, the other materials were sherds. Twenty-three were recovered from level 1: 8 sand-tempered plain and 15 Belle Glade Plain, a comparatively recent, perhaps Period IV, assemblage. From level 2 down came 12 sherds: 10 semi-fiber-tempered specimens (7 came from the 24–30-inch level, 2 from 18 to 24 inches, and 1 between 6 and 12 inches down) and 2 sand-tempered plain sherds, also found in the 18–24-inch level.

This assemblage, over 80 percent semi-fiber-tempered plain, is one of the earliest in our seriation. It is similar to the assemblage in Mid-

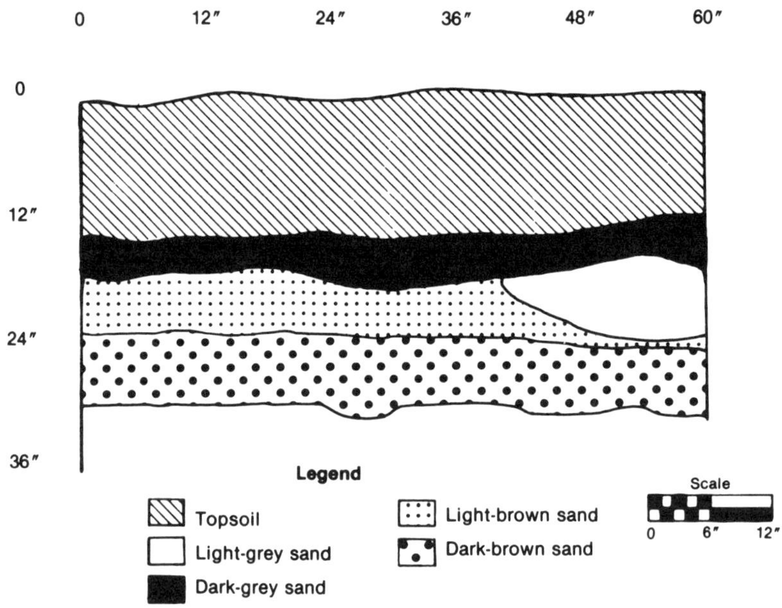

Fig. 9.4. Profile in Mound 12.

den B, associated with the building of the circles and the 450 B.C. radiocarbon date. The function of this early structure, and its later reutilization, seems to have been as a house platform. Probably, as it is today, it was often an island out in the wide river during flood stages.

Mound 13

Mound 13, located on and perhaps the cause of the formation of an old natural levee well out in the meander belt, about 1,000 feet west of Mound 12, does not show up on the map or photograph. It seems to be simply another 2-foot-high and 100-foot-across platform. Erosion, leaching, and deposition of dissolved minerals have produced problems in interpretation.

Excavation, supervised by a Florida Atlantic University student, was limited to a single 5-by-5-foot square. Final depth, well into undisturbed soil, was 38 inches. No profile was drawn because of involvement with sherds and burials that extended out of the square. In yellow-brown mottled sand, 16 to 19 inches from the surface and well above a black muck layer that appeared to be the old ground surface, the remains of at least three humans were found. All were badly decomposed, and the bone fragments were heavily encrusted with iron compounds. The iron crust was also found on the sherds from the lower levels.

Miscellaneous historic junk, including china, glass, coins, and cartridge cases, were found in the top 12 inches of the mound, along with 33 sand-tempered plain sherds and 11 Belle Glade Plain sherds, all suggesting a Period II occupation. Below this assemblage, one small stemmed projectile point and a lot of small, heavily encrusted bone scraps were associated with the skeletal remains. There were also two lots of sherds, most (possibly entirely) from two vessels. One lot was semi-fiber-tempered plain, the second chalky St. Johns paste but with a cord-marked exterior. Cord marking is not a normal part of the St. Johns complex. I see nothing particularly difficult in this association with the semi-fiber-tempered ware. The burials, and the sherds that are probably from whole vessels, suggest early erection or use of this structure as a burial mound. Possibly burials were made through the floor of a house platform. Well after the burials were in place, and after a further accumulation of topsoil during an interval with hammock growth, it was used as a house platform. I dislike leaving the question of mortuary-ceremonial function open. But, though further work was scheduled several times over a number of seasons, each time a rise in water levels made it impossible to carry it out.

Mound 14

Mound 14 is not shown on the site map or the aerial photograph. It is approximately 150 yards west, upstream, from Mound 13 in the same sort of natural levee situation, and it is similar in appearance. Surface collection produced one sherd each of sand-tempered plain and Belle Glade Plain, neither definitive. Location in the meander belt suggests that it should be considered as a part of the earliest, Period I complex.

University of Florida Mound and abutting linear earthwork

Errors on my part caused records on the University of Florida mound to be filed under both Mounds 13 and 14. The confusion is simplified by using the term University of Florida Mound, out of the numbering sequence completely. The mound does not appear on the aerial photograph because of heavy hammock growth. Neither does the abutting linear or another linear that, in uncharacteristic fashion, runs north from a point near the mound about halfway to the Mound 8 complex (fig. 1.1). The north-south earthwork is omitted because we overlooked the need for surveying it during fieldwork. By the time I had noticed the omission, a few years after the completion of the fieldwork, the pipes in that area that were the basic reference points had been removed.

The land on which these structures were built is virtually flat, as is the adjacent savannah, and it is today a hammock with primarily oaks, cabbage palms, and palmettos. Indeed, the linear earthworks owe their preservation, with contours that must resemble the aboriginal ones, to a dense growth of giant palmettos. Some of the supine and tangled trunks stretch out for 15 to 20 feet, with another 3 to 6 feet of the same plants more or less vertical.

I suspect that, when the University of Florida Mound and earthwork were used, the aboriginal environment was more definitely savannah, the same as around the other house mound–linear earthwork complexes. Certainly their construction and maintenance would have been far simpler and less laborious on the open savannah than in dense hammock.

Excavation over parts of two seasons by the University of Florida employed 10 to 12 students directed by Dr. Charles Fairbanks. Unless otherwise noted, excavation was by squares numbered in our basic grid system, with the squares generally aligned to produce trenches across the earthwork or, in the case of the mound, to produce a block that was one quadrant of the mound. The methods of level control and excavation were varied according to problems encountered.

The linear mound, about 60 feet across and approximately 100 yards long, unfortunately was not surveyed because of dense growth. The most useful data on it came from a trench cutting in at right angles and reaching the midline of the earthwork at the 1960 grid line. In the profile, the 20-foot-wide ditch that served as the source of linear fill shows clearly. Most of the fill derived from it and was deposited on top of a barely perceptible old topsoil to form the earthwork. There is some mottling with lighter and darker lenses and small strata, products of recent leaching as well as origin.

Excavation was by "natural" zones. The topsoil had a few sherds of recent mixture. Zone III, primarily the original topsoil below the Zone II fill, contained a mixture of sherds placed with the first fill. The zone consists of material left on the ground surface and some placed on it along with ditch topsoil. The mixture contains some of everything available up until the moment of construction. In a small sample, the percentage of sand-tempered plain sherds is higher than it should be, probably due to Period I or II deposits in the old humus. This situation can also be documented for the house mound to be described. The period of linear mound construction is probably best established by the few sherds from the topsoil that place it in Period IV, the latest period at the site. Even better evidence comes from the abutting round mound, which dates it to the historic period. This well-preserved linear mound, a little over 3 feet high with equally well preserved bordering ditches, is almost certainly an example in good condition of the class of linears washed and plowed down to barely perceptible elevations in the savannah.

One trench was excavated to establish any stratigraphic relationship between the linear and house mounds. No profile was drawn, but written notes substantiate the hypothesis suggested by the low area between the two before excavation. That is, the space between the two mounds was excavated by the Indians well down into the white or light gray sand to a point just over the humite hardpan. This excavation served only as a borrow pit for both mounds, connecting to, or a part of, the one encircling the house mound as well as to the ones flanking the linear earthwork. Since these structures, like Mound 1 and its abutting linear earthwork, were never in contact, the "causeway" hypothesis sometimes advanced and its implications for ceremonial use or prehistoric traffic control are rendered improbable. The lack of physical connection between a ceremonial structure and a ceremonial causeway is even more impressive as evidence against ceremonialism when one considers that the "causeways" lead to everyday house structures, midden areas today, not to structures with any evidence for ceremonial use at all.

The round mound is clearly another deliberately built house platform, built in this case at a spot occupied much earlier in the history of the site. There is old humus under the mound that grades down into white sand, as is normal, except for one small area where a brownish rather than gray topsoil concentrates at the base of the normal topsoil zone. Mound fill above the topsoil is clearly that; it is sterile and is composed of several light gray and tan-gray sand elements.

Although the trenches produced quite a few artifacts, it is clear now that vertical control was difficult. The coherent and consistent samples used on the seriation chart all come from one block of squares covering a quadrant of the mound. This sample is adequate and is consistent with the stratigraphic situation, including a good sample from the premound humus as well as from the premound topsoil. This latter sample, as well as the stratigraphy, demonstrate clearly that the mound was built deliberately and that the midden mixture that occupies the contemporary topsoil can only be a deposit from the living floor of some kind of structure.

The present topsoil, actually excavated as two zones, is one of the latest units on the seriation chart. Its chronological position is further demonstrated by a drilled gold nugget bead from this quadrant sample and by a blue glass bead, an Ichetucknee type or something similar to it, from a nearby segment of topsoil.

Collections from the original humus or topsoil and from a concentrated, brown-colored lower segment of it, labeled zone IV, are of some interest. Both are seriated in figure 7.1. In spite of being in physical contact, and clearly having been in place for centuries before the mound was built, the two deposits are different. Material from the original humus is normal for midden deposits of the period in which it falls. One piece of pipe stem probably comes from the brown deposit below it.

The lower, zone IV midden deposit was only partially excavated. It was a layer of brown dirt at the base of the topsoil. This dirt, distinctive in its brown, powdery appearance, stuck to most specimens, necessitating prolonged cleaning with acid and an ultrasonic cleaner. It looks like a localized humite deposit, suggesting a heavy accumulation of vegetable material in that area.

The collection is odd in several ways. It is high in contorted-laminated ware and has few Belle Glade Plain sherds, but it contains one sherd of semi-fiber-tempered plain. This assemblage is similar to the midden material from the surface of the small platform mound under Mound B, except that there were fragments of several platform pipes with the sherds. Pipes do not occur on the platform mound, only in the Mound A midden.

The size of this sample from only a portion of the deposit, possibly less than one-quarter, strongly suggests that a structure here was contemporaneous with the low platform under Mound B and that it lasted for some time—presumably long enough to be replaced by some occupation at the same time level as the Mound A midden deposits. These Mound A midden deposits should have had the pipe fragments.

I cannot explain the earlier, dense, brown deposit. It resembles the basal humite that underlies the entire savannah, but it must have required special conditions for formation here in the topsoil. Nor, in truth, can I suggest why an early period structure, lasting for some time, was here at all. A great deal of searching and careful shovel testing failed to find more such units of any period, let alone Periods I and II, except for one possibility near the west end of the linear earthwork. It was possibly a midden spillover from Mound A.

Mounds A and B–charnel pond complex

The mound–charnel pond complex, consisting of the mounds, the artificial pond, and an earthen embankment or wall, is located solidly in an oak–cabbage palm hammock on an old natural levee (fig. 9.5). However, pollen data (chapter 8) suggest strongly that this hammock is a recent phenomenon. The low count of oak pollen indicates only a few scattered trees, if that, at the time the complex was built. Instead, it would appear that the area was savannah, distinguished from the present savannah to the east only by 1 or 2 feet of elevation and, probably, by the disturbances of the natural system produced by humans. Quite possibly the oaks there today have intruded into the area, the result of soil systems produced by the aboriginal earth-moving projects and the changes in drainage produced by those projects.

It should be noticed that the units closest to the complex are the University of Florida Mound and related linear earthworks, much later in time, and the Great Circle, completed at a much earlier date. The circle does have one "gate" or "causeway" over the ditch (fig. 1.1), which leads toward Mound B and the embankment around it, only 300 feet away. An opening in the earthwork or wall a bit west of south of Mound B might also relate to the circle or a route to it, but this can only be speculation.

We know that maize was raised inside the circle; in fact it does not appear ever to have had any other function. In later periods, after the mound-pond complex was abandoned, linear earthworks were built, apparently to serve as drained garden plots. But the complex, which contains the most positive evidence found for maize agriculture, does not have a specific structure or location that we can say was certainly, or even probably, used for gardening. As described in the discussion of the Great Circle, it is at least possible that the circle continued to be used into Period II, the time interval during which the complex was used.

This interval would be a long time for use of a garden plot, and enrichment or fertilization, chinampa style, with rich muck full of

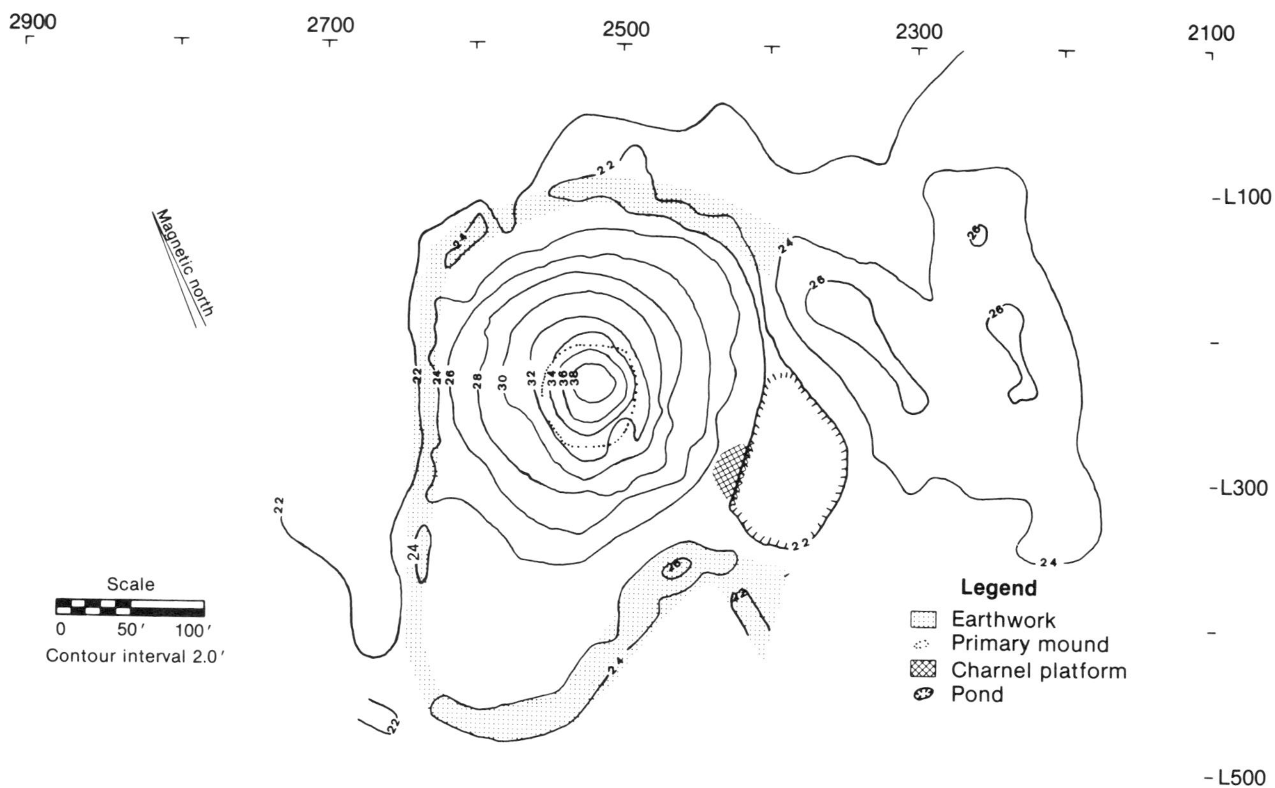

Fig. 9.5. Mounds A and B and pond complex.

tadpoles, minnow, frogs, turtles, and so on to add needed nitrogen to the soil is suggested. If the circle did not serve as a garden plot in Period II, I do not know where the corn we have evidence for was raised.

The physical relationships apparent among the mounds, earthwork, and pond in figure 9.5 suggest that they functioned as a unitary complex. Evidence for this probability emerged early in the excavation program and was soon confirmed. In any event, it was necessary during excavation to treat these units as part of a complex because, in a number of particularly important spots, one could not be investigated without disturbing at least one other.

The simplest structure, apparently, is Mound A on the east. It is a somewhat irregular earth platform, a little over 3 feet high, on average. Sufficient midden material was found on its surface to suggest that it had functioned as a living area, though some confusion was caused by recent occupation by a garden, citrus trees, and garbage dumps. One large pothole produced quantities of mussel shell. Two lobes on the mound are apparent, visible in the contours on figure 9.5; they are a bit higher than the average surface.

Our first test pit cut into one of the lobes and encountered dense, thick midden, suggesting that the lobes were structure sites or something of the sort. Further work revealed the existence of a more complex situation. Other early work at the eastern edge of the pond showed that Mound A erosion and wash into the pond was slight, so it was to be expected that erosion on shallower slopes would be even less.

The pond is an obvious feature, appearing in figure 9.5 as a depression between Mounds A and B. Never physically inviting, the pond before we started major excavation was green, scummy, and evil smelling. It was completely artificial, dug by the prehistoric Indians for ceremonial purposes. It was rather larger than the maps suggest, because wash from Mound B has filled in a large portion of it. It has a nearly flat bottom for most of its area and an elevation of between 16 and 17 feet below sea level, about 5 feet below the average undisturbed ground surface in this part of the site. (The details of excavation are considered later.)

Mound B had an ample amount of vegetation on it, including live oaks of considerable size. These offered some protection against erosion of a construction material that was mostly the native "sugar" sand. Trees had not saved the top of the mound—that part of it above the 32–33-foot contour lines—from the attention of an organized group of pothunters. The apparent symmetry of this upper portion of the mound (fig. 9.5) is due to our efforts when mapping to find those spots protected by tree root masses for measuring points and interpolating between these. One hole still shows on the southeast side. The apparent apron on the south side is also a product of the treasure-hunting activities, although we were not certain of this at the time of mapping.

Mound B, then, before excavation had a rather steep-sided upper cone, if a bit truncated at the top, and lower slopes at a lesser angle. That part at the lesser angle, including the "apron" noted, contains large amounts of wash. This wash is noted here because it affects both the pond, partially filled by the wash, and the embankment around Mound B, which also encloses the pond and forms a sort of courtyard south of Mound B. Along the west side of Mound B, this embankment formed a shelf. Its real nature was certain only after some excavation designed to clear up the point. The embankment, sketched in on figure 9.5, actually continues on at both ends to Mound A, thereby tying both mounds and the pond into a unit.

Excavation

Except for the test pit cut out from one of our trenches, all excavation in this complex—the first test pits, the later trenches, and the final five-year program—was my responsibility. The first two programs sponsored by Lykes Brothers, Inc., and the Florida State Museum employed local labor entirely, readily available in Moorehaven between sugar crops. Extensive and intensive excavation with Florida Atlantic University sponsorship and National Science Foundation funding employed a mixed crew, mixed at several levels. Most of the dirt moving, and a great deal of delicate work, was done by the same laborers from Moorehaven. (I might state, after this work and from over 30 years of experience, that students do not always do superior work and are not always more careful than laborers in spite of attributed superior motivation or, a frequently used phrase, because they "care." A man whose family depends on his paycheck cares also and, if he has spent his life at manual labor, his skills with the tools of field archaeology are superior to those of most students. Actually, most of the laborers I have hired since 1948 developed a great deal of interest and pride in what they were doing.)

Each season we had at the site a number of students. They were housed on the site in a trailer designed as a dormitory, one of three that also provided kitchen, dining space, laboratory, and office. But the students were there to learn how to excavate, to learn as many methods and techniques as possible, including how to cope with the series of crises that make up large-scale field archaeology. Very little of their time, after they had learned the basics, was spent handling a shovel. I regarded them as interns, not as labor per se, although you clearly cannot learn to operate without doing it eventually. A few of them became almost as skilled as the laborers in their use of shovels, trowels, and axes.

Most of the work was done by laborers during the first season on Mound A, and that was probably a good way to proceed. Most of the excavation was actually done by machine, using techniques which a couple of the laborers and I developed by experiment in dump piles and sterile areas. The work recovered a great deal of stratigraphic and topographic data but few artifacts. Some students kept busy with planning, recording, hand-planing walls and floors with the laborers, and similar tasks. If there had been enough students present to have done all of the work, the lack of artifacts might have caused a serious morale problem. This kind of problem is often avoided by planning excavations for instruction rather than for problem solving.

In later years, students worked at the beginning intern level as field assistants, lab supervisors, clerks, draftsmen, and so on. They learned their trade and, mostly, performed well. A separate crew supervised by Audrey Sublett recorded burials, cleaning them and recording the pertinent data while they were in place. Since the wood carvings and the burials encountered were intermingled, excavation personnel were frequently interchangeable. Records were not.

It was neither possible nor, in view of the facts, desirable to excavate the mounds, pond, and embankment as separate units. One problem, erosion into the pond, has been mentioned. Obviously, only observation of water-sorted layers and perhaps developed humus lines on a clean-cut profile will provide information enabling differentiation of wash layers and aboriginally placed fill layers or other structural elements. This sort of problem caused us, at various times, to run trenches from Mound B west across the embankment, east into the partially excavated pond, as well as north of the apparent pond edge, into Mound B. At one point, another row of squares was opened in the pond to move a profile further to the west and to settle a fill or wash question. Mound A at different times had areas cut with trenches running east-west to expose stratigraphic relationships with Mound B and with the pond. Generally, except for these, work in all three was constantly adapted to provide information on questions of physical relationship and time sequence between units as well as on their nature and function.

Work on Mound B began with the removal of the disturbed soil left us by pot and treasure hunters. They had clearly excavated all over the top of the mound, including tunneling under most of the larger trees. I had of course cursorily examined the collection of historic artifacts described in chapter 5 before beginning excavation. The disturbed earth had to be removed. I hoped in the process to find a burial or two which had been missed and thus to recover some associations between artifact classes and human remains.

The disturbed area was staked out, a vertical control system established, and the entire area excavated. All dirt was sifted through ⅜-inch mesh with a power screen and then moved some distance to a dump pile by tractor. The results of all of this were many human bone fragments (later, downslope, we found several reinterments); a lot of fragmentary, heavily oxidized, handwrought iron nails, perhaps from coffins or reused boxes; and a string of tiny shell beads, a few fragments of a Safety Harbor Incised pottery vessel, and scraps of odds and ends. (The final result was the development of considerable disgust on my part: when several members of the group that had done this destructive hunting stopped by after having entered the site illegally, it was a pleasure to arrange for their eviction by armed and deputized ranch personnel.)

One question about the relationship of the Mound B structure and these interments arose during excavation and remains unsolved. I noted several times that the top 3 feet of soil appeared to be darker sand than the fill under it or that further downslope. It seemed probable that 3 feet of local topsoil had been added to the mound after the historic period interments were buried a foot or two deep. If the soil was there when the burials were made, then the burials were about 5 feet deep. Unfortunately, in spite of much work with short profiles, replaned floors, and so on, no determinations could be made. It is, of course, possible that I was observing a 3-foot-thick humus mixture created from a normal humus by pot-hunter activity, but it seemed too dark and uniform for that.

As we cleaned up and removed the mess, a 10-foot-wide trench running on a north-south line was started, more or less through the apparent center of the mound. There was an imperative need for continuous observation of profiles to develop hypotheses concerning the nature and function of zones or layers. At the point when the base of this cut was down to 30 feet above sea level, all soil observed under the disturbed zone appeared to be a uniform, mostly light gray sand. It weathered easily, and it would not hold a vertical profile more than 2 to 3 feet high and that only for a few hours. There were at this level several pot-hunter reinterments of burials from which the artifacts had been stolen. In the profile in fig. 9.6, both the gray sand and the gray sand with charcoal flecks are disturbed. The gray mottled sand to the left, south, is as originally deposited.

The following season, with a full crew, this trenching operation was expanded to the northern and southern limits of the mound. It included, with one jog to line up a right angle, a cut through the earthwork to the south. East-west trenches were also cut, west to see if the shelf were really part of the embankment and east to provide data for mound-pond relationships. The trench to the west provided clear evidence that the shelf was part of the embankment, that it had been built on level ground, and that wash from the mound had filled in behind it.

A longer, interrupted trench to the east, cut down into the edge of the pond, showed clearly that there had been a sequence of events in the mound-pond relationship. The trench started with excavation that sliced through the normal sand soil and the underlying humite hardpan to form the pond. This relationship shows clearly around grid line 2460 in the profile in figure 9.7 in the angle of the upper surface of the hard red-brown humite, which is normally flat since it is a product of leaching and redeposition. Fill then washed in, some immediately as sorted sand and some over a long period as muck, either deposited or developed in place. It interfingers at the mound edge with wash that continued to erode into the pond, a process clearly shown in the profile (fig. 9.7).

After we had completed trenches out to and past the mound periphery in four directions and had completed the removal of disturbed soil on top of the mound, we knew a lot about the top and the fringes of the mound but little about the deeper parts of its center that we thought might have been the focus of earlier activities. This center was excavated as a large single area, starting at 60 by 50 feet. The edge toward the pond kept moving in that direction, eastward, as it was cut down and dirt moved out eastward. The other three sides, including the west side, which was the west wall of the first trench through the top of the mound, were kept as vertical walls. Since slumping continued to be a problem, these sides moved out a bit from time to time.

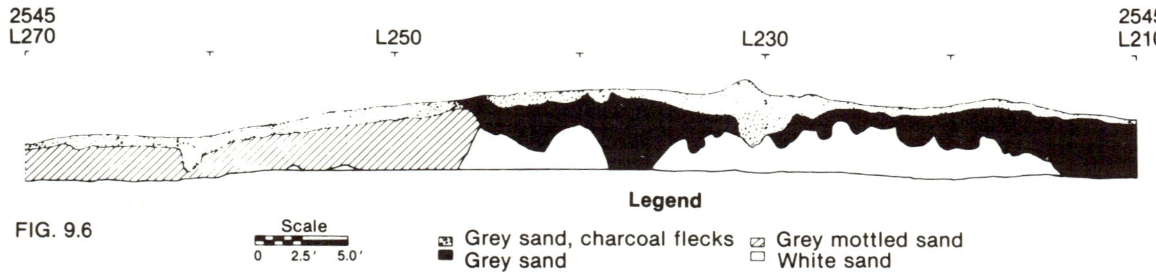

FIG. 9.6

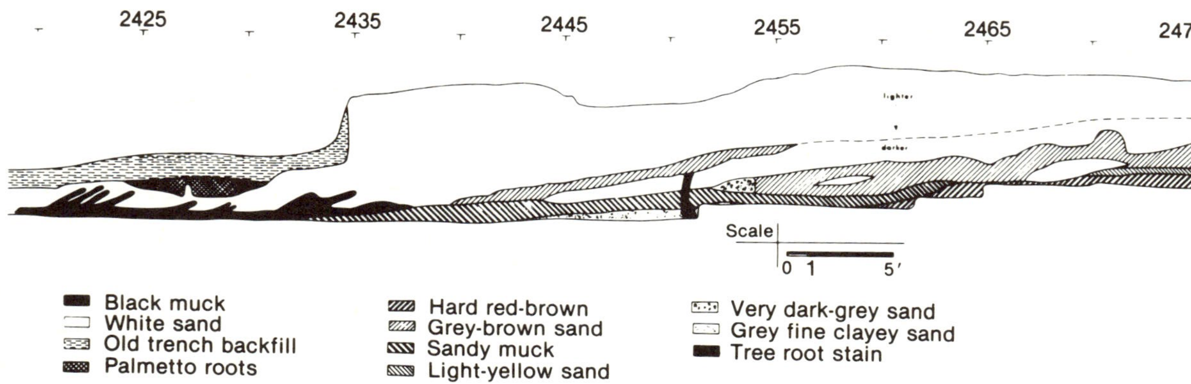

FIG. 9.7

Above, fig. 9.6. Profile of upper part of Mound B. Below, fig. 9.7. Profile of junction of pond and eastern Mound B wash.

Essentially, we excavated the center of the mound through a series of flat cuts, really continuous stripping with the tractor and hand tools. Frequent tests of one kind or another were made, as described, to enable some prediction and adoption of appropriate techniques.

Tractor cutting was accomplished by moving the machine backward and using the back of the front part of the bucket to scrape. When the bucket was nearly full, it was closed and lifted; the load, a little over half a cubic yard on average, was taken to the dump pile. One or two men stayed in front of the tractor to guide the operator while the tractor was scraping. They hand-cleaned another fraction of an inch off the cut while the tractor was depositing the load, allowing us to take the floor of the excavation down continuously in 3- to 4-inch-thick cuts, with continuous observation of a clean surface at each 3- to 4-inch interval.

Of interest to archaeological budget planners, the tractor with three men in this operation replaced an estimated 12 to 15 men with wheelbarrows. They produced clean surfaces and moved the dirt 100 yards away, just outside the working area. The tractor cycle, from the start of one cut to the start of the next, consistently ran 12 minutes.

After cleaning the floor at the 27-to-28-foot elevation, we could see a vaguely circular grayish stain, with a few dark streaks in the middle of the floor. A few well-decayed burials and a few small and rather poorly defined postholes were associated. These burials, and those to follow in this central area, were "discovered" by the tractor, meaning that they were observed after a tractor cut had gone just above them, revealing the brownish stain. In all cases, the only facts recoverable were whether the bones were human, sometimes whether they were adults or children, and usually whether the burial was a bundle or flexed. Most were flexed. There were a few bundles and no extended burials. Since this information was gained, and rechecked, by a clean slice or slices through a stain with a few bone splinters and teeth broken in place, we did not modify our technique. More "precise" methods could have been used, with no gain in information about the artifact-free burials and at an increase in cost by a factor of about 10.

One of these cleaned floors, with burials, postholes, and other features, is shown (fig. 9.8). Other floors, a foot or so higher or lower, varied in burials, postholes, and soil types.

The burials in figure 9.8 and others a bit higher and lower are also plotted on figure 9.11. Postholes, usually small, appeared near many of the bones, and occasionally there seemed to be an alignment. Possibly they remained from some sort of small shelter erected over the remains.

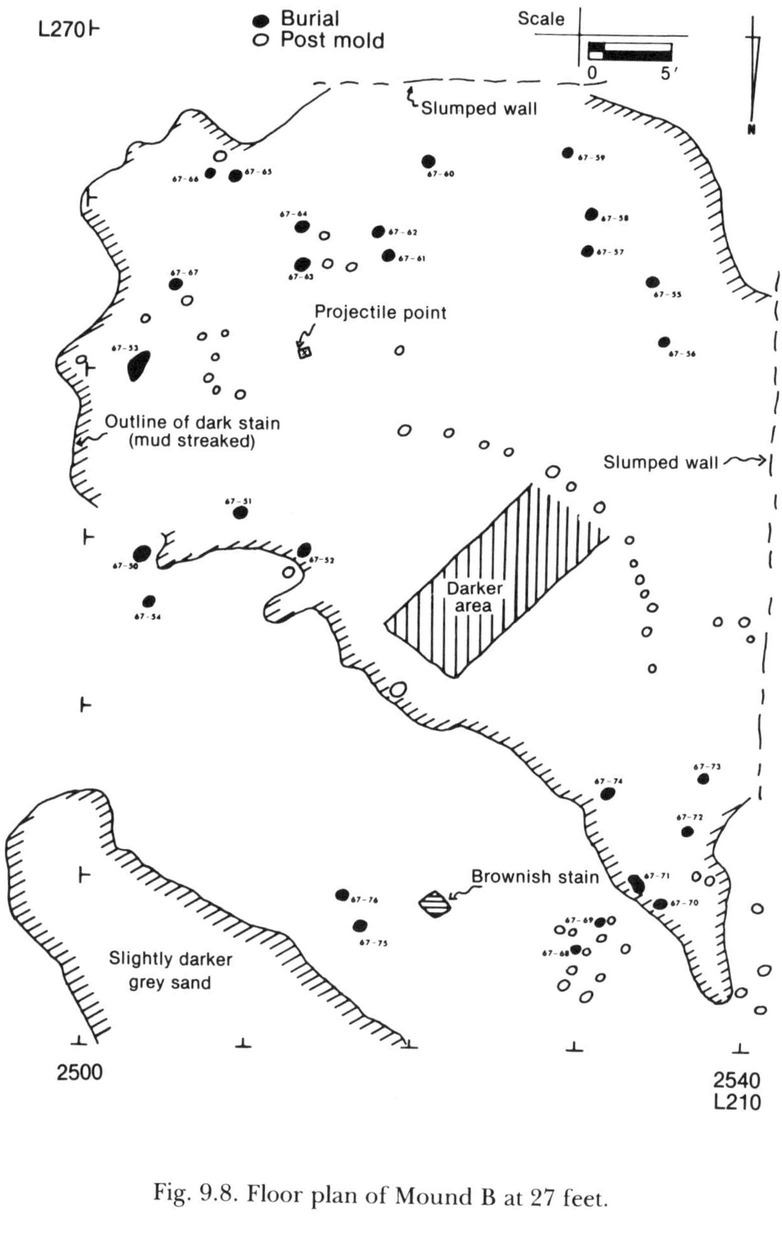

Fig. 9.8. Floor plan of Mound B at 27 feet.

As we continued to excavate this large floor, recording burial locations and frequently hand-cleaning the entire area to double-check, we explored deeper at intervals with postholes using a "bucket" type auger, a number of 5-by-5-foot-square test pits, and, finally, a single 5-foot-wide trench. The burials continued to appear concentrated toward the edges of the cut in a rough circle, associated with the "mud-streaked" sand noted in figure 9.7. At a final floor, scraped by machine and leveled and planed by hand and machine, at 26 feet above sea level, we began to run into conch shells, singly and in pairs. As with human bones, most of them were decayed so that preservation was impossible. Dissection in place demonstrated, by observation of columella remains or the lack thereof, that most shells were *Busycon* dippers but that a few were shells of another species, *Pleuroploca gigantea*, with columella intact. Several *Busycon* shells had intact columellae and could not be dippers. There were also a few projectile points, traces of midden, and a tremendous number of human teeth, invariably broken and fractured in place. Frequent small brown stains seemed to be small human bones and were definitely identified as such in a few cases.

All of this suggested that it was time to change technique. A single 5-foot-wide trench was dug; it cut through the apparent center of the roughly circular area of gray sand with mud streaks. The trench showed that we were, at 26 feet, only a foot above the surface of a roughly flat-topped mound made of a hard, yellow-brown soil mixture (fig. 9.9). There was some midden on its surface and an old humus under it. Test pits and posthole data, some not really understood earlier, demonstrated that its real edges to the north and south were inside our cut and coincided roughly with the apparent limits of the core mound with its mud-streaked gray sand. At this time, the source of the mud-streaked gray sand became clear. The gray did not bother us—gray sand is simply the product of some humus mixed with the normal white sand—but the dark gray to black streaks were a problem. In profile, they appeared as a wavy line 6 inches to 1 foot long and ⅛ to $\frac{1}{16}$ inch thick. Troweled out and viewed from above, each appeared to be a thin, concave deposit of mud.

More or less by accident, we reproduced the phenomenon and then did it again deliberately and carefully. Such mud streaks, or concave lenses, are the product of lumps and wads of sticky black muck from the charnel pond, deposited from people's feet in white or light gray sand. They develop into the thin deposits, either on the surface or, through a process I can reproduce but do not understand, after cov-

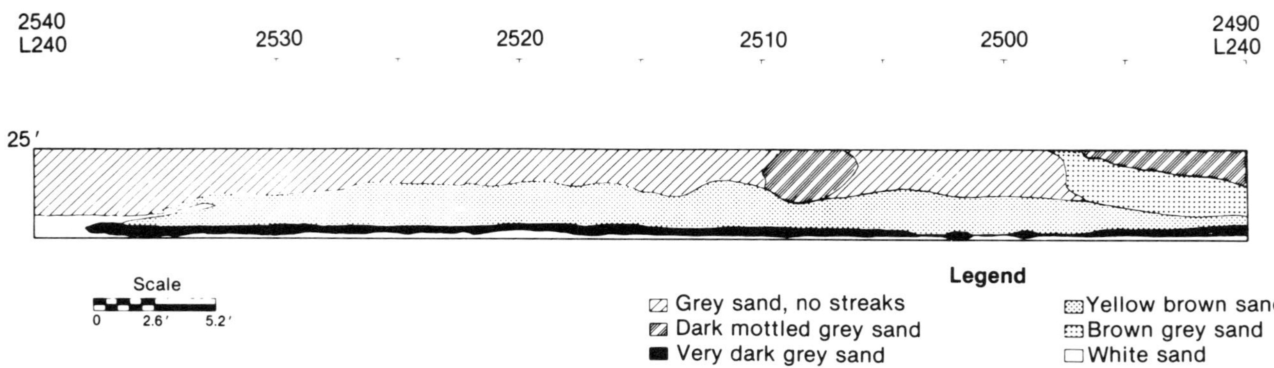

Fig. 9.9. Profile of yellow-brown "primary" platform mound under Mound B.

ering over by more sand. A lot of rain is necessary, but such is inevitable in this area. The lenses are a consistent feature of a layer over the basal, primary, brown dirt mound. The streaked layer is full of the secondary burials in poor shape, placed, as shown in figures 9.10 and 9.11, at elevations from 25 to 29 feet, the thickness of the layer. There were no artifacts with these burials.

Putting the facts and associations together, the only way the mud-streaked sand could have been produced is that people were bringing bodies from the pond. Bundled, flexed burials could easily have been floating around after the collapse of the charnel platform. These, perhaps floating skulls and possibly bundles fished up from the bottom, were put down on the sand being deposited and covered up with more sand. This theory produces the same sources for the muck and the bodies. The 150 or so burials shown in figure 9.11 would have been about half of the platform population. Presumably the others that remained in the pond were missed because they had sunk with the timbers and were entangled in a jumble of bundles, other matting, wood carvings, and strictly structural timbers.

With the removal of this mud-streaked sand with its included burials, using mostly tractor-scraping techniques, our major remaining problem was careful excavation of the brown dirt structure. A foot or so of gray sand on its surface included the conch shells, some midden, and other odds and ends. The structure itself, a platform of sorts, rested on the original humus (fig. 9.9).

Some further suggestion of the ceremonial or sacred character of this platform mound was offered by a deposit (Feature 1) on its eastern edge toward the charnel pond: a single adult human skull in poor shape, the skull cap of an infant with traces of cutting on its margins, seven *Busycon* dippers, three *Venus* clam shells, a set of nested shells consisting alternately of four clam and four scallop shells, two bird-bone tubes, and the cut and worked mandible of a small carnivore. Data from the central trench, combined with the posthole and test pit information, enabled us to continue power stripping to about one foot over the yellow dirt structure and its slopes. Here we shifted from the power tools to the more familiar hand-stripping operation. We were able to perceive the minor changes in artifact class frequencies, from the bare mound surface up, reported on the seriation chart.

Conch shells and conch-shell dippers, bone scrap, and quantities of human teeth were stripped from the structure first. Then the midden was removed. It was distinguished particularly by the absence of the pipes found in Mound A and of the charnel pond basal midden and

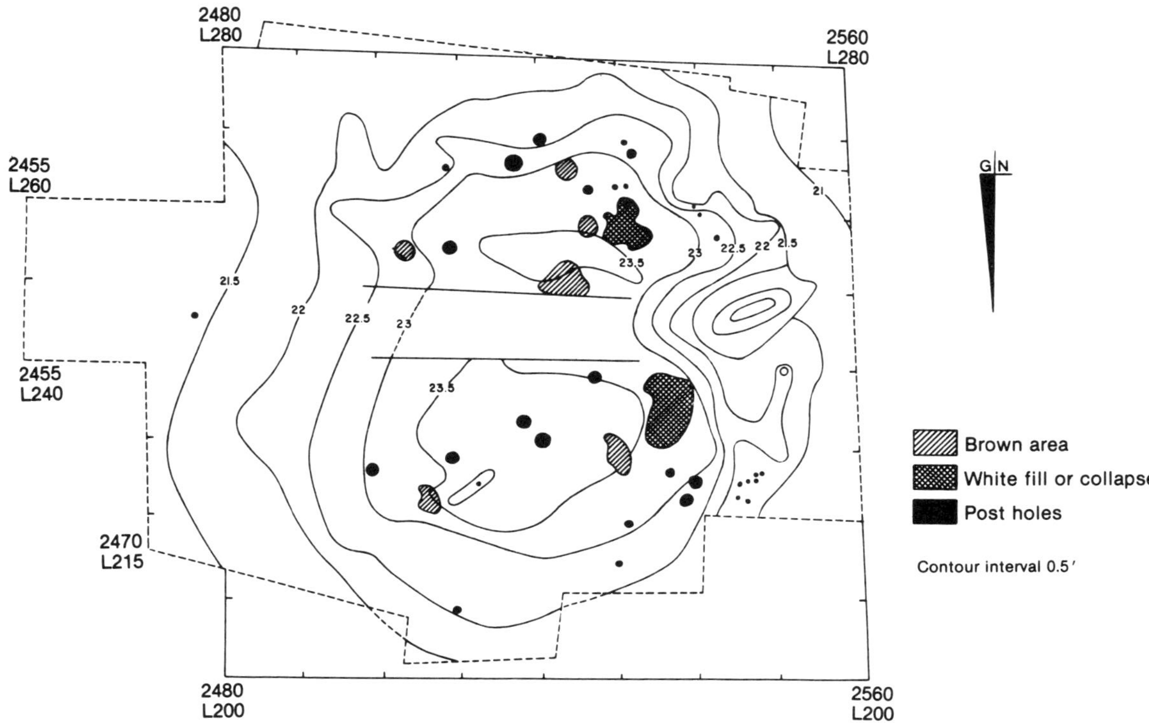

Fig. 9.10. Contours of platform mound and "bathtub."

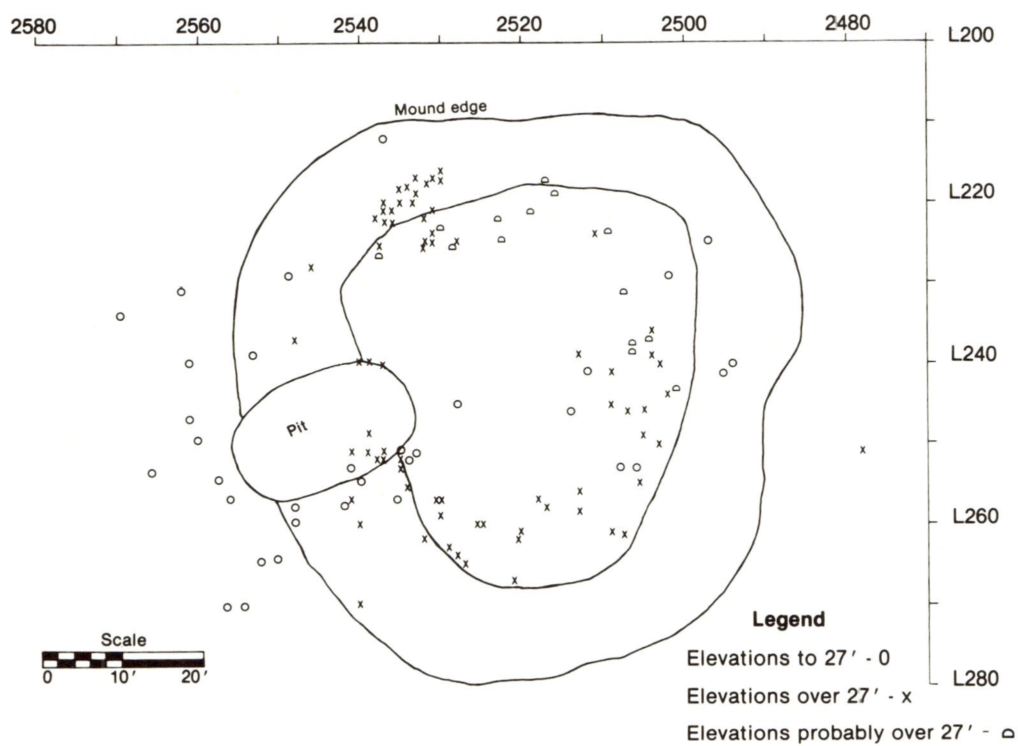

Fig. 9.11. Burials over platform mound.

by the quantities of the peculiar laminated-contorted, Pinellas Plain–like pottery. Also present were some quantity of trade ware, noted earlier (table 3.2). These sherds actually comprise most of the Period II sample. Stratigraphy at the bottom of the pond showed wash from the brown dirt mound, with its trade ware, on the bottom of the pond before the basal midden material was thrown there from Mound A.

As we completed stripping the surface of this platform mound, we could isolate and record a few postholes (fig. 9.10). We also found, just above the midden deposit, the conch shells in figure 9.12. The human teeth were, in most cases, just below it, on the original surface of the mound. We could only record them in part because of rapid drying conditions that led to immediate deterioration. With the teeth, invariably represented only by enamel that was fractured in place, were many smaller human bones. These were brown stains with a "cheesy" bone interior. The conch shells, both dippers and the *Pleuroploca gigantea* shells that might have been trumpets, as well as all the bones and teeth, provide the primary evidence for interpretation of the mound as basically a ceremonial area devoted to preparation of bodies for interment on the pond charnel platform.

The area adjacent to the western side of the mound was stripped to old ground surface, and the details of its relationship to the platform mound and the "bathtub" at its western edge emerged (fig. 9.10). In the process we found more secondary burials at a lower elevation (fig. 9.11), since the fill and burial layer over the platform mound sloped here toward ground level.

The bathtub-shaped pit caused great excitement when it was first observed on a profile that cut its eastern corner. It had the appearance then, and after clearing off its upper surface, of a collapsed tomb. But it was empty when it was filled in, partly with wash and partly with sand deposited for that purpose. Its shape resulted from omission of mound fill at the end toward the mound and extension of wings of mound material for its sides and other end. Chemical tests of slightly darker soil at its base did not produce any compounds that were abnormal and could help in interpretation. In this context, it probably functioned in body preparation, used for holding bodies for a period of decay before bone cleaning.

It is in order to recap here the sequence of events in Mound B, necessarily anticipating some information gained from excavation of the pond itself. Dirt excavated from the pond was used for two purposes: the erection of the 24-to-30-inch-high, approximately platform-

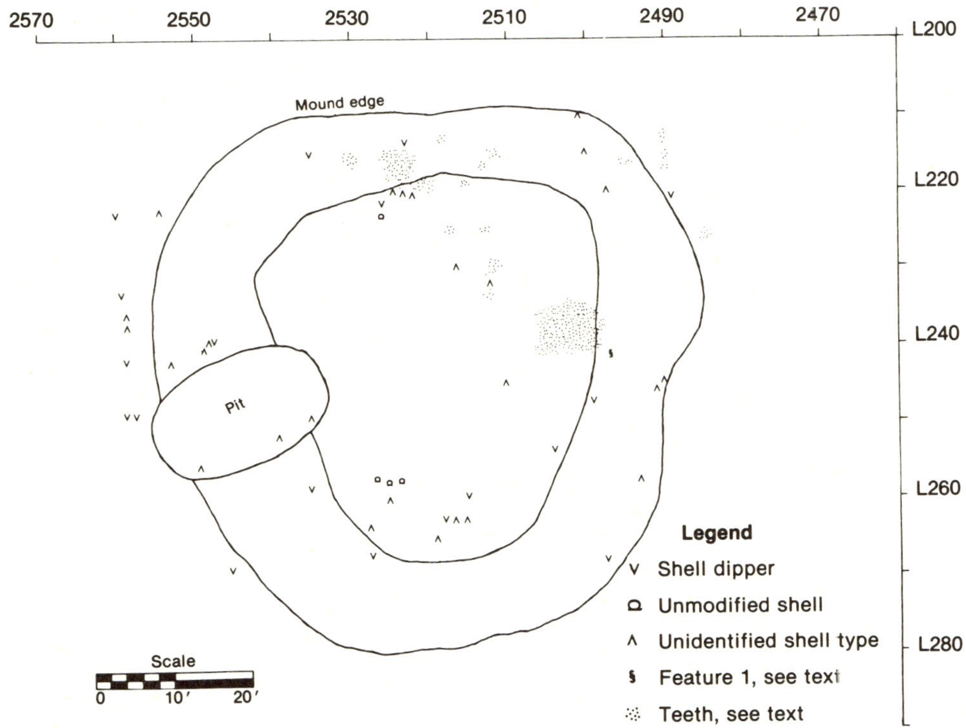

Fig. 9.12. Conch shells, teeth, and other objects associated with platform mound.

shaped, "brown dirt" or primary mound; and the construction of the earthwork encircling the platform and an area around it, particularly to the south, and connecting to Mound A at both ends. These suppositions of purpose are demonstrated by stratigraphic sequences involving both the succession and temporal relationship of strata and their origins. Brown dirt, or yellow, is available only from the hardpan. If we did not have the pond to supply it, we would have to find a borrow pit elsewhere.

At some time, the pond and the structure in it stopped being used. At that time, apparently, the brown dirt platform with its bathtub pit, along with the remains and artifacts on the mound, also became superfluous and were buried. Dirt was carried in, probably from a borrow pit to the south that is visible on the aerial photograph (fig. 1.2). As this dirt was being deposited, bodies recovered from the pond were placed in a continuous sequence in an area roughly defined by the locations of the platform and pit complex. This activity ceased when the mound reached a height of 28 to 29 feet above sea level. From there, to a final height estimated at about 25 feet, 46 feet above sea level, the same clean white sand, but without the mud from the feet of the workers, continued to be deposited. No artifacts or cultural material of any kind was included. The steep conical shape that resulted did not, and could not in this area of heavy rainfall, last very long. It eroded quickly in all directions, including successive washes into the pond, which covered muck, bones, and wooden specimens.

After much erosion and many centuries, the historic burials were placed in the top of the mound. Setting the time for the end of use of the platforms, the brown dirt one under the mound and the wooden one in the pond, at around A.D. 500 suggests that the mound sat for 1,000 years before placement of the historic graves and their gold, silver, copper, and brass grave goods.

Pond

The pond always had some water in it. Our first excavation efforts required the use of pumps, and the need for them continued until we had finished our work and allowed the pond to fill again. It was always flooded because the aboriginal excavation cut through the humite hardpan that underlies the 2 to 4 feet of surface sand in the savannah and provides the base for the surface water table. Water drains along it and into any lower places during dry spells. This means that the excavation of the pond had to be completed while the feature was flooded.

The first excavation, a gingerly excursion into this part of the site, was in the first season of test work and was designed to secure enough information to enable preparation of a grant proposal. The carved wooden eagle that has been in the Florida State Museum for many years appeared to have come from this pond in 1926, according to the scant and somewhat confused information on file. If indeed other wooden objects were to be encountered, we had to consider the requirements for wood preservation.

We started work prepared to move water, with pumps, well points, pipe, and hose on hand. Wood preservation was handled with two vats made from a 55-gallon steel drum cut in half lengthwise and gallons of white glue and carbowax. After experimenting with bits of scrap wood, we did not use the carbowax.

Contiguous squares, developed into trenches with baulks at first remaining down their length for profile control, were excavated by 6-inch levels, mostly with trowels. With few exceptions, everything found was pedestaled to retain associations for as long as possible.

Fortunately, little material was found in one of the first squares, which allowed us to take it down quickly into undisturbed soil. We kept one corner low while we did this and pumped from it frequently. After we completed excavation of the square, the hose intake for a pump was kept inside a strainer in this hole and water from all other excavations in the pond was directed into this pump by control of levels, minor drainage channels, and so on. In the excavation process, we quickly discovered that the lowest parts of wood carvings and human bones, or the lowest points in piles of either one or both, were at a relatively constant elevation of 18 feet above sea level. They were resting on a midden deposit with this level as its upper surface. Midden at the bottom of a pond seemed odd, as did the presence of hardened human feces in the midden, since water is not noted for its preservative action on this type of material. We excavated quantities of the midden, usually in one 6-inch level and whatever thickness less than 6 inches that was required to remove the midden and reach the clay, sand, or gravel that was the bottom of the aboriginal excavation.

With the end of the first season, we withdrew to consider the data in hand and the specimens ready to analyze. The excavated area, with some specimens or part of them sticking out of standing walls, was covered with sheet plastic, 6 inches to a foot of dirt, and allowed to reflood. Within a few weeks, the excavated area and the rest of the hole was once more a scummy, green, evil-smelling pond.

Two years later we were able to tackle the pond and Mounds A and

B simultaneously, a necessity for working out the prehistoric erosion-building-deposition-excavation sequence. The large area of Mound B planed down with the tractor was adjacent to the pond so that elevations that threatened to collapse were being consistently reduced in height as we pumped and dug.

Excavation of the major part of the pond followed, using basically the techniques developed during the first season. Sections, usually 25- or 30-foot-long strips, were opened simultaneously. A profile was maintained on one or more sides, depending on what stratigraphic data were most needed. Clearing muck from bones and wooden specimens was always accomplished in a way that allowed drainage into a sump. The original sump had to be supplemented by a second one. One or two pumps were operated as the accumulated water and the rate of flow made necessary. Each morning, 1 to 2 feet of water were pumped out of the area being excavated, 2 to 4 feet on Monday mornings. Pumps were run during the day as needed, keeping in mind that complete drying out not only would have been impossible but could have ruined the specimens.

One of the pumps had a valve system installed at the output end. This system permitted us to direct part of the water back to areas where it was needed—to spray part of Mound B that was drying too rapidly with lawn sprinklers, to spray wood specimens that were beginning to dry, and, through a garden hose, to use water under pressure to excavate many wooden specimens and some bone ones. Orchard-type sprayers were used in the same way, usually for finer work since the jet pattern was easy to adjust and pressure could be regulated both through tank air pressure and careful control of the trigger valve.

All human bone was studied in place by the late Dr. Audrey Sublett and her team of physical anthropologists and students. In all but a few cases, they cleaned the bone in place, made their in-place observations and measurements, and then removed the bones for final cleaning and the move to the laboratory. Unfortunately, Dr. Sublett's lengthy illness and subsequent death prevented preparation of a report. All notes, observations, and specimens remain in the Florida Atlantic University anthropology laboratory for, I hope and expect, a separate report at some future time. About all I can say here, according to daily but undocumented communication, is that the charnel pond contained the remains of about 150 individuals, based on a count of right mastoid processes. Some partial articulation was present; there were definite suggestions that the degree of articulation was higher before the platform collapsed. It is my own view, in which Dr. Sublett did not fully concur, that the bodies on the platform were probably roughly defleshed, flexed bodies, made into bundles with a wrapping of matting. Sex and age distribution, I was informed, appeared to be normal for a population at this cultural level.

This seems a reasonable place to describe strata, sequences, and events related to the pond in order of deposition and occurrence, determined in various ways as explained. We start with an artificial pond. Its horizontal dimensions were on the order of 60 to 70 feet long, the length of the "D" shape on figure 9.5, and about 40 feet in breadth. Its lowest point was 16 feet above sea level. Since average land elevation in that part of the site is 21 to 22 feet, the depth of the pond was a bit over 5 feet. Usually water would have filled it only part way, to a little above the humite level, for a depth of 4 feet.

The purpose of the pond was to provide the culturally correct environment for a charnel platform; evidently the water was a ceremonial requirement. We must assume that the platform was built immediately after the completion of the excavation of the pond, although unfortunately we have no precise data on this possibility. The pond base was just on or above layers of clay and gravel that could not be pumped dry. I think it is worth emphasizing that the excavation of that part of the pond below the brown humite hardpan must have been completed in a water-filled hole. The chances of a drought in the recent past having dried out the entire Lake Okeechobee basin below a humite formed as the result of saturation are not only remote but virtually impossible.

Descriptions of all pieces of wood found in the pond that appear to have been shaped were presented in chapter 4. Their locations within the pond are shown in figure 9.13; there are also some probably shaped but not illustrated pieces. The location diagram served in part as the basis for the artists' reconstruction of the platform (fig. 9.14). The individual artists' reconstructions of the identifiable specimens and photographs of the carvings themselves are also found in chapter 4.

We cannot demonstrate absolutely that the carved wooden figures were parts of a platform. They certainly did fall down with the human bones, resting on the muck layer at the bottom of the pond. They also had bases long enough, with or without tenon adaptations, to reach into the bottom of the pond and hold the bird and animal representations above water as shown in the reconstruction. Mixed with the recognizably shaped fragments, there was a great deal of thoroughly rot-

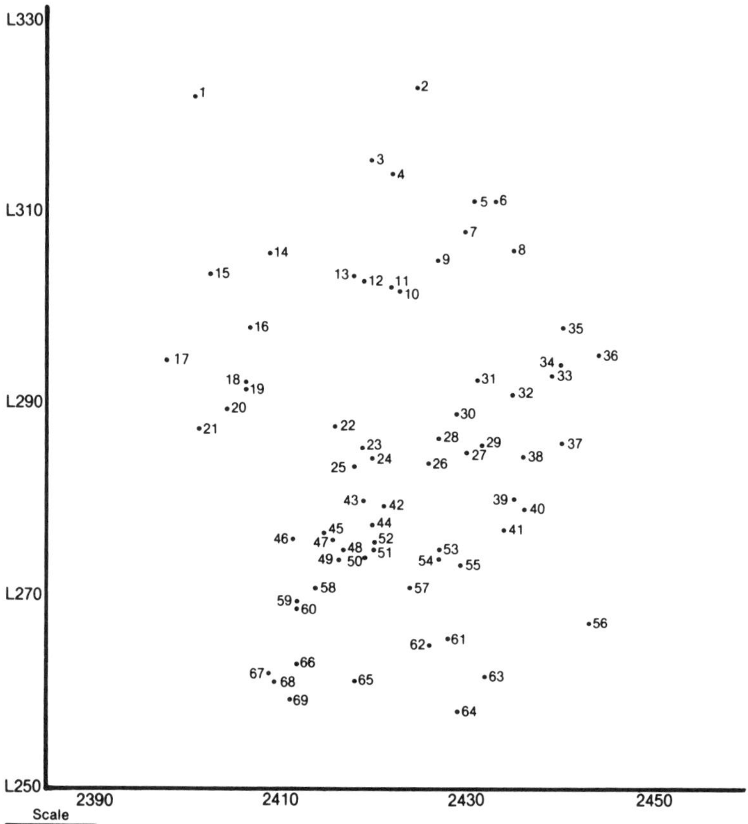

Scale

0 5′ 10′

No.	Ref.
1	4.11,C
2	—
3	4.2,C
4	—
5	—
6	4.4,B
7	—
8	4.2,B
9	—
10	4.1,B
11	—
12	4.1,B
13	—
14	—
15	4.11,A
16	—
17	4.6,A
18	4.3,G
19	4.3,G
20	4.10,B
21	4.10,A
22	4.3,F
23	—
24	—
25	4.2,C
26	4.4,A
27	—
28	4.6,F
29	—
30	—
31	—
32	4.4,C
33	4.9,C
34	4.5,D; 4.10,D
35	4.9,D
36	—
37	4.5,C
38	—
39	4.4,E
40	—
41	4.9,A
42	4.6,C
43	4.6,B
44	4.6,H
45	4.3,E
46	4.1,A
47	—
48	—
49	4.3,H
50	4.5,B
51	4.4,D
52	4.5,A
53	4.7,B
54	4.7,B
55	—
56	4.7,A
57	4.7,B
58	4.2,A
59	4.6,G
60	4.7,D
61	—
62	—
63	4.10,C
64	4.7,C
65	4.6,D
66	4.9,B
67	—
68	4.9,E
69	—

Fig. 9.13. Location in pond of carved wooden specimens.

ted wood. Piles of carved wood, human bone, and rotted wood were as thick as 18 inches, even 24 inches in a few spots. There were also a fair number of recognizable and apparently unmodified pieces of tree trunks and branches and a number of tree trunks with attached, flat root masses. At least one of these flat root masses near the north end of the accumulated material was extensively charred, as were carvings and human bone in this area. All of the evidence together—the wood recovered or observed, plotted, and returned to the pond—makes plausible a platform that held up the bones and used the carvings as described in chapter 4.

When this structure collapsed, apparently because of fire at the north end that destroyed structural integrity, the bottom of the pond was already covered with two artifact-bearing deposits. The first of these, sandy and laminated, was clearly derived as slope wash from the Mound B area (fig. 9.7). The sherds, labeled "Mound B wash" on figure 7.1 where they are early, were nearly identical to the collection from the surface of the brown dirt platform mound. This resemblance is shown by the relative proportions of major types and variants present and by the trade sherds. They are a major part of the Period II trade sherds listed in table 3.1.

The second deposit, which overlies the first in spots along the north side, is much thicker, more extensive, and of a curious origin. Soft and mucky, it was clearly midden material with a heavy sherd and bone component, supplemented by small quantities of fresh- and salt-water shell fragments, lumps of soft, sandy, gray-white material, pipe fragments, and a lot of human feces. Some of the feces were very soft and virtually unrecoverable; others were very hard. We assumed, at first, that the deposit accumulated during the use of the platform, that people threw stuff in, including the fecal specimens. Some are clearly the products of constipation and others of diarrhea.

Excavation of about one-quarter of the deposit was managed, mostly done with trowels, working into a 10–12-inch face to remove two levels. This approach seemed to work reasonably well as long as the pumps continued to function. It was only after complete processing of the specimens in the laboratory that the origin of this pond-bottom midden became apparent. The bulk of this material (called "Mound B–pond basal midden" in the seriation chart) fits into the development of the Mound A midden at a specific time, as reflected in that chart. This time was when the feces were being exposed to lime that was being burned on Mound A. Since this hardening could not have taken place in the pond, it appears that the basal muck is the product of a massive Mound A housecleaning: All of the material was thrown into the pond.

After this episode, life continued as before, both in the pond and on Mound A. The collection sample in figure 7.1 labeled "Mound B pond-wood-bone level" suggests some deposition from Mound A

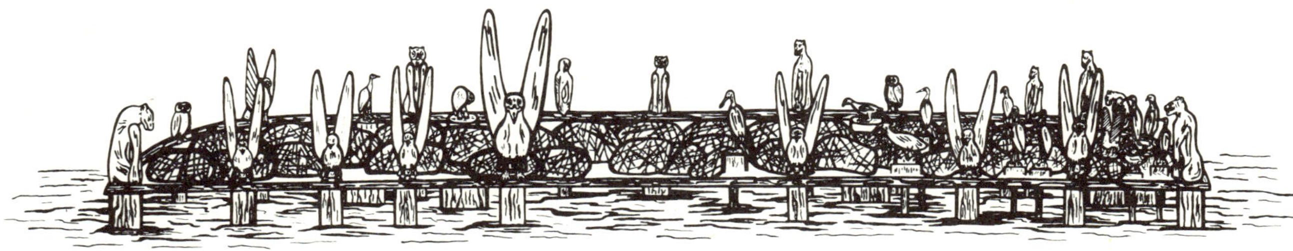

Fig. 9.14. Reconstruction of charnel pond platform.

after the platform had collapsed and almost certainly after the final cap had been added to Mound B, terminating the ceremonial functions of the complex.

Mound A

A 5-foot-wide trench was cut into Mound A in the 1966 season. The mound was excavated in 6-inch levels to undisturbed basic soil to determine its probable nature and its relationship to the pond and to Mound B and to allow planning for large-scale work.

A profile drawing of a long segment of this trench (fig. 9.15) demonstrates a number of things. Most of the exposed midden, the dense hard midden and shell, is on sand with an elevation of a little under 22 feet, close to the normal elevation of the terrain so that, even though there is some drop to the east, there does not appear to have been a pre-midden artificial structure here.

Several trenches were dug to the south, shorter ones to the north, and one back to the pond edge to the west; the trench illustrated in figure 9.15 was excavated all the way across the mound to the east. All of these trenches were designed to give information about structure and depositional history. Most of them gave us this information, but artifact-bearing deposits or strata either were missing or were thin, except for the first one encountered. Results from other deposits are included in the summary remarks at the end of this section.

We then opened up an area to the south of the east-west trench, extending to the south from the richest deposits on the profile. A large area, 60 by 25 feet at its greatest extent, was excavated on a continuous basis, with some shifting of boundaries with time and an increase in information. Figure 9.16 depicts a profile through the deposits to the south and a fairly typical clean floor, in this case at a high level, just below the humus of 25.1 feet above mean sea level. Neither the ash area nor the burial, a recent interment of an adult female without grave goods or ornaments, provided much information, but the exposure is typical of what we had to work with and what was recorded. The total area was dug with a continuous shovel-peeling technique with the floor kept level, completely clean, and under observation at all times. All of the dirt, midden mostly, was mechanically sifted. The midden was tremendously rich. Inspection of totals on the seriation diagram (figure 7.1) demonstrates that sherd samples ran to 5,000, 6,000, and even 7,000 sherds. By volume, there was at least three to four times as much animal bone. With the midden were occasional human deciduous teeth, indicating that people really had chil-

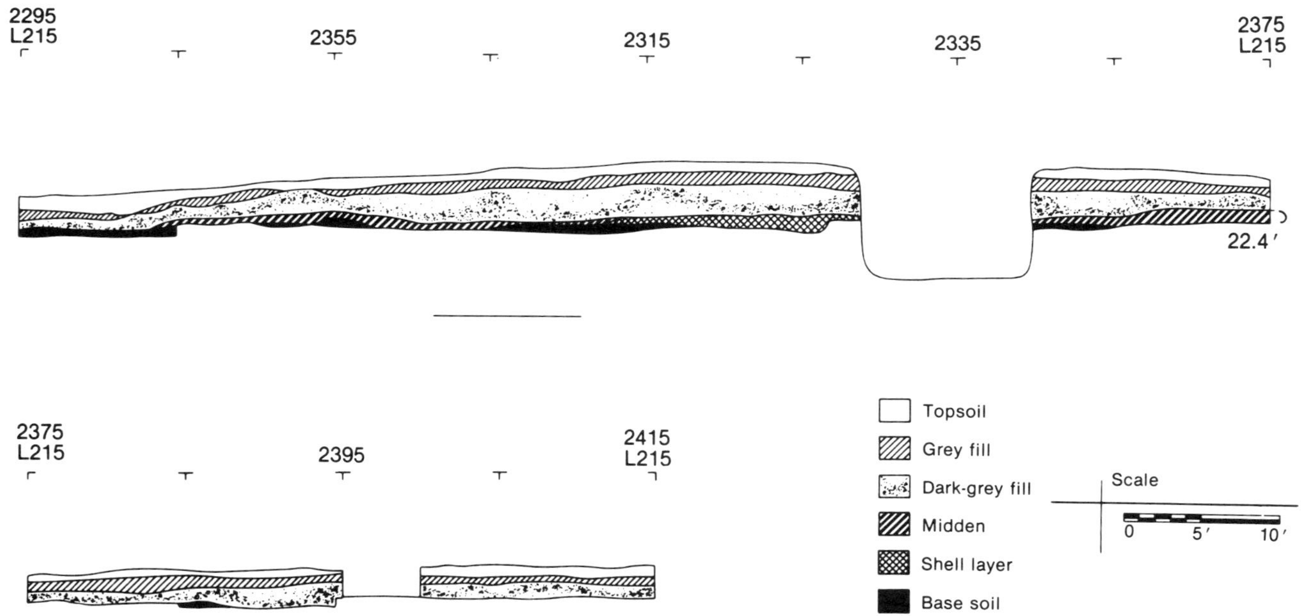

Fig. 9.15. Profiles on 215 grid line in Mound A.

dren there, and occasional odds and ends of broken human bone, definitely deposited with animal bone, usually deer, and discarded in the same way. Cannibalism seems probable. Artifacts other than sherds—shell tools, pipes, some stone grinding tools, and a few other items—were recorded individually with precise vertical and horizontal coordinates taken and recorded. I could not find any meaningful clusters or associations.

At what seemed to be appropriate intervals, the floor was leveled, cleaned, and inspected carefully for structural remains such as postholes. It is my contention that posthole alignments can easily be missed (and usually are) in 5-foot trenches or pits. They show up with the increase in contrast and visibility on larger prepared surfaces.

Unfortunately, no real post molds could be found until we had cut all the way through the midden, when they became obvious on and in the immediate pre-occupation surface. Most of them had been filled in, as the posts rotted, with midden debris partially cemented together by lime, a mixture characteristic of the lower part of the midden. The post molds observed and plotted at this lowest level probably come from all of the buildings erected over many years. Efforts were made to sort out "cement" postholes from others filled with less hard substances and to sort by varied depth, but none of this was helpful. The distribution suggests definitely oval or circular houses about 30 feet in diameter with 18–24-inch spacing between posts.

An unusual feature of the Mound A midden deposit was that large quantities of lime had been made in pits by burning shells. In the floor plan, the lime pits appeared as circles. The centers of these circles were hard lime mixed with some sand, which, chemically, approaches a fair grade of plaster. Inspection of the material under a binocular microscope demonstrates its derivation from shells; incompletely calcined shell fragments can be seen in large quantities. The "plaster" faded into a ring of shells, more thinly dispersed as one moved out from the center. Most of the shells were river mussels, but there was also marine shell scrap, particularly conch and *Venus* clam. All of the lime pits excavated were used for lengthy, if variable, periods of time as shown by thin lenses of midden intruding into, at times through, the center lime deposits. This intrusion showed that lime and midden accumulated at about the same rate while the total deposit increased its elevation by a foot or more.

As we sliced horizontally through these circular deposits, the reason for the presence of hard human feces became apparent. Defecation seems to have taken place on the edge of the lime. The chemical ac-

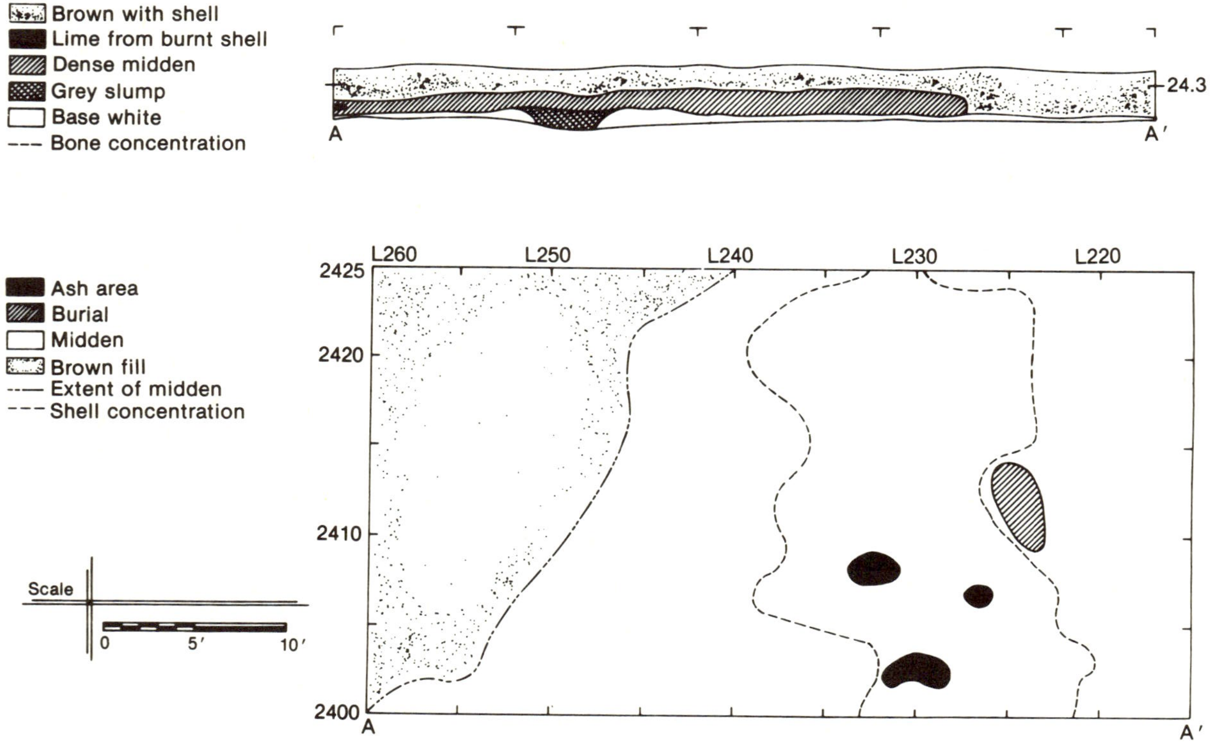

Fig. 9.16. Profile and floor in Mound A.

tion of fresh quicklime kills odor, a purpose for which it is used today, and it chemically altered the feces. Whether elimination of odor was intentional is questionable. Unfortunately, this alteration did not preserve vegetable material in recognizable form. Small bone fragments were present. The feces have been analyzed for pollen content (chapter 8).

Lime penetrated the midden. The lowest part of the deposit was almost solid, extending downward into the "concrete" post molds. This hardening is similar in effect to what often takes place in shell middens. Here we lack an adequate supply of shells, but the action could take place more rapidly with finely powdered lime that would go into solution easily. Further, lime solution made for the purpose to be discussed had to be discarded somewhere.

I suggest that the lime was made for the treatment of maize, that stored, dry, and hard maize was soaked in a lime solution to soften it. In the process, the maize swelled and the soft outer skin could be removed. Although this soaking is the first step in the production of masa in Middle America, there is not evidence here for the production of tortillas. Rather, since we do have pestles, the familiar mush, sofkee if you will, of the eastern United States appears to have been the final product. I realize that this treatment does not produce hominy or hominy grits, which are made in the eastern United States by a different treatment with wood ashes, that is, with lye. I suggest that, rather than being an independent invention, the hominy–wood ash treatment developed from the lime-masa, a process millenia old in Central America by the time it appeared in Fort Center. The evolution requires only constant decrease in the proportion of shell or rock for lime and an increase in the amount of wood to produce more ash. The use of either ashes or lime yields a similar product. How many of the white-to-gray lenses labeled as "ashes" in middens in Illinois and Ohio were really lime, recognized as such by some of the earliest mound excavators?

To summarize, Mound A began its existence with the deposition of midden on the ground surface adjacent to the pond. Radiocarbon dates as well as seriation techniques demonstrate that it existed in the same time interval as Mound B but slightly later and that it continued to develop after the brown dirt platform under Mound B no longer served domestic functions or habitation. It certainly was in existence during the time that the pond was functioning as shown by the midden deposited at the pond's base. Some use of Mound A as a living area continued until well along in Period III.

However, most of the elevation that makes up Mound A on figures 1.1 and 9.5 appears to have had other functions. To the north and south, parts of the mound are associated with the earthwork that encircles the ceremonial areas. Some of the structure to the east and west is sterile fill—like the earthwork-related areas—added late in the history of the structure to increase its area. Test pits and trenches were dug to determine the function of these areal increases, and we constantly examined floors and walls of cuts for answers. I can say only that increases in Mound A's size were apparently considered desirable or necessary or both several times in Periods II and III and so were built. No specific data could be found.

The dense midden area of Period II, adjacent to the pond and the charnel platform, level with the functioning area of Mound B to which it was connected by earthworks, probably had a sacred function. Its earliest levels follow the midden deposits on the little platform mound in the enclosure, adjacent to the pond. Probably the few ceremonial specialists who had produced the midden deposits on the Mound B brown platform mound—deposits related to only one or two dwelling units—moved to Mound A. I am inclined to view the two to four dwelling units found on Mound A at all times as housing for ceremonial specialists. They began the use of pipes at the site, and it appears at least possible, perhaps even probable, that a part of their sacred function was providing lime for others. At that time there were a few other people on the site or in other areas in use, represented by Midden A deposits and the deposit under the University of Florida Mound.

The Mound B area, particularly the brown platform with its built-in "tub," continued to serve ceremonial functions, as attested by the presence of the tub, the large quantities of human bone scrap and teeth, and the conch shells, be they dippers, trumpets, or symbols of some sort. When we remember that strict contemporaneity is certain among the pond, this platform, and the earthworks—a complex clearly functioning for mortuary ceremonialism—the move to Mound A is surprising. But stratigraphy and seriation document that it did happen.

The ceremonial aspect of Mound A is demonstrated by the occupancy that began there when it stopped on the brown platform mound, by the earthworks encircling the brown platform and the pond end at Mound A on both sides, tying it physically to that complex, and by the deposition of large amounts of garbage—midden—in the pond and under the charnel platform before its collapse.

The dwelling units on Mound A apparently housed religious functionaries, probably the equivalent of the Choctaw Buzzard Men, and their families, who cleaned bones from decomposed human bodies. That the people living on Mound A were families is demonstrated rather neatly by occasional finds of deciduous teeth. These people operated the ceremonial center activities for a considerable number of persons scattered through the desirable bits of microenvironment on the sand lands around the lake. Our evidence suggests that, during Period II, the site was used as a ceremonial center with a resident population of ceremonial specialists of several families. This activity, continuing over some centuries, would have produced all of the bodies on the platform, including those moved to Mound B after the collapse of the platform. The lack of rank and status differentiation among the charnel house pond bodies is because all of the persons so disposed had status as ceremonial-mortuary specialists. The people they served in their duties as specialists—providing lime for treatment of their corn and probably pipes and tobacco—lived elsewhere, in the small midden sites on higher land throughout the sand country.

If other centers such as Big Tony's Mound or Ortona were in operation at this time, then Fort Center served only a fraction of the Belle Glade culture population.

Great Circle

The "Great Circle" is one of the dominant features of the site (figs. 1.1, 1.2). It is about 1,200 feet in diameter, and the ditches that form it average 25 to 30 feet wide and 6 feet deep. Dirt from its excavation seems to have been thrown on either side but with a distinct preference for the interior.

There are two "causeways" formed by unexcavated segments. They do not show well on the site map with its 2-foot contour interval, but they are plain on the ground and clearer on a 1-foot contour interval map. One of them is immediately east, or northeast, of the near circular depression on the southeast side of the circle; the ditch curls out and into the depression, usually a pond, leaving the causeway before the ditch resumes a bit further along. The other is near the eastern limit of the circle, approximately opposite Mound B.

The aerial photograph (fig. 1.2) shows traces of two other, somewhat smaller, overlapping but not concentric circles. Traces of these circles and their intersections with each other are represented on the map by the odd and otherwise inexplicable changes in elevation in the interior of the Great Circle. These elevation features are both ditch and old ditch spoil traces.

Planning excavation of something this size, to increase our ability to test hypotheses, is a bit of a problem. Four efforts of varying character were made, preceded by a thorough inspection—a survey, if you will. On my hands and knees I looked at every inch of soil visible and inspected the dirt from gopher burrows, minor erosion channels, and all other disturbances. After a chopping device pulled by a crawler tractor had removed some of the huge palmetto clumps, I looked again. Over the years, all of the students, archaeologists working at the site, visitors, and visiting archaeologists, including Jim Ford and Mike Coe, looked too. No artifacts of any kind were ever found except in the riverbank middens.

During the first test programs, I put 20 feet of a 5-foot-wide trench into a low rise, believed to be a mound, near the center of the circle. There were 2 feet of sand, leached white, over the original surface with its humus near the center of the rise. The sand was artificial, but there was no indication of its function. In retrospect, the "mound" is a spoil remnant from one of the older, small ditches.

Some years later we dug four 5-by-5-foot pits in the eastern side of the circle, into spots picked as exceptionally high or low. Results suggested extensive soil rearrangement in the area, again apparently a product of digging the smaller circles. Of the soil samples taken, three produced maize pollen (samples P-116, P-267, and P-301). One of these, P-116 could conceivably be a product of recent contamination, although I do not believe that it is. The others are definitely prehistoric (chapter 8). Unfortunately, while the samples demonstrate prehistoric maize growing, they cannot be dated with any certainty. Since the soil movement in that area seems to have been a product of small circle construction, this sample probably related to the time of that construction.

A third effort to secure data that could help us with problems of dating, of construction method and sequence, and of the function of the circles was undertaken late in the work at the site. The 1,000-foot-long trench shown in figure 1.1 was cut across a major part of the circle, using the tractor. The base of the trench was on the humite layer except in one 20-to-40-foot segment near the L600 stake, where the humite was missing, a lack attributed to earlier small ditch construction. While the trench was being dug, all dirt was piled on the west side of the cut by the tractor, and the east side profile was hand cleaned for study. At least one set of soil samples representing all visible strata was taken at each 100-foot station.

Still, no artifacts were found. There was definite evidence of the small circle construction in the L600 to L800 area. Cuts and fills as well as the missing humite could be seen clearly on the profile and on the floor. Certainly the trench and the test pits demonstrated that the traces of smaller circles visible on the aerial photograph were real and that maize had been grown in the circle in prehistoric times.

The most useful and immediately pertinent information on the circles, their age, and their construction sequence was produced by Charles Fairbanks and his students during the 1967 field season, prior to the excavation of the long trench. A series of well-designed and -executed cuts intended to provide the needed information did just that. The comments following are from a 1967 "in-house" report by Fairbanks, edited only by omission, as indicated. The profile accompanying this report (fig. 9.17) has been edited a bit from the field copy, mostly by adding symbols to replace a number code for strata and lenses.

After noting that the smaller circles visible on the aerial photograph are less clearly defined than the big circle, and thus might be older, Fairbanks states:

> We began the investigation of these ditches in an attempt to define their period of construction and use, as well as to attempt some functional explanation of their use. . . . A trench 5 feet wide was cut across the entire visible ditch about 100 feet from the creek. . . . A second 5 foot cut was made beside the first. . . .
>
> Our first discovery was that the visible ditch was paralleled by a precedent ditch to the west which was invisible from the surface. . . . There seems to have been some weathering of the [earlier] ditch profile while it was open, although this could not have been very long. Subsequently, the ditch was filled with the dirt excavated from the later ditch to the east. . . . The eastern, later ditch is clearly intrusive to the western ditch as its fill strata overlie the earlier strata. . . .
>
> We cut another series of profiles across the two ditches 100 feet further west and 400 feet south of the first cut. . . . At the most southern cut almost no artifacts were found in the basal deposits of either ditch, although they were so abundant in the bottom of the younger ditch near the creek. [See Midden B–

> ditch" units on the figure 7.1 seriation chart, especially the Period I units.] This presents a problem. The source of the bone and the sherds in the base of the ditch near the creek is clearly the midden there. From the distribution of the bone and sherds it is apparent that they accumulated in the ditch while the midden was forming rather than being washed in from an already existing midden. [Radiocarbon date I-3556, 450 BC ± 105, is on a sample from one of the lowest midden lenses in the latest ditch. Pollen samples with maize are from similar lenses or layers with about the same stratigraphic position.] The extreme scarcity of sherds or bones in the earlier ditch indicates that the midden was not forming to any extent during the open life of that ditch. In the southern cuts we found several sherds of semi-fiber-tempered plain and two steatite sherds in the top of the subsoil at the base of the earlier ditch. . . . An estimate of age for this earlier ditch would be in the transitional period, not later than 500 B.C.

To sum up, the two small, overlapping circles were dug, sequentially, early in the history of the site. They were followed by the Great Circle. Our radiocarbon date and dates for complexes related to the material from the ditches suggest that all circles were completed by 450 B.C. Probably only semi-fiber-tempered pottery was being used when the smaller circles were originally excavated by the Belle Glade people.

The complete lack of any structures or artifacts except those in the riverbank midden areas has a bearing on circle function. Use of them for ceremonialism or fortification, or anything else, would have left some evidence. It is not there. The traces of maize pollen in several spots are almost certainly pertinent; that is, the circle ditches were built for an economic function, to aid in maize production. Drainage off the hardpan in the encircled area and into the ditches makes functional sense in the basin savannah environment. Some enrichment of gardens with nitrogenous muck from the ditches is possible. It is not possible to estimate the length of time during which the earlier, small circles were used. The Great Circle seems to have been used as a garden area from several centuries B.C. until at least the end of Period II, a tremendously long period. Some discussion of origins and relationships and their implications in this early terraforming effect will be found in chapter 11.

Midden A

Midden A, a deposit of black dirt midden, has small quantities of mussel shells, with occasional lenses or pockets of packed shell. These occur in all of the midden deposits on the site. This deposit is about 120 feet long and a maximum of 50 feet wide, and the greatest thickness observed was 5 feet. However, as the site map and aerial photo suggest, there has been, and continues to be, heavy erosion caused by the creek cutting into the outside of a bend during periods of high water. It seems probable that midden dimensions were greater in the past, particularly the width of the deposit.

Stratigraphically, the deposit is most unremarkable. A black topsoil, full of roots, sits on a uniform, dark-gray midden that comprises most of the deposit. There is some calcium deposition in the lower part of the midden where it sits on an old, slightly darker topsoil, which in turn rests comformably on the normal fine, white to light gray sand. The unchanging physical nature of the bulk of the deposit suggests steady accumulation, unmarked by human or natural incidents.

For the duration of the project all student crews worked either in this deposit or in Midden B before moving to other units. Florida Atlantic University teams excavated one large test pit that intersected one dug by John Goggin many years earlier (Goggin 1952a). Colgate University crews explored a great deal of the deposit with pits, trenches, and one cut to face up the deposit where creek erosion had left a nearly vertical face. University of Florida crews also dug pits and trenches.

Most excavation was by arbitrary levels. The University of Florida teams made efforts to work by observed "zones" in several instances, but this scheme did not work well here because of the nature of the deposit.

Representative artifact data will be found on the seriation chart (fig. 7.1) and in the list of trade sherds (table 3.1). The samples included are from one trench that was excavated so that, even though excavation was by arbitrary levels, the topsoil, higher midden, lower midden, and material from the old topsoil could be combined and provide temporally pertinent samples. Further data come from arbitrary levels in one test pit.

A lot of excavated material is not reported here, for several reasons. Many samples were very small and came from units that could not be combined with others for various reasons. Some large samples clearly

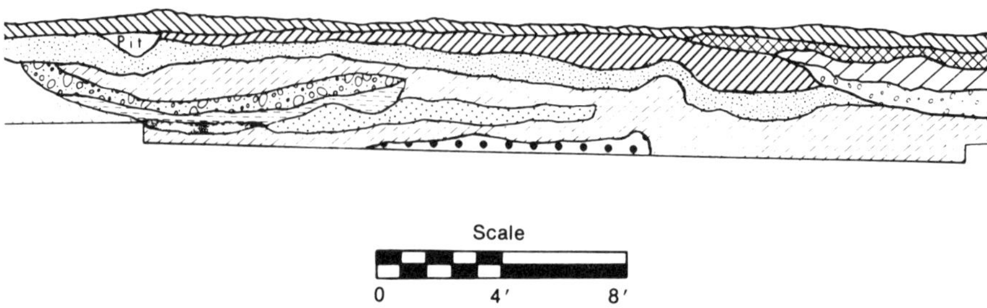

Legend

- Topsoil
- Light-tan sand with iron concretions
- Light-tan to white sand with iron concetions
- Tan sand with iron concretions
- Light-tan sand
- Chocolate-brown sand grading to light-tan sand
- White to dark-brown sand with iron stains
- Medium-brown sand
- Dark-brown sand
- Brownish-grey sand

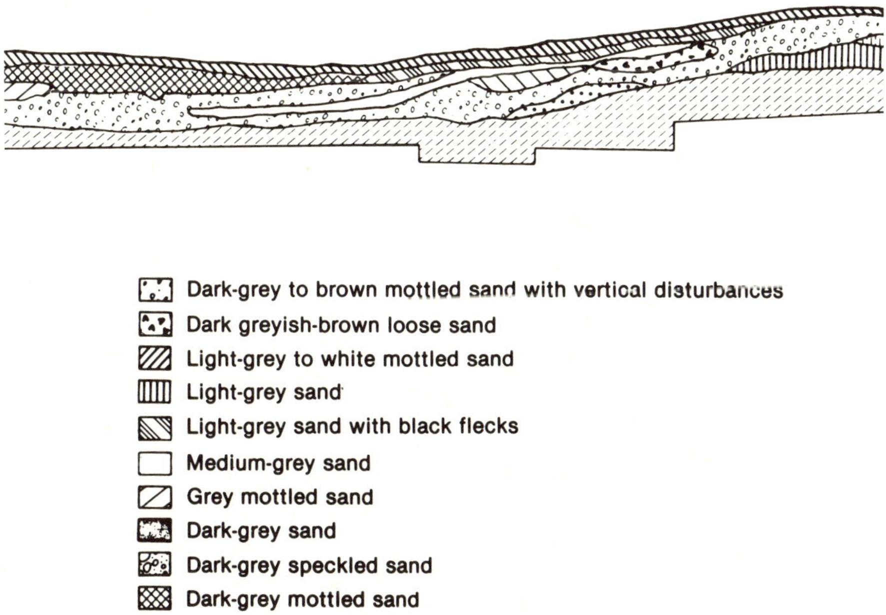

Fig. 9.17. Opposite and above, north profile across circular trenches and Midden B along grid line L525, 3959–3896.

covered very long periods of time and were not in any way comparable to most of those used in seriation. Finally, a number of collections were scrubbed so vigorously that removal of the surface eliminated the possibility of distinguishing between Belle Glade Plain and sand-tempered plain.

The lowest midden deposit, on the old humus, was associated stratigraphically with the charcoal sample that yielded the A.D. 180 ± 110 date. The complex, stratigraphic position and date relate nicely. This first Midden A occupation, early in the occupation of the site, apparently did not last very long. After some centuries of disuse, midden began to accumulate again, and it continued slowly and steadily until nearly the end of occupation at the site.

The data suggest use of the location by a single family at most. Equally possible, I think, is that there was frequent but not continuous use of the location, by people living elsewhere, for fishing, turtle spotting, and other food procurement activities. The locale has always been relatively high, probably overlooking deep pools in the river much of the time, and it provides a commanding view over much of the river meander belt. Such food procurement activities have gone on here in recent times, providing some of the midden accumulation in the contemporary topsoil. The following list of materials from the topsoil in a single 5-by-20-foot trench may make the point: unburned charcoal briquets, pipe stem, 38-caliber, 44-caliber, and 12-gauge shells, 3 buttons, 1 piece of glass, a 6-inch spike, a bottle cap, a metal ferrule, and a can top.

Midden B

Midden B is a series of more or less connected deposits of varying width and depth. It stretches along the riverbank from just east of the intersection of the west side of the Great Circle ditch and the river to a point about 100 feet west.

Colgate University excavated a fair-sized segment of the deposit near its western limits. Levels were combined in the analytical process, and the combined samples appear in the seriation chart (fig. 7.1) as "Midden B topsoil," etc. The chart suggests a long span of intermittent occupation.

The University of Florida excavated segments of the midden as part of a complex effort to date the Great Circle ditch and to gather information on building methods used and on the relationship of the Great Circle to the smaller circles. (Further description of these excavations can be found in the section on the Great Circle.) The midden samples that were used for seriation are listed in figure 7.1 as "Midden B ditch" units from several locations and depths. They range in time from Period III to, for most samples, Period I. This westernmost area seems comparable to Midden A. An early, short occupation is followed, after a long time, by continuous but low-intensity use.

10

Settlement Patterns

THE Fort Center site represents about one-half square mile of terrain. Middens and earth structures run roughly east and west with the axis of Fisheating Creek for a mile and are distributed over a north-south area about one-half mile in width. This area contains three environmental components: river meander belt, open savannah, and oak–cabbage palm–palmetto hammock. In the meander belt and savannah environments, over a period of several centuries beginning more than 2,000 years ago, the aboriginal residents built and used combinations of earthen mounds and other earthworks, products of both their social systems and their economic adjustments to the wet environments of the Lake Okeechobee Basin.

With the control afforded by our fine-grained seriation, cross-checked by radiocarbon dates and other nearly absolute dates afforded by trade sherds from dated sequences, we can relate the man-produced features to one another and to the natural systems. The results are archaeologically perceived patterns that actually existed and functioned.

The aboriginal utilization of this area with its well-defined features—mound structures of different types, earthworks of several kinds, circular ditches, and several midden deposits—makes discernment of patterns somewhat simpler than is usual in the Southeast. Relationship of patterns to ecosystems is no more difficult when the excavated data are in hand. Prognosticating in advance of the data or without temporal control can (and has) led to error.

Description of patterns and adaptations is by the same four periods indicated on the seriation chart (fig. 7.1). That these are arbitrary divisions along a continuum must be realized, and, as inspection of the chart shows, even our own four-part division does not guarantee that all units in a specific period existed at once.

Period I

Period I lasts from several centuries earlier than 450 B.C. (I-3556) to A.D. 200. The radiocarbon date is associated with the building of the most recent circular ditch. At a guess, the early end of the period, associated with pure semi-fiber-tempered pottery components, is near 800 to 1000 B.C.

Structures definitely from this period are the Great Circle ditch and two smaller and earlier ditches, each 300 feet in diameter. These smaller ones are visible in part on the aerial photograph and were verified by several trench cuttings. The earliest deposits in Midden B, the earliest in Mound 3 (which initially was probably a midden deposit rather than a mound), and the building and use of Mounds 12 and 13 and probably 11 and 14 belong in this period.

All of the mounds except Mound 3 seem to have been simple house platforms, and Mound 13 was used for burial as well. Midden B at this time, like Midden A a bit later, seems to have been produced by use of a low natural levee for living purposes in lieu of building a mound. All of these units, mounds and middens, are in or on the edge of the river meander belt (fig. 1.1). In fact, all of them, with the possible exception of Mound 3, have suffered some creek erosion over the years. It appears that at any one time the site contained one or more single-family dwellings, either on the edge of the river meander belt or out in it. Large parts of this belt were flooded much of the time, and if the situation then was similar to that in the present, flooding could have occurred for weeks at a time in most months of the year. The old meander patterns and the location of the mounds and middens certainly indicate that this is an old situation.

The use of house mounds is, of course, a technique permitting life to go on during flooded periods, but why were the dwellings not built in higher locations? There were no building sites completely out of flood range, but certainly population pressure was not forcing builders to use marginal locations. And, equally certain, the turtle and fish that provided most dietary protein and, I suggest, a large part of the bulk of the diet were readily available in these "island" locations.

I have no way to judge whether the Great Circle was ever complete on the north side, where the creek appears to have cut off the northern edge. The midden that was present seems to have contributed odds and ends of debris to the last ditch, suggesting that the circle ditch was open on this side between the two points where today it is incomplete.

The bases for placing all three circular ditches in Period I, both radiocarbon analysis and stratigraphy, have been explained (chapter 9). Two hypotheses have been advanced for the function of these circles. (1) They could have been ceremonial, as set forth most explicitly by John Goggin and William Sturtevant (1964). This use is highly improbable, particularly the notion of any "Calusa" input for the ditches, and there is no supporting archaeological evidence, even circumstantial, that the ditches were ceremonial. (2) They could have been for agricultural purposes. The builders would have drained the soil encompassed by the circles by cutting ditches below the hardpan and allowing water to drain along the hardpan into the ditches, a phenomenon observable along the creek today after a flood recedes; the causeways are for access to the gardens in the interior of the circle.

The second hypothesis is supported by the need for drained garden plots if agriculture was to be practiced in this environment and by the presence of maize pollen in soil samples from points inside the ditches and the contemporaneous midden.

In summary, the earliest settlement pattern at Fort Center consisted of (1) one or more dwelling units placed on high places or house mounds in or directly adjacent to the river meander belt and (2) a circular ditch that provided drained land for maize horticulture. The first two circles were about 300 feet in diameter, and they were replaced by one 2,100 feet in diameter. No reason for the size increase is known or proposed.

Period II

Period II dates from approximately A.D. 200 to about A.D. 600–800. Focus of the site during this period was the ceremonial center, composed of features covered by fill under Mound B, and Mound A and the pond with the wooden structure in it. A low earth wall enclosed an area of some size containing all of these structures and attached to Mound A at its ends. Mound A was the location of one or two dwelling units during the later part of the period. Inside the earthwork was the carefully dug pond, and in it a wooden charnel platform. Near the pond, and also inside the low earthwork, was a low earth platform; both this platform and the encircling earthwork were made from earth taken from the pond during its excavation by the Indians. At the end of the brown earth platform opposite the pond was a carefully shaped oval depression formed by the platform and the "wings" extending from it.

The brown earth platform served a number of functions. First, one or more persons lived on it for some time, depositing midden material that differed in artifact content from any other on the site. The platform appears temporally ancestral to the earliest complex on Mound A. Second, there were deposits of human bone and teeth, suggesting that body preparation and bundling for deposit on the wooden platform in the pond took place here. There may have been one or more buildings associated with these activities.

A single ceremonial deposit, Hopewellian in nature, was found on the slope at the edge of the platform nearest the pond. Finally, after the midden deposit was made but before the mound was covered over to become Mound B, more bones, more teeth, conch shells, conch-shell dippers, and, finally, a layer of earth along with bodies from the charnel house were placed on and over the mound.

Mound A was composed in part of midden deposited in connection with several dwelling units. Most of the mound, and most of the midden, are tightly related physically and temporally to the ceremonial features in the area delimited by the low earth wall. One activity that took place here, in or about the round or oval houses, was lime burning. Except for one other unit noted, it is also the only place on the site where pipes were smoked. Clearly, there are distinct ceremonial implications for these activities.

It is clear, I think, that the earth enclosure, the earthen platform, the pond, the wooden platform, and the dwelling units on Mound A functioned as a ceremonial complex. There are no data to suggest anything other than a mortuary cult, although of course such a cult implies religious beliefs of somewhat greater depth and complexity than a mutual funeral society. The dead on the charnel platform are probably the remains only of the religious specialists who lived and functioned in this center.

Two other items suggest possible agrarian overtones to the religious complex: the burning of shells into lime—some burning may have taken place in Middens A and B, but, quantitatively, it was far more significant in Mound A; and the discovery of large quantities of maize pollen in the lime-based pigment strips adhering to a carved wooden eagle in the charnel platform, a quantity far too large to be accidental.

Physically, the low earth wall ties these units together into a single complex. Mound A completes the boundary on the east side, across the pond. The remains of one individual were found in the wall, where one of our trenches cut through it directly south of the earthen platform on the far side of a large open area. It appears to have been included during construction, not intruded later. We made a number of cuts through the wall, by tractor and by hand, at a number of other points, and no more such remains, nor any artifacts, were found. They may have existed, but the primary function of the wall seems to have been to delimit an area, and any other use was distinctly secondary. Careful inspection of the contour lines (fig. 9.5) shows that a gap, a gateway of a sort, existed at the "corner" of the wall to the south.

The southern part of the enclosed area, south of the brown dirt platform, is a sort of courtyard. It had from 8 to 38 feet of Mound B fill and wash over the northern part of it. We were expecting evidence of some ceremonial function, but several trenches and pits produced no such evidence, in fact nothing at all except the undisturbed original humus on the old ground surface. I suppose the ambiguous term "ceremonial courtyard" must be applied.

There were minor traces of occupation on the site not specifically connected with the ceremonial units. Midden B had occupation early in Period II and Midden A late, and there was some occupation of the Mound 3 location. Probably each represents an occupation for some part of the period, as suggested by the seriation chart. Any of the occupations could have been occasional and short term, products of the use of the riverbank for food gathering.

A single occupation, considerably more intense, was found on the old ground surface under the University of Florida Mound. This deposit could represent a dwelling unit. Under it, in and at the base of the original humus, was a more specialized deposit containing, along with sherds, the only platform pipe fragments found outside of Mound A—certainly evidence for a single-family dwelling, possibly with ceremonial overtones, out on the flat ground, an aberrant location at this site. Much searching, peering into gopher holes, and digging random shovel tests in the whole hammock area failed to produce any more such deposits. A few scattered sherds on the ground surface near Mound A and a few more near the University of Florida Mound were picked up and included in the fill of the linear earthwork, but these samples were very small.

Period II was definitely one of heavy agricultural production, as demonstrated by the maize pollen and the lime. On the question of where maize might have been raised, the circles functioned earlier (Period I), and the linears sufficed in Period III. There could have been continued use of the Great Circle. Admittedly, producing corn on the same plot for centuries guarantees a small yield, but in this environment new fields could not simply be cleared. Terraforming was not an eccentricity but a requirement.

Fertilization as a by-product of cleaning out circular ditches is possible. The muck that accumulates in the ditches, particularly after a flood, is practically protoplasmic, wiggling with great quantities of fish and amphibian small-fry and eggs. The nitrogen content at least should be most useful in maize growing, and the tiny bones might provide some phosphorus. Certainly the ditches had to be cleaned occasionally if they were to function.

But corn might not have been raised on the site at all during this period. If the inhabitants were ceremonial specialists who produced lime as one product with magical qualities, they may have been supplied with corn by parishioners from other sites.

Period III

The structures that are definitely from Period III, A.D. 600–800 to A.D. 1200–1400, include most of Midden A, a small part of Midden B, and the later occupation (postceremonial center usage) of Mound A. The designation of this period on the seriation chart (fig. 7.1) was based on perceptible changes in the smooth flow of development of ceramic styles, particularly, in this case, the introduction of certain rim forms, even though the quantities were too small to show. As it happens, it is also a period between the extensive ceremonial endeavors centering around the pond–Mound B earthwork complex and the later development of characteristic linear earthworks with small mounds for dwellings adjacent to one end.

There is no new settlement pattern. Life went on in the same structures in the same places. We do not have positive evidence for corn growing, but it is present in the next period so we can assume its continued use through Period III.

The settlement pattern may be characterized as a family or two living on what were, by then, old deposits that gave them some elevation. Perhaps they experimented with gardening in higher natural elevations.

Period IV

The later date of Period IV, A.D. 1200–1400 to A.D. 1700, is based on the single radiocarbon date for Mound 3 deposits and on the fact that historic objects of Spanish origin or reworked from Spanish metal were found in two contexts on the site. Units that functioned in this period are most of the Mound 3 riverbank structure, all of Mound 1 and the adjacent linear earthwork, all of the University of Florida Mound and abutting linear earthwork, probably Mound 5 and the linear earthwork that stretches toward Mound 3, and, because the other mound–linear earthwork complexes belong here, probably Mounds 2 and 8 with their linear earthworks.

Each mound except Mound 3, which had a checkered career, is a vaguely round platform a little over 30 feet across the top, just large enough for a single structure. The shape and size were most obvious in Mound 1, with midden confined to what is essentially the contemporary topsoil. The University of Florida Mound was really similar, but the picture was confused by inclusion of older material. It had been scraped up to form the mound, along with dark topsoil and midden, from the area that was to surround it.

Dating, in addition to the radiocarbon date, is from historic material in the topsoil midden on top of the University of Florida Mound, yielding a point on the seriation chart as sixteenth to seventeenth century. The large amounts of historic material with burials inserted in the top of Mound B also, of course, demonstrate nearby occupation during the historic period.

11

Conclusions

THE Fort Center site, with components located at various points in three ecosystems and covering an area about one mile long by one-half mile wide, was in existence for over 2,000 years. House mounds, agricultural earthworks, midden deposits, and ceremonial structures were built and used at different times. Consequently, there were over time a number of definable settlement patterns or, perhaps better, a continually changing pattern. The Okeechobee Basin environment surrounding the site is wet and frequently flooded, and the construction of earth structures and the resultant settlement patterns during the occupation of the site were adaptations to this situation.

The first occupation recorded is some centuries prior to 450 B.C., perhaps, we estimate, as early as 1,000 B.C. This aboriginal population developed, I believe, from that already present in the area; that is, the adaptations were new, the human stock was not.

I have presented at length elsewhere (Sears 1977b) the hypothesis that much of the settlement of Florida, at least that in the wet, fresh-water zone from the southern end of the state well up into the northern St. Johns area, is a product of people moving from northern South America through the Antilles well in advance of the Arawak migration. There is some evidence in support of this theory: the use of conch-shell tools in the Archaic period in the St. Johns region; the frequent presence of conch-shell celts and adzes in early contexts in inland South Florida; and the fact that Timucua, the dominant linguistic stock of peninsular Florida, is believed to be of South American derivation (Granberry 1971) (its closest relative is apparently Warau, spoken in the Orinoco delta).

A constant relationship is suggested between northern South America and South Florida. At some time, as James A. Ford suggested (1966), fiber-tempered pottery, and later its decorated variants, were introduced by the same route as that advocated for tools and language. Northern South America is also (Denevan 1970), as I have suggested elsewhere, the home for various terraforming techniques that enable savannah agriculture.

By the date 1,000 B.C., suggested as the time of beginning settlement at Fort Center, we find available, thanks to the South American savannahs and the Antillean route, a well-adapted population, making fiber-tempered pottery in simple bowl forms. These forms remain characteristic of South Florida throughout its history, a strong contrast to the vessel forms of the mainland eastern United States. This aboriginal population possessed more than pots: They cultivated maize, which could be stored to stabilize and seasonally equalize their food supply, and they had a technique for growing it in the savannah, making circles that provided drained fields and possibly a source of fertilizing muck.

To summarize and to facilitate consideration of techniques and influences that stabilized and changed the Fort Center culture, I will use the culture periods defined earlier. These periods, divisions of a cultural continuum, have been delimited largely on the basis of the seriation of ceramic samples from most possible contexts at the site. Each subdivision is marked by the introduction of a new culture trait. These periods have also been verified by radiocarbon dates and by relating some units and periods to others in Florida and in the eastern United States, units and periods that have both absolute dates and sequences available to assist in temporal control. After summarizing the major features of each period, I will, where appropriate, offer some thoughts on interpretation and on relationships to other cultures in Florida and elsewhere in North America.

Period I

The beginning of Period I, the initial occupation of the site, occurred well before our radiocarbon date of 450 B.C. The date 1,000 B.C. is suggested for the earliest levels of the site, which apparently contain only semi-fiber-tempered pottery. The people of this period lived along the riverbank and on small house mounds well out in the creek meander belt. Proximity to the belt, the source of most fish and turtles, seems to have been particularly important. In view of the rather thin deposits and the length of the period, it seems likely that there were not more than one or two families on the site at any one time and that they possessed a slowly changing material culture.

All three circular ditches were built and used in this early period. Conceivably, the two earlier structures, sequentially built and utilized, only 300 feet in diameter, could have been built entirely by residents of the site. I think that the latest model, still pre–450 B.C., 1,200 feet in diameter, exceeds the capabilities of the few people at the site unless they used the finished and functional part of it and continued to excavate over a long period of time. In any event, our hypothetical use of the circles as drained agricultural plots is supported by the presence of a number of pollen samples containing maize pollen from the circle interior and from midden deposited along the riverbank at the ends of the Great Circle.

During Period I, the fiber-tempered pottery bowls had the fiber content reduced and the sand content increased. By the end of the period, a time chosen, of course, on the basis of this change, most of the pottery was the sand-tempered plain ware. There was some use beginning of the laminated-contorted ware that, temporally and functionally, appears to be a stage in the development of fiber-tempered pottery into sand-tempered pottery. The sand-tempered pottery was beginning to be popular, and possibly the distinctive Belle Glade Plain finish truly made its appearance, not simply in a statistical sense.

We have few artifacts from this period other than pottery. The few projectile points were almost certainly imported from northern Florida as complete objects. Most hunting, other than catching turtles, which can be run down on land or in shallow sloughs, was probably managed with cane or hardwood points. There were, of course, some bone tools.

In contrast with the next period, there is absolutely no evidence for differential treatment of persons, individually or as a class. Possibly there was some interment in a mound, but such burial treatment may have been afforded the entire population.

One might ask why horticulture was practiced in fields drained by circular ditches, even if the premise is accepted that some form of terraforming was necessary in a wet environment with frequent flooding and a groundwater table only 24 to 30 inches down. In view of the pollen and other evidence for maize growing and processing in the next period, I can suggest only that it was successful. Probably the technique originated in the savannahs of northern South America. Similar circular ditches exist in Colombia (Denevan 1970). I doubt that they were independently invented in Florida at the comparatively late date of 1,000 B.C.

All three of the circles, used in sequence from perhaps 1,000 B.C. until some time closer to 450 B.C., are earlier than any of the Adena circles in eastern Ohio and adjacent areas. The latest one is also certainly larger than most, if not all, of the Adena circles. Other circular ditches have been found on aerial photographs in locations where they appear to be associated with Hopewellian manifestations, in Louisiana and Illinois particularly. I believe that there is a relationship. The circles in the savannah country in Florida, with antecedents in the savannah regions of South America, are functional, and it appears almost certain that they came into Florida with the maize that was raised in them.

Thus, a complex moved into Florida that included, although it was not restricted to, the earthworks and maize. I suggest a hypothesis, which could not be tested any further at this site, that the circles and the maize moved together to the Midwest as parts of a complex that was functionally interrelated in the minds of the practitioners. Corn has been recovered from Adena contexts. In the Midwest of the United States, the functional circles became ceremonial and developed other forms and variations, most of which could not have been functional anywhere.

Other than this suggested relationship, we have little evidence for contact during Period I with other Florida cultures, let alone cultures farther away. Certainly contact with the St. Johns region, an area possibly occupied by old relatives, is apparent in the rather large quantities of St. Johns Plain pottery and a few sherds of earlier Orange fiber-tempered ware. Too, the projectile points had to come from the north, and certainly chert is available in many locations near the St. Johns River. However, I do not see in this period any real influence of the St. Johns region, or any other culture area, on the Belle Glade culture, then in its developmental stages. Nor do I see any indication of the reverse. At the end of the period, a few people had settled down on the site and were tilling corn in the Great Circle, a structure probably shared with people from other midden sites in the immediate area. With techniques for exploiting the fauna of the marshes and with stability provided by a corn crop, the culture was well adapted.

Period II

A century or two after the birth of Christ, the focus of activities at Fort Center changed in a new direction, one maintained for six or eight centuries. This shift marks the beginning of Period II. All of the people on the site were directly involved with the operation of the ceremonial center, which consisted of the pond and its charnel platform (with its carved wooden birds and beasts), the small brown platform mound (under Mound B) with its bathtub-shaped pit for preparation of bodies prior to their interment on the wooden platform in the pond, a habitation complex on Mound A, and a low earth wall that surrounded all of these units and was attached to Mound A at both ends.

While all of these structures had ceremonial functions, at least at the mortuary level, people also lived on the site. We estimate that, initially, there were one or two families living on the brown platform mound and two to four families who lived for a long time in the habitation area of Mound A.

We have few faunal remains from the midden on the surface of the brown dirt platform mound. Like the human remains there—both under, in, and on the midden deposit—they tended to be somewhat cheesy stains. Nor was there any evidence for maize, although certainly it was present.

Mound A people ate well. Tremendous quantities of bones of turtles, fish, deer, turkey, and other fauna were found, along with an assortment of other odds and ends, including human remains. We also have positive evidence that maize was present, and this evidence is magnified in importance by the lime burning that took place—giving us reason to believe that lime was produced for making dry, stored corn palatable.

The pottery from the two habitation areas, changing through time, was utilitarian. We did find, however, that most of the trade sherds from the site in these units or in lenses of sand had washed down onto the bottom of the pond from the habitation areas. Such pottery included specimens of Crystal River, Deptford, Cartersville, Pasco, and St. Johns wares, the last including copies of Deptford forms and decoration. Emphasis on trade ware in a ceremonial context suggests that the trade pottery was itself sacred, that it was acquired for ceremonial function. Such function, too, may be ascribed to the chert, shell, and sharks'-teeth tools from Mound A midden deposits. Except the worn and polished projectile points, all of them are normal for the Glades area, which lies, for the most part, south and west of Fort Center. More to the point, their occurrence is almost limited to Mound A, suggesting their use in the operation and maintenance of the ceremonial center. Perhaps they were imported primarily for use in making the carved wooden figures.

There were, for example, no shell tools on the brown platform mound. It did have shell dippers, absent from Mound A, and complete *Busycon* and other large conch shells, which, regardless of whether they were trumpets, were certainly ceremonial in function. There is a great deal of evidence that the brown dirt mound had as its primary function the preparation of bodies for placement on the wooden charnel platform. This evidence includes small scraps of human bones or small bones and tremendous quantities of teeth. A deposit of human skulls, skull caps, conch-shell dippers, and bird-bone tubes, a distinctly Hopewellian-sounding assemblage, was found on the east slope of the mound and is certainly indicative of ceremonial function.

Mound A, although a habitation site, also seems to have served primarily ceremonial purposes over the long period during which it functioned. This span includes that period marked by the removal of part of the midden, most of the material then on the house floors perhaps, and its redeposition on the bottom of the pond under the charnel platform. Activities took place on Mound A that did not occur on other apparently contemporaneous units, such as some part of Mound 3 and Midden A: lime burning in large quantities, the manufacture and use of monitor and obtuse angle elbow pipes, and, judging by the concentration of tools, wood carving. Some pipe fragments were found in an apparently contemporary but distinctive deposit *under* the later University of Florida Mound. Hints of lime burning were found in Midden A but not on the scale of the Mound A deposits.

The pond, deliberately excavated to depths below the water table, and its platform, made in large part with elaborately carved birds and beasts as structural members, are clearly ceremonial. The platform collapsed after a substantial portion of it—including carved figures, structural timbers, and human remains—burned and some remnants became heavily charred. The remains of 150 individuals, representing a normal population distribution of ages and sexes, fell into the bottom of the pond where, mixed with timbers and carved wooden figures, they rested on a level base composed of the redeposited midden.

The episode initiated a continuous mound-building effort, during which about 150 more bodies were placed in the mound fill that was being deposited over the brown dirt mound. This fill, and further sterile fill, transformed the area into the 25-foot-high Mound B, which extended out to the wall to the east and to the edge of the pond to the west. There was also some sand added to Mound A at this time to level and extend it.

Three hundred people sounds like a large number, but our seriation and the radiocarbon dates indicate that the ceremonial center functioned for some centuries. I think it probable that these bodies are the remains of all of the people who, as a category that included children, carried out socially required ceremonial functions while living on the brown platform mound and on Mound A. All of the inhabitants of Fort Center during the time of this ceremonial center episode constituted a single social class that had sacred status.

If this theory is correct, then this ceremonial center functioned for a society occupying an area larger than we thought, around the lake and up the Kissimmee River. According to recent reports, some related activities were going on at the Belle Glade site, where deep, mucky deposit has produced many human skeletal remains. There was no wood associated, so this may be another of the increasing number of water depositories for human remains that are being found in the interior, freshwater regions of South Florida.

At this time, there were no other large sites, unless some of the other earthwork assemblages were functioning simultaneously. Until more work is done, we will not know whether that was the case. There are many small sites, single-house mounds with midden deposits on natural levees and other kinds, throughout the savannah region.

The economic system supporting the center and the people occupying all of the small sites acquired stability through dependable maize crops. The maize was undoubtedly dried for storage, and our evidence demonstrates that it was then prepared for human consumption, as needed, by soaking it in a lime solution. Perhaps the personnel at the ceremonial center exchanged lime for corn, since there is not a clearly defined place for corn growing at Fort Center during this period. If the few families spent a good deal of their time in rituals for the benefit of the entire culture and spent more time preparing their own dead for burial, their specialization could easily have required that their food supply at least be supplemented by those who benefited from the ritual.

It is not difficult to visualize a group of people whose mana—power—was so strong that their bodies had to be isolated by the water in the pond, a matter of prudence on the part of the society. The extensive use of conch-shell dippers and conch shells, and the ceremonial cleaning of the living area that took place at least once during its occupation, are reminiscent at least of the historic busk ceremonies.

Contacts with the St. Johns area and certainly with the Crystal River area and site are clear and certain. In both instances, the presence of trade sherds suggests that the contact was at a ceremonial level.

Tetrapods, simple stamping, and check stamping in the St. Johns region at this time are limited in their occurrence to burial mounds and the sacred aspects of the culture. At Crystal River itself, the ceramic complex that produced the trade sherds found in sacred context at Fort Center is a part of what I have defined as the Yent complex (Sears 1962). It seems probable to me that the earth wall around the burial mound at the Crystal River site was similar in function to the one at Fort Center. I would not be surprised if a small platform mound were to be found under the rebuilt and enlarged Crystal River burial mound, a hypothesis I hoped would be tested during the minor excavations that preceded development of the site as a park.

The similarity of the brown platform mound to a structure observed mostly in profile at the Mandeville site in Georgia (Kelly, Kellar, and McMichael 1962) is not unnoticed, and ceremonial pottery similar to Fort Center's is also present at that site. Another such platform existed at the base of the Crooks Mound, another Hopewellian manifestation (Ford and Willey 1940), and again there are a few similarities in artifacts. I think that such platforms were a necessary part of Hopewellian ritual or ceremonial centers and that they became mortuary centers only when they were being entombed—practitioners, specialists, platforms, paraphernalia, and all.

I have suggested before that most major Hopewellian centers (Sears 1971a) were really ceremonial centers that may or may not have been converted to mortuary function when their ritual use ended, especially some of the Ohio sites, which have a great deal of evidence for ritual and almost no burials. Comparisons with Fort Center and with each other at the right level of generalization are worthwhile but cannot be done at present.

Nor can I use the space here that would be required to refute effectively the hypothesis that mud, flat-weed horticulture provided an effective economic base for the Hopewell interaction sphere. Again, I have made my views clear elsewhere, although they have been largely ignored in the most recent compendium of Hopewellian knowledge (Brose and Greber 1979).

The hypothesis, based on the presence of sometimes misidentified charred weed seeds found in contexts where such weeds would proliferate and fall into the fire anyhow, is not adequate to explain increases both in population and in social complexity at the time. Trade in status symbols, without explanation of social need for status symbols and their similarity in many different societies, is not accounted for by pointing to an interaction sphere. Why did it exist? The weeds were there, and I presume they were occasionally used throughout the late Archaic period. Something had to be added to produce "Middle Woodland" after forest efficiency had been achieved.

There is no doubt that Fort Center is not alone in the possession of maize, a "tropical cultigen" if you wish. There is some evidence for its presence in most Hopewellian complexes. The finding of a grain or two of pollen, an ear of corn, or a few kernels in Ohio, Illinois, or Kansas tells us that it was present. If more corn cannot be found, while the weeds can, is it the fault of the prehistoric Indians or of archaeological technique?

I continue to believe that the viable hypothesis is one that has corn, a storable food, as a foundation for an economic system. The crop moved from one culture to the next with a religious-ritual system that accounts for its movement and permits us to trace the spread of the total system. All of this—crop, garden, dry corn treatment, and ritual—is the Hopewell phenomenon.

I have had my say and have contributed some positive information and data that I hope will be used. Where the data do not fit preconceived concepts and cultural reconstructions, possibly some alteration will produce valid reconstructions.

Period III

Period III might be regarded as a necessary evil, that period of time (and of minimum cultural change) between the last use of the ceremonial center and the beginning of use of the new system of house mounds and attached linear earthwork garden plots of Period IV. The same people, with essentially the same culture, continued to occupy the site, and in the same places, Mound A and Middens A and B.

There was little change in artifacts during Period III. The quantities of sand-tempered plain pottery continued to decrease, and Belle Glade Plain had a considerable relative increase. St. Johns Check Stamped pottery began to appear, supplementing a few sherds of the chalky plain. But both are found in small quantities, indicating minimal contact with the St. Johns culture.

Even the economic structure is unclear, except for continued use of fauna from the total environment with the usual emphasis on turtle. Since we found some evidence for maize in the next period and a great deal of it in the preceding, we may assume that it continued to be grown and used in Period III. But we do not know where—possibly on high natural levee areas and old earthworks.

Period IV

Period IV is marked by a number of features. Changes in ceramics that provide, through seriation, our time scale can be characterized in this period as the presence of a small amount of sand-tempered plain pottery and a large amount of Belle Glade Plain ware. By this time, both types, though drab and utilitarian, were technically excellent. Most pottery specimens are hard and ring when struck; surfaces are uniform and rims neatly finished. The firing technique used to produce hard pottery also produced light gray, even nearly white or light tan, inner and outer surfaces. A series of new rim forms became popular, particularly expanded flat and comma-shaped varieties.

The same number of families—one or two at a time—lived on the site. A new housing mode seems to have been introduced: Small, well-made house mounds were built out in the open savannah. With them appeared a new form of earthwork, another introduction, I think, from South America's long linear earthworks used for corn agriculture. We do have maize pollen from the linear earthwork abutting Mound 1 and from the small linear earthwork abutting on Mound 8. The samples are, I think, unequivocal, coming as they did from long-buried surfaces.

The historic artifacts associated with a few burials in the top of Mound B and a few more artifacts in the midden on the University of Florida Mound document that Period IV is well in the historic period. A single radiocarbon date from the stylistically contemporary late occupation of Mound 3 provides corroboration.

After the characterless Period III, Fort Center and, perhaps specifically, Mound B were once more a focus for authority of some sort. The objects buried with the few people on Mound B, characteristic of this time in southern Florida, seem to be symbols or badges of rank. Since Mound B is the only large mound available for reuse in many miles, the people who were buried may not necessarily have come from Fort Center, and certainly they functioned as parts of a much larger social system than the one existing on the site.

There is no doubt, I think, that Fort Center was a part of the sixteenth- and seventeenth-century Calusa empire, described in some part by Fontaneda (1945), whose description has been expanded and explained by Goggin and Sturtevant (1964). The historic objects from the site, in form and style, seem to be part of the distribution of such objects that coincides with area of the "empire." This is particularly true of the metal badges with engraved spiders or jaguars. The distribution of the twenty-three badges known to date in South Florida coincides with the area of Calusa political overlordship as described. But there is certainly a major concentration inland of the gold and silver objects, particularly the symbols. The three from Fort Center are the largest and heaviest known, suggesting the importance of the inland region. I see no reason to believe that the Calusa, apparently a small but highly organized society from the Caloosahatchee estuary, ever came inland to Fort Center or anywhere else for ceremonies, as has been suggested.

Until more work has been done at the major earthwork sites, with good temporal controls, such suggestions can have no validity. Certainly at Fort Center the major earthworks are pre-Calusa and probably had a 5-foot stand of palmettos on them by A.D. 1500.

Fontaneda stated that there were only a few people in a few small villages around Lake Okeechobee. One of them may have been the one at Fort Center. He said that the inhabitants had a kind of bread made out of roots, which they could not get when the water was high. He does not mention corn at all, but would he have recognized it if he had seen it?

I have ended with a question. We are still in the stage where a little research produces as many questions as it answers. For my part, I have found each new set of questions even more fascinating than the old ones. But I hope indeed that answers, and questions, will continue, not just jobs and "reports" filed with agencies that happen to have money.

References

Alexander, T. R., and Crook, A. G.
1974 Recent Vegetational Change in South Florida. In *Environments of South Florida: Past and Present*, edited by P. J. Gleason, pp. 61–72. Miami Geological Society, Memoir 2.

Allen, Ross.
1948 The Big Circle Mounds. *Florida Anthropologist* 1:17–21.

Armistead, W. J.
1949 An Indian Saw. *Florida Anthropologist* 2:47–48.

Barghoorn, E. S.; Wolfe, M. K.; and Clisby, K. H.
1954 *Fossil Maize from the Valley of Mexico.* Harvard University Botanical Museum Leaflets 16 (9).

Barkley, F. A.
1934 The Statistical Theory of Pollen Analysis. *Ecology* 15:283.

Binford, Lewis R.
1962 Archaeology as Anthropology. *American Antiquity* 28:217–25.

Brew, John O.
1946 *Archaeology of Alkali Ridge, Southeastern Utah.* Papers of the Peabody Museum of American Archaeology and Ethnology 21. Cambridge, Mass.: Harvard University.

Brose, David A., and Greber, N'omi, eds.
1979 *Hopewell Archaeology: The Chillicothe Conference.* Kent, Ohio: Kent State University Press.

Brown, James A., ed.
1971 *Approaches to the Social Dimensions of Mortuary Practices.* Memoirs of the Society for American Archaeology 25.

Bullen, Ripley P.
1952 *Eleven Archaeological Sites in Hillsborough County, Florida.* Florida Geological Survey, Report of Investigations 8. Tallahassee.
1953 The Famous Crystal River Site. *Florida Anthropologist* 6:9–37.
1959 The Transitional Period of Florida. *Southeastern Archaeological Conference Newsletter* 6:43–53.
1968 *A Guide to the Identification of Florida Projectile Points.* Gainesville: Florida State Museum.

Bullen, Ripley P.; Jahn, Otto; and Brooks, Mark J.
1974 Some Tests at the Zellwood Site (0–17) beside Lake Apopka, Florida. *Florida Anthropologist* 27:62–66.
Bullen, Ripley P.; Partridge, William L.; and Harris, Donald A.
1970 The Safford Burial Mound, Tarpon Springs, Florida. *Florida Anthropologist* 23:81–118.
Cook, S. F.
1964 The Nature of Charcoal Excavated at Archaeological Sites. *American Antiquity* 19:514–17.
Cushing, Frank Hamilton.
1897 Explorations of Ancient Key Dwellers' Remains on the Gulf Coast of Florida. *Proceedings of the American Philosophical Society* 35:329–448.
Denevan, William M.
1970 Aboriginal Drained Field Cultivation in the Americas. *Science* 169:647–54.
Dragoo, Don W.
1964 The Development of Adena Culture and Its Role in the Formation of Ohio Hopewell. In *Hopewellian Studies*, edited by J. R. Caldwell and R. L. Hall, pp. 3–34. Illinois State Museum, Scientific Papers 12. Springfield.
Faegri, K., and Iverson, J.
1964 *Textbook of Pollen Analysis*. New York: Hafner.
Fewkes, Jesse Walter.
1924 Preliminary Archaeological Explorations at Weeden Island, Florida. *Smithsonian Miscellaneous Collections* 76(13):1–26.
Fontenada, Do. d'Escalante.
1945 *Memoir of Do. d'Escalante Fontenada Respecting Florida, Written in Spain about the Year 1575*. Translated with notes by Buckingham Smith; edited by David O. True. Coral Gables, Florida: Glade House.
Ford, James A.
1962 *A Quantitative Method for Deriving Cultural Chronology*. Pan American Union, Technical Manual 1. Washington: Pan American Union.
1966 Early Formative Cultures in Georgia and Florida. *American Antiquity* 31:781–99.
Ford, James A.; Phillips, Philip; and Haag, William.
1955 *The Jaketown Site in West Central Mississippi*. American Museum of Natural History, Anthropological Papers 45(1).
Ford, James A., and Willey, Gordon.
1940 *Crooks Site, a Marksville Period Burial Mound in LaSalle Parish, Louisiana*. Department of Conservation, Anthropological Study 3. New Orleans: Louisiana Geological Survey.
Frison, George C.
1968 A Functional Analysis of Certain Chipped Stone Tools. *American Antiquity* 33:149–55.
Furey, John F.
1972 The Spanish River Complex. Master's thesis, Florida Atlantic University, Boca Raton.
Gleason, Henry A.
1963 *Manual of Vascular Plants*. Princeton, N.J.: Van Nostrand.
Goggin, John M.
1949a Cultural Occupation at Goodland Point, Florida. *Florida Anthropologist* 2:65–91.
1949b Cultural Traditions in Florida Prehistory. In *The Florida Indian and His Neighbors*, edited by J. W. Griffin, pp. 13–44. Winter Park, Florida: Rollins College.
1952a Archaeological Notes on Lower Fisheating Creek. *Florida Anthropologist* 4:50–66.

1952b *Space and Time Perspective in Northern St. Johns Archeology, Florida.* Yale University Publications in Anthropology 47.

Goggin, John M., and Sommer, Frank H., III.

1949 *Excavations on Upper Matecumbe Key, Florida.* Yale University Publications in Anthropology 41.

Goggin, John M., and Sturtevant, William C.

1964 The Calusa: A Stratified, Nonagricultural Society (with Notes on Sibling Marriage). In *Explorations in Cultural Anthropology: Essays in Honor of George Peter Murdock,* edited by Ward H. Goodenough, pp. 179–219. New York: McGraw-Hill.

Goodrick, R. L.

1974 The Wet Prairies of the Northern Everglades. In *Environments of South Florida: Past and Present,* edited by P. J. Gleason, pp. 47–52. Miami Geological Society, Memoir 2.

Granberry, Julian.

1971 Report—Final Collection of Texts, Vocabulary Lists, Grammar, of Timucua for Publication. *Yearbook of the American Philosophical Society* (1970), pp. 606–7.

Griffin, John W.

1946 Historic Artifacts and the Buzzard Cult in Florida. *Florida Historical Quarterly* 24:295–301.

Griffin, John W., and Smith, Hale G.

1948 *The Goodnow Mound, Highlands County, Florida.* Contributions to the Archaeology of Florida 1. Tallahassee: Florida Park Service.

Irwin, H. T., and Barghoorn, E. S.

1965 *Identification of the Pollen of Maize, Teosinte and Tripsacum by Phase Contrast Microscopy.* Harvard University, Botanical Museum Leaflets 21(2).

Kelly, A. R.; Kellar, J. H.; and McMichael, E. V.

1962 The Mandeville Site in Southwest Georgia. *American Antiquity* 27:336–55.

Kohler, Timothy.

1975 The Garden Patch Site: A Minor Weeden Island Ceremonial Center on the North Peninsular Florida Gulf Coast. Master's thesis, University of Florida, Gainesville.

Larson, Lewis H.

1980 *Aboriginal Subsistence Technology on the Southeastern Coastal Plain during the Late Prehistoric Period.* Gainesville: University Presses of Florida.

Lewis, T. M. N., and Kneberg, Madeline.

1946 *Hiwasee Island: An Archaeological Account of Four Tennessee Indian Peoples.* Knoxville: University of Tennessee Press.

Long, Robert W., and Lakela, Olga.

1971 *A Flora of Tropical Florida.* Coral Gables: University of Miami Press.

MacLaury, James

1968 Archaeological Investigations on Cat Island. Master's thesis, Florida Atlantic University, Boca Raton.

McPherson, B. F.

1974 The Big Cypress Swamp. In *Environments of South Florida: Past and Present,* edited by P. J. Gleason, pp. 8–17. Miami Geological Society, Memoir 2.

Martin, Paul S.; Quimby, G. I.; and Collier, D.

1947 *Indians before Columbus.* Chicago: University of Chicago Press.

Milanich, Jerald T.

1971 *The Alachua Tradition of North Central Florida.* Contributions of the Florida State Museum, Anthropology and History 17.

Milanich, Jerald T., and Fairbanks, Charles H.

1980 *Florida Archaeology.* New York: Academic Press.

Moore, Clarence B.

1899 A Cache of Pendant Ornaments. *Journal of the Academy of Natural Sciences of Philadelphia* 11:187–91.

1901 Certain Aboriginal Remains of the Northwest Florida Coast. Part 1. *Journal of the Academy of Natural Sciences of Philadelphia* 11:419–97.

1903 Certain Aboriginal Remains of the Central Florida West Coast. *Journal of the Academy of Natural Sciences of Philadelphia* 12:361–463.

1907 Crystal River Revisited. *Journal of the Academy of Natural Sciences of Philadelphia* 13:407–27.

1918 The Northwestern Florida Coast Revisited. *Journal of the Academy of Natural Sciences of Philadelphia* 16:514–77.

Nance, J. D.

1971 Functional Interpretation from Microscopic Analysis. *American Antiquity* 36: 361–66.

Phelps, David S.

1965 The Norwood Series of Fiber-Tempered Ceramics. *Southeastern Archaeological Conference, Bulletin* 2:65–69.

Phillips, Philip.

1970 *Archaeological Survey in the Lower Yazoo Basin, Mississippi, 1949–1955.* Papers of the Peabody Museum of American Archaeology and Ethnology 60. Cambridge, Mass.: Harvard University.

Prufer, Olaf H.

1968a *Ohio Hopewell Ceramics—An Analysis of the Extant Collections.* Museum of Anthropology, Anthropological Papers 33. Ann Arbor: University of Michigan.

1968b The Hopewell Complex of Ohio. In *Hopewellian Studies,* edited by J. R. Caldwell and R. L. Hall, pp. 35–84. Illinois State Museum, Scientific Papers 12. Springfield.

Ritchie, William A.

1961 *A Typology and Nomenclature of New York Projectile Points.* New York State Museum and Science Service, Bulletin 384. Albany.

Rouse, Irving.

1951 *A Survey of Indian River Archaeology, Florida.* Yale University Publications in Anthropology 44.

Sears, E., and Sears, W.

1976 Preliminary Report on Prehistoric Corn Pollen from Fort Center, Florida. *Southeastern Archaeological Conference, Bulletin* 19:53–56.

Sears, William H.

1958 The Grant Site—Br–5. *Florida Anthropologist* 11:114–24.

1960a Ceramic Systems and Eastern Archaeology. *American Antiquity* 25:324–29.

1960b *The Bayshore Homes Site, St. Petersburg, Florida.* Contributions of the Florida State Museum, Social Sciences 8.

1962 The Hopewellian Affiliations of Certain Sites on the Gulf Coast of Florida. *American Antiquity* 28:5–18.

1963 *The Tucker Site on Alligator Harbor, Franklin County, Florida.* Contributions of the Florida State Museum, Social Sciences 9.

1967 Archaeological Survey in the Cape Coral Area at the Mouth of the Caloosahatchee River. *Florida Anthropologist* 20:93–102.

1971a Food Production and Village Life in Prehistoric Southeastern United States. *Archaeology* 24:322–29.

1971b The Weeden Island Site, St. Petersburg, Florida. *Florida Anthropologist* 24: 51–60.

1973 The Sacred and the Secular in Prehistoric Ceramics. In *Variation in Anthropology—Essays in Honor of John McGregor,* pp. 31–42. Illinois Archaeological Survey.

1977a Prehistoric Culture Areas and Culture Change on the Gulf Coastal Plain. In *For the Director: Research Essays in Honor of James B. Griffin,* pp. 152–84. Museum of Anthropology, Anthropological Papers 61. Ann Arbor: University of Michigan.

1977b Seaborne Contacts between Early Cultures in Lower Southeastern United States and Middle through South America. In *The Sea in the Pre-Columbian World*, edited by E. Benson, pp. 1–15. Washington: Dumbarton Oaks Research Library and Collections.

Semenov, S. A.
1964 *Prehistoric Technology*. New York: Barnes and Noble.

Steinen, Karl T.
1971 Analysis of the Non-Ceramic Artifacts from a Hopewellian Affiliated Site in Glades County, Florida. Master's thesis, Florida Atlantic University, Boca Raton.

Thomas, David Hurst.
1978 The Awful Truth about Statistics in Archaeology. *American Antiquity* 43: 231–44.

Whitehead, D. R., and Langham, E. J.
1965 Measurement as a Means of Identifying Fossil Maize Pollen. *Torrey Botanical Club, Bulletin* 92:7–20.

Willey, Gordon R.
1949a *Archeology of the Florida Gulf Coast*. Smithsonian Miscellaneous Collections 113.
1949b *Excavation in Southeast Florida*. Yale University Publications in Anthropology 42.

Wing, Elizabeth
1977 Factors Influencing Exploitation of Marine Resources. In *The Sea in the Pre-Columbian World*, edited by E. Benson, pp. 47–64. Washington: Dumbarton Oaks Research Library and Collections.

Witthoft, John
1967 Glazed Polish on Flint Tools. *American Antiquity* 32:383–88.

Index

An italic page number indicates that the reference is to a table or illustration on that page.